"With all that is happening in the world, there has never been a more critical time for this important book! In *Beyond Hashtag Activism*, Mae Cannon brings her years of experience and expertise to call us beyond concern to an authentic commitment to racial justice, gender equity, and global hope. This book is a very practical resource for anyone who wants to actively participate in God's story of reconciliation and social healing. I highly recommend it!"

Brenda Salter McNeil, author of *Roadmap to Reconciliation* and *A Credible Witness*

"Dr. Cannon deftly navigates many *big* issues—such as poverty, justice, and climate change—and shows the interplay between these complex problems. Often, justice issues are treated in isolation, and people must choose which is the most urgent. But Cannon shows the delicate interplay between various justice issues like poverty, race, climate change, and gender justice. Each chapter provides tangible next steps for Christians who want to put their convictions into meaningful action."

Nikki Toyama-Szeto, executive director of Evangelicals for Social Action at the Sider Center

"In my fifty years of being an activist pastor, this is the best resource I've read to equip individuals and congregations for improved discussion and strategies on important issues. Dr. Cannon is not only a credible theologian, she's a skillful writer who keeps us engaged and learning, even from those with whom we disagree. Kingdom thinking takes in truth from everywhere to make real progress anywhere."

Joel C. Hunter, former senior pastor of Northland, A Church Distributed, and chairman of the Community Resource Network in Central Florida

"I have known Dr. Rev. Mae Elise Cannon a long time, and she is eminently qualified to speak on this important and broad subject matter. Mae has a deep love of Scripture, commitment to the church, and resolution to pursue justice in all arenas. In *Beyond Hashtag Activism*, Mae carefully explores growing divisions within evangelicalism within the realm of justice, and she develops an interdisciplinary and intersectional approach for exploring justice—at both a global and domestic level. This book will grow your understanding, deepen your resolve, and send you into the world as a more effective ambassador for justice."

Daniel Hill, pastor, author of *White Awake* and *White Lies*

"On issues that are diverse and complex and at a time when divisions have never been wider, Mae Elise Cannon provides an incredibly valuable resource to educate, compel, and equip Jesus followers for meaningful social justice advocacy. Mae speaks with authority and authenticity from her years of personal global engagement. I encourage you to listen and learn . . . and then prayerfully commit as God calls you to action."

Santiago "Jimmy" Mellado, president and CEO of Compassion International

"In *Beyond Hashtag Activism*, the Rev. Dr. Mae Cannon sounds a clarion call to Christians and faith communities to engage in biblically grounded, Christ-centered ministries of justice to address the critical domestic and international crises of our day. This book will both challenge and inspire readers and congregations to act in strategic ways that are effective in taking on the challenges that cause many to feel powerless. Cannon provides ways that we can connect with others who are putting their faith into action and reminds us of the danger of what happens when we fail to act. *Beyond Hashtag Activism* calls for thoughtful reflection and action and at times calls us to repentance and reparation. This is a resource that should be placed in the hands of every person who asks, 'What can I do?'"

Christopher Pierson, senior pastor of Gary United Methodist Church, Wheaton, Illinois

"*Beyond Hashtag Activism* is a book for the decade. There are many books on singular issues swirling around today, but Dr. Cannon takes us on a holistic journey of justice woven together with the same thread that reflects the Holy Scriptures. It is a lifestyle not a pick-and-choose. The historical, theological, and biblical depth is profound, coupled with present-day complexities, making it inspirational reading and a resource for personal and global transformation now and in the future."

Jo Anne Lyon, ambassador, general superintendent emerita, The Wesleyan Church

"Mae Cannon is right: this world is not as it should be. In these pages she offers a way forward for moving from the nightmare we both create and perpetuate to God's dream of a better future for us all. Both thoughtful and practical, this is a book well worth reading . . . then reading again."

Michael B. Curry, presiding bishop of the Episcopal Church

Beyond Hashtag Activism

Comprehensive Justice in a Complicated Age

Mae Elise Cannon

An imprint of InterVarsity Press
Downers Grove, Illinois

InterVarsity Press
P.O. Box 1400, Downers Grove, IL 60515-1426
ivpress.com
email@ivpress.com

*InterVarsity Press® is the book-publishing division of InterVarsity Christian Fellowship/USA®, a movement
of students and faculty active on campus at hundreds of universities, colleges, and schools of nursing in the
United States of America, and a member movement of the International Fellowship of Evangelical Students.
For information about local and regional activities, visit intervarsity.org.*

*All Scripture quotations, unless otherwise indicated, are taken from The Holy Bible, New International
Version®, NIV®. Copyright © 1973, 1978, 1984, 2011 by Biblica, Inc.™ Used by permission of Zondervan.
All rights reserved worldwide. www.zondervan.com. The "NIV" and "New International Version" are
trademarks registered in the United States Patent and Trademark Office by Biblica, Inc.™*

*While any stories in this book are true, some names and identifying information may have been changed
to protect the privacy of individuals.*

Cover design and image composite: David Fassett
Interior design: Jeanna Wiggins
Images: ivy plant: © ranasu / E+ / Getty Images
       textured paper: © troyek / E+ / Getty Images

ISBN 978-0-8308-4589-7 (print)
ISBN 978-0-8308-3644-4 (digital)

Printed in the United States of America ♾

*InterVarsity Press is committed to ecological stewardship and to the conservation of natural resources
in all our operations. This book was printed using sustainably sourced paper.*

Library of Congress Cataloging-in-Publication Data
A catalog record for this book is available from the Library of Congress.

P	25	24	23	22	21	20	19	18	17	16	15	14	13	12	11	10	9	8	7	6	5	4	3	2	1
Y	37	36	35	34	33	32	31	30	29	28	27	26	25	24	23	22	21	20

To the board and members

of Evangelicals for Justice (E4J)

May we never give up on the hope

of the Good News of the gospel

and the knowledge that one day God's kingdom

of love and justice will come

(Hosea 12:6)

Contents

Introduction

#MeToo. #LikeAGirl. #WeAccept. The internet and social media have changed the face of social justice advocacy with hashtag campaigns. These movements have accomplished much in raising awareness about important justice issues like global poverty and gender discrimination. Hashtag activism can be understood as the social media world's engagement of thousands of internet users who express their opinions, stand in solidarity around certain issues, and show support for causes they care about via different social media platforms like Twitter, Facebook, Instagram, and other venues. Hashtag activism is a great place to start, but our social justice advocacy must move beyond the limits of likes, sharing, and click rates.

Beyond Hashtag Activism seeks to enter into social media realities while calling readers and the church toward a more comprehensive perspective on justice issues. Much has changed over the past decade in terms of Christian engagement with social justice in the United States. On the one hand, American Christians have made significant progress through the support of international development organizations like World Vision and Compassion International in addressing the realities of global poverty. For example, the number of children under five dying every day from preventable causes has decreased over the past several decades by half—from more than thirty thousand children a day to around fifteen thousand children a day.[1] On the other hand, much work is still to be done.

Today, Christians in the United States have never been more divided on issues of social justice. In a 2018 letter called "The Statement on Social Justice and the Gospel," conservative evangelicals claimed social justice is dangerous to the core tenets of the gospel.[2] In contrast, a gathering of progressive evangelicals met in Chicago in September 2018 to commemorate the forty-fifth anniversary of the signing of the "Chicago Declaration of Evangelical Social Concern (1973)."[3] With the election of President Trump to the Oval Office, racial and political divides have become more extreme between Bible-believing evangelicals of color and white evangelicals, many of whom are sometimes identified as "Trump evangelicals." As evangelicals of color become increasingly disenfranchised with "white Christianity," many are throwing in the towel on movements toward reconciliation.

Beyond Hashtag Activism enters into these realities within evangelicalism in the United States. It articulates a holistic reading of the gospel of Jesus Christ that is inclusive of core principles of social justice, including responding to the needs of the poor in the United States and around the world, addressing the realities of racial inequities and white supremacy, acknowledging and calling for change in the mistreatment of women domestically and internationally, and wrestling through questions on the horizon that the evangelical church will have to address.

Certainly "comprehensive justice" is an audacious claim. This book doesn't cover all that there is to cover on questions about the church, civil society, advocacy, activism, and biblical justice. Rather, it seeks a comprehensive, interdisciplinary, and intersectional approach to many of the most critical aspects of domestic and global injustice—instead of viewing them in isolation from one another—as we ask how God might call us to respond as Christian individuals and as the church. Our individual solutions to complex problems are not enough. The only way the church will be able to effectively respond to any type of injustice is to pursue comprehensive methodologies that look at the common themes, trends, and dynamic aspects of broken and unjust systems. A comprehensive approach must be employed to bring change and healing to people, places, and communities where power is abused.

Part one lays a foundation of what the Bible has to say about God's heart for justice. Chapter one considers what social justice looks like in the twenty-first century and recounts some of the history of justice within the evangelical tradition. It then discusses holistic prophetic advocacy, including social, legal, spiritual, political, and economic means. Chapter two delves more deeply into political advocacy. How should politics and our faith interact? And what does it mean to have a healthy Christian ethic in our engagement with religion and politics?

Part two emphasizes justice issues in global and domestic poverty. Chapter three looks at how to integrate our Christian faith and get involved in responding to the needs of the world's poor. Progress has been made on eradicating extreme poverty around the world, but much work needs to be done. Chapter four looks at how poverty manifests itself differently in the United States. Material deprivation, the "crisis of despair" that has led many to opioid addiction and suicide, healthcare, and the growing gap between the rich and the poor in the United States all play a role in domestic poverty.

Part three focuses on race. Chapter five begins by defining terms like *white supremacy, white fragility,* and *racism,* and then wrestles with the shifting demographics of America and how the white community is responding. Chapter six documents events from the murder of Trayvon Martin to the racial unrest in Ferguson, as well as the rise in shootings around the United States that have terrorized schools, movie theaters, mosques, and churches. The church must seek to understand racial violence, police brutality, and the age of incarceration. Chapter seven addresses the global immigration crisis, refugees, and battles at the border between the United States and Mexico. Immigration continues to become a more polarizing issue, from the influx of refugees fleeing from violence and poverty to the highly debated immigration policies that guard our own borders. Chapter eight focuses on global racial and ethnic violence, highlighting historic and contemporary global conflicts and explaining how Christian organizations are seeking to address the resulting humanitarian desperation and respond to the devastating effects of ongoing war.

Part four focuses on gender issues of oppression and injustice around the world. Chapter nine addresses the realities affecting women in the United States, from the #MeToo movement to sexual discrimination and violations in the workplace, general society, and the church. Chapter ten highlights places where women continue to be legally identified as second-class citizens with significant impairments on their freedom and human rights, addressing topics such as sex trafficking, violence against women, body image realities, and the question of abortion.

Part five highlights divides in the twenty-first century. Chapter eleven discusses justice issues that relate to marriage and sexuality. How might Christians and organizations seek to maintain biblical integrity and faithfulness to the gospel while also advocating for the rights of all people? This chapter highlights personal stories of those impacted by debates around sexuality and LGBTQ+ inclusion, and looks deeply at biblical arguments across the spectrum of views. Chapter twelve looks at the complex and deeply rooted conflicts around Israel and the Middle East, covering topics such as the Palestinian Christian community, realities of life for Palestinians living under occupation, human rights concerns, and the humanitarian crisis in Gaza. The chapter also addresses anti-Semitism, Christian-Jewish relations, Christian Zionism, and Palestinian liberation theology. The final chapter focuses on religious freedom and how it affects many faith communities in the United States and around the world. This chapter calls readers to stand up against bigotry, anti-Semitism, Islamophobia, and any belief that condemns or brings harm to other faith traditions.

The intersection of these diverse and complicated issues reminds the church that the world is not yet fully redeemed. Every time we recount the Lord's Prayer, saying "Thy kingdom come, thy will be done," we are acknowledging the reality that the *shalom* of God is not yet fully present here on this earth. We see only glimpses of hope and triumph and goodness. As believers and followers of Jesus, we are called to never give up hope, and to persist in our belief that injustice and oppression are not the end of the story.

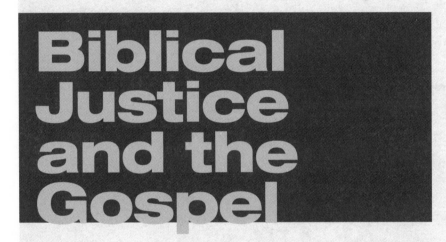

PART 1

Biblical Justice and the Gospel

God's Justice and Prophetic Advocacy

The Lord loves righteousness and justice;
the earth is full of his unfailing love.

PSALM 33:5

DURING THE SUMMER OF 2018, I fulfilled a years-long desire to spend a week on the Isle of Iona off the western shores of Scotland. Iona *(Ì Chaluim Cille* in Gaelic) has a long spiritual history dating back to the sixth century when an Irish monk named Columba settled there and founded a monastery. My journey to Iona was long—three legs via plane from Washington, DC, to New York City, to London, and finally to Scotland. After an overnight in Glasgow, I had another full day of travel, taking a several-hours-long train ride from Glasgow to Oban, a ferry for almost an hour from Oban to Craignure on the Isle of Mull, an additional two-hour coach bus ride (on mostly single-lane roads!) from Craignure to Fionnphort, and finally a quick ten-minute ferry ride from Fionnphort to the Isle of Iona. Needless to say, I felt most grateful to finally arrive!

With every mile traveled toward this sacred place where I went to meet with God, the troubles and realities of the world became more obscure. I actually believe the ridiculously long journey to Iona is a part of the sacredness of retreating there; the distance seems spiritually significant. As the final ferry approached the landing terminal, I became overwhelmed by the harsh beauty of the place. When I had seen pictures, I thought they had been doctored because the water was so overwhelmingly brilliant and so vibrantly turquoise. Sparkling. Clear. Pure. White sand beaches line the very short length of the island. (I later learned that one of the most beautiful beaches is called "White Strand of the Monks" *[Traigh Bhan Nam Monach]*, commemorating where several of Columba's followers were slaughtered during a Viking invasion. Even in such a sacred place, the violence of the world had broken through.)

Iona has been called a "thin place" by many—a place, as Tracy Balzer puts it, "from earth to heaven" where the line "between the spirit world and the physical world" is paper thin.[1] She describes a thin place as "any place that creates a space and atmosphere that inspires us to be honest before God and to listen to the deep murmurings of his Spirit within."[2] On the island, there is not much to do besides worship, be still, and meet with God. I wrote in my journal that evening, "Why do I feel closer to God here? Perhaps because Iona is a *thin place* closer to heaven and the spiritual realm than some of the 'thick' places in the world."

The kingdom of God, which we often can glimpse in those *thin places* of the world, encapsulates the fullness of God's heart for justice. Justice is the promise that one day the world will be made right. The book of Revelation reminds us that the kingdom is a place where there are no tears, where Christ will be glorified and the brokenness of the world will be fully healed:

"Never again will they hunger;
   never again will they thirst.
The sun will not beat down on them,"
   nor any scorching heat.
For the Lamb at the center of the throne
   will be their shepherd;
"he will lead them to springs of living water."
   "And God will wipe away every tear from their eyes." (Rev 7:16-17)

This is a picture of God's divine justice. Through Christ, the brokenness of the world has been redeemed, and one day justice will completely prevail.

The Bible is a book about justice. Kingdom justice. Biblical justice. And social justice. For God did not send his son Jesus into the world to condemn the world but to reconcile the world to himself. John 3:16 is the heart of the gospel. Christ came to save the lost and broken so that the world might be reconciled to God and once again made right, the way God intended for it to be.

I've become increasingly convinced that the gospel of Christ cannot be fully expressed without both salvation and justice being integrated and pursued. Biblical justice is the manifestation of the full gospel of Christ. We see this throughout the Scriptures from God's initial view of creation as "good" and his proclamation that Adam and Eve, man and woman together in community, not only reflect the image of God (*imago Dei)* but are deemed by the Creator as "very good" (Gen 1:31). The prophets continually talk about justice and how worshiping and honoring God is directly linked to the pursuit of justice. And justice is certainly woven intricately throughout the entirety of the gospel. Consider Luke 4—Jesus' very first recorded sermon in the Gospels—where he proclaims the words of Isaiah: "The Spirit of the Lord is on me, / because he has anointed me / to preach good news to the poor." His words would have reminded those listening of the promises of the Year of Jubilee from Leviticus 25, which was a vision of how God intended the world to be—free from slavery and oppression, where blindness exists no more, the impoverished are released from economic poverty, and captives are set free.[3] Jesus was declaring himself the fulfillment of the Year of Jubilee.

The gospel cannot be dichotomized into only spiritual provision or only material deliverance. Both—the spiritual and the material—are necessary components of the good news of salvation. Proclaiming Christ without responding to the needs of those who are poor and oppressed is inadequate. Comprehensive biblical justice is the scriptural

mandate to manifest the kingdom of God on earth by making God's
blessings available to all humankind.

Christian Clashes over Justice

In early 2018, a Christian movement known as Red Letter Christians
(RLC) that includes evangelicals and others came head to head with Jerry
Falwell Jr. and his stalwart right-wing convictions at Liberty University.
RLC and its leaders—people like Shane Claiborne and Tony Campolo—
hosted a "Red Letter Revival" April 6-7, 2018, in Lynchburg, Virginia,
near Liberty. The goal of the revival was to address the "toxic Christianity" that manifested in white evangelical support of President Trump
and his policies. "In word, worship and witness, this 'revival of Jesus and
Justice' will stand in stark contrast to the distorted Christian nationalism
that many white evangelical leaders have become known for," an RLC
statement read in part. "It is a gathering for people of faith or no faith
who are curious about Jesus and troubled by the state of evangelicalism
in America."[4] In 2019, RLC hosted a subsequent Red Letter Revival with
a similar emphasis.

The initial 2018 event took place over the course of a weekend,
drawing together about 300 people in a high school auditorium.
Speakers included founder of Freedom Road Lisa Sharon Harper, author
and pastor Jonathan Martin (who was escorted off the Liberty campus
for suggesting a peaceful protest), and activist and founder of the Moral
Mondays movement William Barber. Prior to the event, Claiborne requested the opportunity to pray with Liberty students and Falwell Jr.
(the university's president), but "Liberty police also sent him a letter . . .
threatening fines and jail time if he visited the Liberty campus to pray."[5]
What extreme division could cause a conservative Christian university
to threaten arrest and legal action and ban a group with whom they
disagree from praying with them on campus?

The clash between Liberty University and Red Letter Christians is
just a small glimpse of the growing divides and chasm of political difference between white conservatives and the more progressive

evangelical movement, which is often inclusive or led by leaders of color. Statistics show more people today will get married across religious divides than political ones. Harsh partisanship is present in Washington, DC, and increasingly "the left" and "the right" are at what seem to be irreconcilable odds.

Evangelicalism has never been more divided in the United States. Since the 2016 election, one of the most prevailing questions of our day has become "what does it mean to be evangelical?" due to the fact that the overwhelming majority of *white evangelicals*, more than 80 percent, voted for Trump to become president.[6] These questions are all the more relevant leading into the 2020 elections.

There has been a merging and redefining of the religious right and those historically understood as fundamentalists with the term *evangelical* today. Mark Labberton writes in *Still Evangelical?* that "beliefs about God, Jesus, the Bible, conversion, and the afterlife" aren't distinguishing enough features to "explain the growing division between some evangelicals and others."[7] White evangelicals voting for Trump and evangelicals of color all claim to follow the same Jesus yet often could not be further apart in their understanding of social realities like racism, immigration, incarceration, gender, and many other issues.

Labberton, explaining the division, says the "gloves have come off" when it comes to "conservative social anxiety over an ever-wider reach of an ever-wider liberal and secular government agenda; cultural war debates about abortion and homosexuality and potential Supreme Court nominees; threats to US safety because of terrorism and the role of Islam; economic and social elitism that isolates and ignores the cries and struggles of middle- and lower-class citizens, particularly whites; roiling anger and fear over issues of immigration and race, especially killings of unarmed, young black men, further unsettling a narrative of America as exceptional, Christian, and white."[8] Many of Trump's policies like the Tax Cuts and Jobs Act (TCJA) have sought to address these fears of middle class white Americans. At the same time, Trump's presidency has allowed the fears of white Middle America to rise to the surface and be expressed more openly, and at times viciously as evidenced by the Brookings Institute report that found "substantial evidence that Trump has encouraged racism and benefited politically from it."[9]

The 2018 "Statement on Social Justice and the Gospel," led by John MacArthur, provides a glimpse of another clash over the definition of evangelicalism. The signers concurred that social justice is dangerous to the core tenets of the gospel, stating, "We deny that true justice can be culturally defined or that standards of justice that are merely socially constructed can be imposed with the same authority as those that are derived from Scripture. We further deny that Christians can live justly in the world under any principles other than the biblical standard of righteousness." The statement condemned postmodern ideologies such as "intersectionality, radical feminism, and critical race theory."[10] It is important to note that MacArthur's views on justice exploded in the news again in October 2019 when he made an incredibly controversial response to a question about his thoughts regarding gender and preaching about the Southern Baptist Bible teacher Beth Moore. MacArthur criticized the Southern Baptist Convention as "caving" and said that Moore should "go home."[11] MacArthur's comments further expanded the chasm between like-minded conservative evangelicals and more centrist evangelicals like New Testament theologian Scot McKnight, who strongly condemned his words.[12]

Intersectionality may be defined simply as a framework that identifies how "interlocking systems of power impact those who are marginalized in society."[13] In other words, how does racism play a part in our application of criminal justice? Does gender inequality affect other systems and structures of power? These interconnected relationships must be deconstructed and acknowledged if we want to address systemic injustices, rather than just respond to symptoms of the problem. While one may not agree with the origins or use of the term, we must acknowledge the reality of how systems interact and intersect, and how power structures and their abuse affect the marginalization of people groups and certain segments of society.

In contrast to the MacArthur statement, "The Chicago Invitation," written by the group convened to celebrate the forty-fifth anniversary of the "Chicago Declaration of Evangelical Social Concern (1973)" in September 2018, highlighted "diverse evangelicals" continuing the journey, committed to the "biblical mandate," and lamenting the "current crisis in evangelism, which jeopardizes the reputation and witness of the Christian church."[14] I was a drafter and original signer of "The Chicago Invitation" and concur that evangelicalism seems to have been co-opted by one segment of a political party, and that we have "fallen short of the Biblical values and commitments proclaimed in the gospel." Evangelicalism in the United States today will die if we do not remember and return to a full commitment of the gospel that is manifested both in love and in justice (Psalm 101:1).

Protest and Resistance

In November of 2017, one of DC's most influential leaders, Barbara Williams-Skinner, and a number of other pastors and faith leaders congregated together, many dressed in clerical garb, in the lobby of the Hart Senate Office Building to protest the tax cut bill that would have had a large effect on health care for Americans. Some of them were there as part of the #2000verses social media campaign, and their protest included reading out loud verses from the Bible about serving the poor and condemning the making of unjust laws. Skinner said to the senators, "People will die from a tax bill that reflects a reckless disregard for human life because millions will be thrown off health care; and struggling Americans of all races and backgrounds will be treated as collateral in a race to give the rich a tax cut they do not need."[15]

The protest came after a letter by a number of faith leaders from a variety of traditions was published to call for a stop to the tax reform bill, noting its injustice to the poor and how disproportionately it would affect people.[16] As the protest continued, the Capitol Police repeated several times, "This is your last warning," and cautioned that further action would be taken if the protestors did not cease their disruptive activities. The several minutes of prophetic shouting, reading of verses, and other pastoral declarations resulted in the arrest and removal of twelve faith leaders, including Barbara Williams-Skinner and Jim Wallis, founder of Sojourners. Their protest is an example of prophetic advocacy.

Breaking the law is not a new trend within Christianity. In fact, there is a long history of defying societal laws in order to live out God's love for others. One of Martin Luther King Jr.'s most famous pieces was his "Letter from Birmingham Jail," written while he was serving out an arrest because of his protests against the lack of civil rights for black Americans. King and others lived and breathed the Old and New Testament stories of those who decided to live for God rather than recognizing the power of the governmental authorities of their day. First-century martyrs, Martin Luther, and Dietrich Bonhoeffer all spoke out against oppressive authoritarian regimes in favor of God's law. The few distinct Bible passages that tell God's people to submit to the government are not blanket demands to uphold every law every time.[17] In fact, Peter and the apostles reminded their followers that "we must obey God rather than human beings" (Acts 5:29).

Identifying the laws that do more harm than good and also standing in defiance of those laws in a way that continues to reflect God's love for all people is important. Shane Claiborne describes this type of prophetic spiritual action this way: "Good resistance work holds up a mirror to the world and changes laws. When you see militarized police spraying nonviolent protesters in Birmingham or Standing Rock, it makes you ask questions about who is on the right side of history."[18] Many faith leaders have used nonviolent civil disobedience as a means of standing against these kinds of laws. And while Claiborne recognizes that not everyone has the privilege to ignore the possibility of jail time, he explains, "Our times demand courageous action. King used the following metaphor: Traffic laws are good things, but when a fire is raging, the rescue team runs the red light. When a person is bleeding, the ambulance speeds through red lights, and other cars get out of the way."

The reality is that those who are the most buried and suffocated by oppression and injustice often don't have a choice about whether or not to engage. People of color don't have a choice about whether or not to engage in the realities of racism because they suffer from overt forms of oppression and microaggressions on a daily basis in white dominant contexts. An African American or Latina mother sending her young son off to school has to care about police brutality because she fears whether or not her baby boy will come home that night. People living in poverty don't choose whether or not to care about economic realities because if they don't wrestle with the effects of poverty, they won't have food for their families. Women threatened with sexual violence don't have a choice about whether or not they should care about gender equality and justice.

However, even in the midst of these gross injustices, oppressed communities are often the most profound places to find hope.

Prophetic Advocacy

Prophetic advocacy includes both spiritual and practical methodologies of directly responding to injustices we witness in the world. But what is advocacy? And what does it mean to be an advocate of biblical justice?[19]

Many people say advocacy is about speaking up for others. On the one hand, this is true; advocacy is about elevating the voices of those who are often marginalized and whose voices aren't heard in mainstream or broader society. However, we must be attentive to the pitfalls of believing that we have the ability to "speak for those without a voice," as this presumes people are incompetent or unable to speak for themselves. We must be sensitive to protect others' individual autonomy while also not being oppressive in our attempts to advocate on behalf of those who may be suffering as victims of injustice.

In some ways, advocacy also includes the redistribution of resources. Often those who are being violated in some way do not have access to wealth, power, and information. Good legal advocacy, for example, is the provision of wisdom and knowledge about the law that allows for protection or recourse in the quest for justice. The redistribution of power involves curbing the abuse and seeking to right imbalances of power. One example of this is tied to a famous quote attributed to historian and moralist Lord Acton in 1887: "Power tends to corrupt, and absolute power corrupts absolutely. Great men are almost always bad men."[20] What did he mean by "great men are almost always bad men"? Lord Acton was arguing that the more power and privilege one human being possessed, the more tempted that individual would be to abuse that power by taking advantage of others, and he cited the authorities of his day as examples of people who lived out his theory. He did not believe there should be exceptions to judgment against moral vices like murder, violence, and theft, even if those acting unjustly were the king or the head of the church. Lord Acton cited Queen Elizabeth's reputed command that her sister Mary Queen of Scots be murdered as an example where neither king nor queen (nor Pope) should be above the law.[21] For Acton, the powerful should be held accountable to justice, just as those on lower tiers of society. Advocacy seeks to address these kinds of imbalances of power.

Ultimately, advocacy in pursuit of justice provides a mechanism by which people can seek to bring about change in the world. It is part of the process of how the world can be made right, the way God intended it to be. Each of us has a critical part to play in advocating for the world to be different, better, and closer to God's original design as revealed in Genesis 1–2, the Year of Jubilee in Leviticus 25, and Jesus' ministry. Christians are to express our faith by being intercessors and advocates for the least in society. Advocates are change agents who work to secure justice on behalf of those experiencing injustice who might not have the power to change their current circumstances.

Prophetic advocacy is about the transformation of attitudes, hearts, and behaviors on an individual level as well as transformation on a systemic level. Entering into confession and lamenting the brokenness of the world changes us. As we groan in our spirits in response to places of deep pain and suffering, the Holy Spirit joins us in our lament. We are not alone. In our submission to better understand these realities and by confessing our limitations and weaknesses, we increasingly enter into a posture of being able to be molded and transformed more into the image of God—the God of all compassion and justice, who loves the world and will one day make it completely right.

Martin Luther King Jr. captured this idea of holistic change at both the individual and systemic levels in his vision for the *beloved community:* a picture of what relationships between men, women, and God's creation should one day become. And Augustine talked about the "city of God" as not only a metaphor but also a glimpse of what the world might look like if kingdom ethics are fully applied and manifested. Prophetic advocacy describes our work to help the world be made right as God intended, where the wrongs of the world might be redeemed and brokenness fully restored. We see this call in the Lord's Prayer, the parables of Jesus, and the Beatitudes, as well as throughout the Prophets. Christ-followers live out obedience to God when we advocate for justice.[22]

Prophetic advocacy can take several different forms, but there are five primary types of advocacy: spiritual advocacy, social advocacy, legal advocacy, political advocacy, and economic advocacy.[23]

Spiritual Advocacy

Spiritual advocacy includes seeking to meet with God and come into alignment with his will on behalf of others and the world. We know God cares for the poor and oppressed. Proverbs 14:31 says, "whoever is kind to the needy honors God." The Holy Spirit models for us what it means to intercede and intervene on behalf of others, as Romans 8:26-27 reminds us: "the Spirit intercedes for God's people in accordance with the will of God." We can follow this model and intercede on behalf of others in prayer and supplication. The power of effective prayer must not be underestimated. Ephesians 6:12 says our battle is not against flesh and blood but "against the rulers, against the authorities, against the powers of this dark world." Simply put, spiritual advocates pray. We pray for and with people, inviting others to pray alongside us.

Spiritual disciplines such as worship, silence, and solitude are all helpful ways we can meet with God and beseech him to intervene and address injustices we have witnessed. We can also use music as a way to invite people in. My book *Just Spirituality: How Faith Practices Fuel Social Action* talks about how worship and spirituals are a way of crying out for justice and new realities. One of the most impactful experiences of my life was marching across the Edmund Pettus Bridge in Selma, Alabama, with men and women who had been there decades before during Bloody Sunday. We sang "Ain't Nobody Gonna Turn Us Around" and "We Shall Overcome." These and other spirituals prophetically put to song the truth that our current realities are not the end of the story.

Social Advocacy

Social advocacy is the process of standing with, walking with, and accompanying those who are victims of injustice. It can mean speaking up when someone in your presence makes a comment that is offensive or demeaning to someone else or toward a particular people group. In public situations where an individual or a group is being ostracized, left out, or neglected, it can also mean walking across the room and extending hospitality, kindness, and welcome.

Social action, often rooted in Catholic social tradition, includes some of the richest history of Christian social advocacy. Consider the profound impact of activists like Sojourner Truth, Mother Teresa, Óscar Romero, and William Wilberforce. These world changers committed themselves to living out social justice in the public sphere and challenged some of the gravest injustices of their day, including slavery and the abuse of the poor.

Social media tends to be a place in the public square today where there are lots of conversations about justice issues—often in highly contentious ways! In some situations, writing a blog or Facebook post that highlights injustice and issuing an invitation to respond can be courageous. Telling stories, showing pictures, and raising awareness can often touch people's hearts and help them begin to learn and care about important justice issues. Some people call this kind of advocacy "hashtag activism" because of the # used on Facebook, Twitter, Instagram, and other forms of social media. However, we must not become complacent and believe that social advocacy and "clicking a box" on social media to say we care about an issue is the only role we are called to play. When done well, social advocacy raises awareness about ignorance and misperceptions and stands in the gap on behalf of those in society who are often overlooked and underrepresented.[24]

Legal Advocacy

Some of the most inspiring social justice work today centers around legal advocacy: a person or organization helping someone navigate the legal system. Leaders like Bryan Stevenson and the Equal Justice Initiative (EJI) are one example, as they work to free inmates who have been falsely accused and convicted of crimes. Consider Stevenson's book *Just Mercy* or watch the Hollywood movie by the same title to learn more about his work. Over the course of EJI's thirty years of work, more than 125 inmates on death row have been exonerated.[25] Prison Fellowship International (PFI) is another example. A number of other human rights groups around the world challenge the application of laws that they believe limits an individual's or a certain people group's legal rights. Al-Haq, located in the city of Ramallah in the West Bank of the occupied Palestinian territories (oPt), is an NGO whose work includes the documentation of human rights abuses, research, and studies on "interventions on breaches of international human rights and humanitarian law" in East Jerusalem, the West Bank, and Gaza. Al-Haq "undertakes advocacy before local, regional, and international bodies."[26]

Many individuals and communities around the world have limited access to adequate legal representation, making legal advocacy a critical component of effectively addressing injustices.

Political Advocacy

Political advocacy seeks to shift regional, state, and national policies, righting unjust aspects of our governmental structure through the political system. People can advocate for systemic change by voting or by visiting or writing government representatives on both the state and federal level. US citizens need to remember the important impact we can have by engaging in political advocacy.

Many organizations provide templates of letters and other user-friendly tools that make contacting your elected officials less intimidating. Likewise, Christian justice groups often provide advocacy training on how to effectively talk to your elected officials about policies and how they often impact the most vulnerable within our society. Bread for the World is one of the best NGOs encouraging American Christians and churches to engage in political advocacy in response to global hunger. World Vision also provides robust advocacy opportunities in addressing global poverty, sex trafficking, immigration and refugees, and other international issues. We must not forget that US government policies greatly affect not only our own backyards but also the world. When the US Congress passes legislation related to appropriations and the federal budget, the international community is deeply impacted. And US foreign assistance often means the difference between communities having their basic humanitarian needs met through access to food, water, and housing, or not. Many Christian and evangelical communities still wrestle with why and how the church should engage constructively in political advocacy. This struggle is addressed in the next chapter.

Economic Advocacy

My mentor John Perkins always says, "Justice is an economic issue." The ways we choose to invest our financial resources and spend our money encapsulates some of the greatest power we possess. Economic advocacy includes things like fundraising, making conscious purchasing decisions, and being well informed on how our financial investments (including pensions, stocks, retirement plans, etc.) are utilized. It can also mean engaging in movements that include economic nonviolent actions such as boycott, divestment, and sanctions (BDS). Many activists protesting the apartheid in South Africa used and advocated for BDS against the apartheid regime and policies. Some historians argue that the global sanctions against South Africa constituted one of the most important tools in shifting power and resulted in the fall of apartheid.[27]

In 2018–2019, legislation was proposed in the US Congress that came to be known as the Israel Anti-Boycott Act. The initial bills proposed would have made it illegal for US citizens to participate in a United Nations– or European Union–sponsored commercial boycott against Israeli companies that do business in Israel or the occupied Palestinian territories. The initial legislation did not become federal law, but many states have enacted anti-BDS legislation of their own. The US Constitution protects the right of individuals and groups to engage in nonviolent protests via economic means including the right to boycott. The protection of the constitutional right of free speech in the right to boycott is fought for heavily by the American Civil Liberties Union (ACLU). When boycotts are applied to Israel, the situation is particularly complex. Some boycotts call for a full boycott of Israel and others only boycott settlement products from the occupied Palestinian territories (oPt) of East Jerusalem, the West Bank, and Gaza. Regardless of one's personal convictions about the occupation, boycotts should be a federally and state-protected right and economic-advocacy tool within the United States.

Each of the above five types of advocacy comes with its own unique challenges and obstacles. Yet one of the greatest obstacles to effective advocacy includes the emotional cost and "compassion fatigue." With literally hundreds of different issues of injustice in our towns, communities, cities, states, country, and world, how can we not be overwhelmed? Jennifer Butler, founder and CEO of Faith in Public Life, told me that, instead of being overwhelmed, she feels great hope and is encouraged in her ongoing work to remember that at least we can do something. We can all contribute in meaningful ways, she reminded me. We are not victims of our circumstances and predetermined outcomes.

Rather, each of us has skills, assets, talents, and resources that can be used to make a difference. My friend and human rights activist Jessica Montell, who works for a human rights organization in Jerusalem, told me that Jewish tradition says that it is not our task to finish the work, but we are all obligated to engage in some way or another. This idea comes from *Pirkei Avot* 2:21 when Rabbi Tarfon said, "It is not our responsibility to finish the work of perfecting the world, but you are not free to desist from it either."

Four Best Practices

We should be encouraged by the reminder that our work makes a difference. When we take up a cause and stand alongside others, we are advocating for change in the world. Over my years of church ministry and leading nonprofits committed to holistic ministry and justice, I've identified four best practices that are critically important in helping our advocacy be more effective.

First, our efforts should have a clearly defined goal that is specific and targeted. In an era of intersectionality and so many connections between movements, advocacy can sometimes be completely sabotaged because a group tries to address every injustice under the sun all at once. I believe there is a time for integrated approaches and the pursuit of holistic justice. However, without a clearly defined goal for our advocacy, there's often no clear channel through which our energy and momentum can be utilized. As a result, movements can easily fizzle out and become too diffuse to actually be effective.

Second, *advocates should also be pragmatic* in their efforts to accomplish their stated goal. Some time periods demand prophetic voices who call out the need for different realities. The goal of advocacy, however, is to tactically bring about a specific change. Time and time again, I see the methodology of well-meaning activists rest on moral principles and on being "on the right side of history." I certainly hope my work also contributes to that reality! But advocacy is so much more effective when we set aside the "need to be right" and instead think about pragmatic ways to build bridges with those with whom we disagree. If there is a specific policy we are trying to address, many times a pragmatic approach will constitute a much more effective methodology for getting things done.

I am not saying we should throw out our moral compass and engage in utilitarian tactics where the end justifies the means. I've just come to believe wholeheartedly that evangelical and other Christian justice movements could gain a lot more traction by setting aside some of our hubris and adopting practices that are pragmatic as we seek justice and pursue new realities. Some questions we should ask include "Where can we get traction?" and "What are some immediate steps of progress or 'wins' we might be able to accomplish on an issue?"

One of my favorite stories of pragmatic advocacy is that of William Wilberforce and his contributions to ending the slave trade in England. Slavery was not ended (at least initially) because people in Great Britain unanimously agreed it was egregious and a sin against both God and humankind. Rather, Wilberforce and other evangelical Quakers in the abolition movement won the fight because they were pragmatists. The Foreign Slave Trade Act, which outlawed the slave trade to the French colonies, passed overwhelmingly quickly, but it had more to do with the United Kingdom's interest and concerns regarding the French Revolution than with a moral condemnation of the slave trade.[28] It took twenty years for the British Parliament to pass the Slave Trade Act of 1807. And years more before slavery actually ended.[29] Nonetheless, some of the greatest successes that moved the needle in bringing an end to slavery were pragmatic wins, rather than moral ones.

There is a dynamic tension between this reality of prophetic witness and pragmatic activism. I sometimes say that prophets are the worst advocates. But we definitely need prophets! Their ability to courageously go ahead of others and speak the truth while inspired by the Holy Spirit creates space for effective pragmatists to follow in their stead, painstakingly working on mundane details in the advocacy space that make a real difference and can often have profound effects. Both are critical components in our fight against injustice. May prophets and pragmatic advocates bless each other in their critical work toward effective advocacy.

The third best practice in being an effective advocate is to *get your facts right*. Over the years, I have seen some major advocacy campaigns become derailed because of hyperbolic exaggerations and not getting the numbers precisely right. Take, for example, the grave injustice that has been perpetrated in the Middle East against a farmer and the land he has owned in his family for more than three generations. The one-hundred-acre Nassar family farm near Bethlehem, now known around the world as Tent of Nations, has been in the family since 1916, when the land was purchased during the reign of the Ottoman Empire. Owned by Palestinian Christians and surrounded by Israeli settlements, the farm continues to stand as a form of peaceful resistance against the surrounding pressures of Israeli land confiscation.[30] But, despite having decades of documentation of land ownership from every era since the Ottoman Empire, including when Bethlehem was under the British Mandate, then Jordanian rule, and now Israeli rule, the Nassar family has been fighting to keep their land for more than twenty years. The case has even reached the Israeli Supreme Court.

In the middle of these realities, in 2014, the family woke up to a piece of their land having been demolished by the Israeli military.[31] One side says the land is "contested land"; the other says it belongs to their family as it has for generations. The portion of the land that was demolished was a fruit orchard grove and some olive trees. When the case hit the international news, the Nassar family and many other mainstream media services reported 1,500 trees were damaged, while other news outlets claimed it was only 300 trees.[32] Soon the primary question became how many trees were damaged. Some opposing groups who believed that the Palestinians exaggerated their numbers showed pictures from Google Maps where they counted the trees. The family explained that they included the number of grapevines that had also been destroyed, which made the number much higher than just apple and other fruit trees. Whatever the reality was, the main point of the story was not the number of trees, but rather that the demolitions were unjust in the first place. The debate about the numbers took attention away from the injustice itself.

Finally, success in the advocacy space requires *fortitude, persistence, and longevity.* The only way to truly be a successful advocate is to stay in the game and not give up. We may be encouraged by the reminder that it is our responsibility to do our small part, but even more encouraging is the fact that God is the one who will take the seeds we have planted and make them grow. In 1 Corinthians 3:6, Paul says, "I planted the seed, Apollos watered it, but God has been making it grow." May our diligence and ongoing efforts over weeks, months, years, and decades be effective as we seek to submit our efforts toward justice to God. Not one of us can do everything, but all of us can do something. May we be faithful in whatever that something is that God has called us to do. And our prayer, our persistent hope, is that God will take the efforts of our hands and make them grow.

For Further Study

Cannon, Mae Elise. *Just Spirituality: How Faith Practices Fuel Social Action.* Downers Grove, IL: InterVarsity Press, 2013.

——. *Social Justice Handbook: Small Steps for a Better World.* Downers Grove, IL: InterVarsity Press, 2009.

Cannon, Mae Elise, Lisa Sharon Harper, Troy Jackson, and Soong-Chan Rah. *Forgive Us: Confessions of a Compromised Faith.* Grand Rapids: Zondervan, 2014.

Cannon, Mae Elise, and Andrea Smith, eds. *Evangelical Theologies of Liberation and Justice.* Downers Grove, IL: InterVarsity Press, 2019.

Johnston, Robert K. *Evangelicals at an Impasse: Biblical Authority in Practice.* Atlanta: John Knox, 1979.

Labberton, Mark, ed. *Still Evangelical? Insiders Reconsider Political, Social, and Theological Meaning.* Downers Grove, IL: InterVarsity Press, 2018.

Lee, Hak Joon, and Tim A. Dearborn, eds. *Discerning Ethics: Diverse Christian Responses to Divisive Moral Issues.* Downers Grove, IL: InterVarsity Press, 2020.

Offutt, Stephen, F. David Bronkema, Krisanne Vaillancourt Murphy, Robb Davis, and Gregg Okesson. *Advocating for Justice: An Evangelical Vision for Transforming Systems and Structures.* Grand Rapids: Baker Academic, 2016.

Rah, Soong-Chan. *Prophetic Lament: A Call for Justice in Troubled Times.* Downers Grove, IL: InterVarsity Press, 2015.

Sider, Ronald J., and Ben Lowe. *The Future of Our Faith: An Intergenerational Conversation on Critical Issues Facing the Church.* Grand Rapids: Brazos Press, 2016.

Suttle, Tim. *An Evangelical Social Gospel? Finding God's Story in the Midst of Extremes.* Eugene, OR: Cascade Books, 2011.

Swartz, David R. *Moral Minority: The Evangelical Left in an Age of Conservatism.* Philadelphia: University of Pennsylvania Press, 2012.

Westfall, Cynthia Long, and Bryan Dyer, eds. *The Bible and Social Justice: Old Testament and New Testament Foundations for the Church's Urgent Call.* Eugene, OR: Pickwick Publications, 2015.

Zabriskie, Marek, ed. *The Social Justice Bible Challenge: A 40 Day Bible Challenge.* Cincinnati: Forward Movement, 2017.

Questions for Discussion

- What did you grow up being taught in your local church or in your personal background about justice and the Bible?

- How do you understand the core tenets of the gospel? Where do you see (or not see) the role that justice plays? Do any particular Scriptures come to mind?

- What have you heard about "evangelicals" recently in the media? What do you wish they were saying, or do you feel like that paints an accurate picture of what it means to be an evangelical? Do you like the term or do you think a different identification, if any, should be used?

- Does the term *social justice* make you uncomfortable? Why or why not? Do you see biblical justice and social justice as being one and the same? Why or why not?

- What are some specific areas of injustice that speak most closely to your heart? What provoked this particular interest or passion?

- Is there a specific type of advocacy in which you feel gifted or with which you particularly resonate? Why or why not? Is there an area of advocacy you wish to learn more about or grow in?

- Identify the power, privileges, or advantages in your own life. This is not an exercise in feeling guilty but rather in making you more aware of the places where your power affects those who might not possess these things. Or are there areas of your life where you haven't had power and privileges? Process what those experiences have taught you and how you relate to power and advantages today.

Politics and the Gospel

Endow the king with your justice, O God,
the royal son with your righteousness.
He will judge your people in righteousness,
your afflicted ones with justice. . . .
He will defend the afflicted among the people
and save the children of the needy,
he will crush the oppressor.

PSALM 72:1-2, 4 (1984 NIV)

IN 2018, I HAD THE OPPORTUNITY to meet with some senior level staff members at the Trump White House. In my introduction, I described my role as an evangelical pastor and some of the work we do to address global poverty in the Middle East, as well as my background and evangelical credentials. One of the White House staff interrupted: "But what churches do you work with?" I have a relationship and work (behind the scenes) with one of the evangelical churches where Vice President Mike Pence sometime attends when he is in DC. I knew the "right" answer and responded accordingly. Seemingly assuaged, the White House staff member continued, "We wanted to know what box to put you in."

This black and white question of "are you on our side or not?" was both pragmatic and disturbing. It's one example of the distressing evidence of how integrated the fundamentalist and conservative evangelical theo-political agenda has become within the current administration. In other words, conservative/fundamentalist evangelicals are given a voice, influence, and an audience with people in positions of power, and other Christians (let alone people of non-Christian faith traditions and backgrounds) are not.

Another example of this occurred during a meeting I was in at the State Department shortly after President Trump's inauguration. When introducing myself to one of the senior advisers on faith-related issues, I mentioned that I was ordained in the Evangelical Covenant Church (ECC). She responded, "Does that mean you are an evangelical like me? Or an evangelical like the Lutherans?" She clearly presumed that Lutherans do not hold or maintain the same evangelical credentials as the mostly white conservative evangelicals who have shown so much support for the current administration. My response reverted back to what I learned a long time ago in Sunday school: "I am not sure. But I do love Jesus!" That seemed to suffice. And despite our politics differing significantly, she and I have come to develop what I believe to be an authentic relationship and friendship that centers on our common faith in Christ, and I am grateful for the doors she has opened for our political advocacy.

On the one hand, the separation of private faith and spirituality for evangelicals and political interests in the public square has had one of the most devastating effects on the gospel of Christ as a witness in the US context. Many churches strongly believe Christians have "no business" talking about politics and government policies related to social issues in the context of church life and ministry. This "wall" between the church and politics within the evangelical world has negatively impacted Christian influence in the public square. Because of many churches' silence on politics, Christians who do engage politically often do so without consideration of how our theology and witness impacts our political perspective and compels our engagement. Over the past several years, I have grown in my understanding of how politics and the church might healthily intersect. And I've come to understand more about why and how the conservative evangelical community has viewed political engagement as peripheral to the core tenets of the gospel, despite the direct correlation between the rise of the New Right and conservative Christian support of the Republican Party during the Bush era and under the presidency of Donald Trump.

Politics and Fear

The personal life of our current president has included abundant indulgence and decisions made in self-interest, the gaudy display of the accumulation of individual wealth, braggart diatribes about exploits against women, and other morally questionable life choices. He also regularly denigrated women during his 2016 campaign, such as when he accused journalist Megyn Kelly of asking inappropriately pointed questions because she was menstruating. "You could see there was blood coming out of her eyes," Trump said. "Blood coming out of her wherever."[1] How could such a person—one who claims he never asks God's forgiveness (the implication being that forgiveness is not needed, because he doesn't ever do anything wrong)—so win the hearts and minds of the vast majority of white evangelical voters?

Evangelical historian John Fea argues in his book *Believe Me: The Evangelical Road to Donald Trump* that the 81 percent of white evangelicals who voted for Trump—a higher percentage than voted for George W. Bush, John McCain, and Mitt Romney—overlooked all of his indiscretions because of his conservative Republican policy commitments. Trump's "Make America Great Again" campaign (a slogan borrowed from Ronald Reagan) included promises that appealed to the conservative voter, such as pulling the United States out of the Paris climate agreement, moving the US Embassy in Israel from Tel Aviv to Jerusalem, electing a conservative to the Supreme Court, building a wall between the United States and Mexico, "bombing the hell out of ISIS," and protecting and defending Christian heritage "like you've never seen before." Fea argues that the evangelical road to support of Donald

Trump has been "marked by the politics of fear, power, and nostalgia" and should have been predicted based on previous evangelical political engagement related to moral issues.[2]

Trump's rise to power is only symptomatic of the real underlying issues that remain prevalent in our society: racism that has been buried just underneath the surface like a dandelion whose roots have never been adequately torn from the ground; sexism, which allows for the perversion and distortion of loving and mutual relationships between men and women; bigotry, which demands the "othering" of people who are different or outside of the elitist norm; and classism, which loves wealth, power, and control and uses them as means to exert influence and self-protect against inner feelings of inadequacy and fear.

Donald Trump has given voice to white American fear that has been buried and undiscussed for decades—for example, fear that foreigners will take white Middle American jobs, fear that Arab militants will attack and destroy the democracy of the United States via terrorist attacks, and fear that the cost put on US society for immigrants will be paid on the backs of white Americans. And these fears are just the beginning. In my opinion, the majority of these fears are unfounded, but regardless of what we think of them, it is important to understand that they exist. Trump tapped into these fears of white Americans and manipulated them for his benefit in his rise to power.[3]

The same fear motivated the rise of the New Right, which emerged during the Reagan and Bush eras and increasingly linked white evangelical Americans to the Republican Party. But the roots of this trend developed much earlier:

> In the decades following World War II, evangelicals, especially white evangelicals in the North, had drifted toward the Republican Party—inclined in that direction by general Cold War anxieties, vestigial suspicions of Catholicism and well-known evangelist Billy Graham's very public friendship with Dwight Eisenhower and Richard Nixon. Despite these predilections, though, evangelicals had largely stayed out of the political arena, at least in any organized way.[4]

In large part, following the civil unrest in the United States during and after the Vietnam War era, including but not limited to civil and women's rights, the politics of white evangelicals increasingly became motivated by fear. Fea describes the primary motivators of these fears as "nativism, xenophobia, racism, intolerance, and an unbiblical view of American exceptionalism."[5]

Despite clear and strong associations between conservative American Christians and the Republican Party, white evangelicals have held a long and firm belief in the separation of church and state. Even today, few white evangelical churches hear sermons from their Sunday pulpits on citizenship and the role Christians should play in the US political system. The separation and isolation of theology, biblical study, and practices of the church from addressing political questions of the day does not mean American evangelicals are not incredibly engaged in politics outside of Sunday morning. Rather, white evangelicals have shaped their political engagement based on a few moral issues such as abortion, the death penalty, and gay marriage. For this demographic of evangelicals and conservatives, politics is "off limits" when it comes to religious piety, except for around a few specific issues that have been cherry picked by those in political power. As public society has become increasingly liberal, American conservative Christians have increasingly become isolationists and retreated while developing even more stalwart convictions around these issues. In other words, white conservative Christians vote on a few select moral issues and convictions, but they neglect to engage in the political square when it comes to other social justice issues like the treatment of minority communities, racial disparity and white supremacy, and discrimination based on gender or sexuality. It is important to note that while the church on Sunday is largely silent about politics, there is a plethora of the church "showing up" on Capitol Hill and in the halls of power in Washington, DC. Consider events like the National Prayer Breakfast, which every president has attended since Eisenhower, and weekly prayer meetings on both the Senate and House sides of the Capitol. These dynamics of Christian influence over the powerful and elite in politics are addressed significantly, albeit critically, in the book *The Family* by Jeff Sharlet and in a Netflix documentary by the same name.

Politics and the Church

What should the relationship between the church and politics look like? Different theories have existed since the time the early church was born at Pentecost. Augustine's *City of God* is a foundational work defining the relationship between the church and state. He wrote about an earthly temporal city and a heavenly city, which modeled how people should get along within society here on earth. For Augustine, the ultimate goal would be achieved once the heavenly city could be established on the earth. More recent books such as *Unsettling Truths: The Ongoing, Dehumanizing Legacy of the Doctrine of Discovery* by Mark Charles and Soong-Chan Rah criticize Augustine's theory for espousing a doctrine of Christian empire and justifying abuse and mistreatment of "infidels" who chose not to submit to Christian political leadership.[6]

In the twentieth century, political theorist Leo Strauss wrote prolifically about what he called the "theologico-political problem."[7] In Strauss's view, the core problem is where authority should be centered. He asked questions about what scope political authority should maintain, whether or not political authority should be grounded in revelation or reason, and who should hold the ultimate authority within society.

Even more recent, the book *The Church's Social Responsibility: Reflections on Evangelicalism and Social Justice* tells the fascinating story of interactions about these questions regarding the church and politics between oil magnate J. Howard Pew; Carl Henry, the first editor of *Christianity Today;* and theologian Richard Mouw.

In 1966, Pew wrote an article called "Should the Church 'Meddle' in Civil Affairs?" in which he ultimately concluded that the church should not intervene but rather should focus on its highest priority and ancient mission of "changing hearts of men and women" and "render[ing] unto Caesar the things that are Caesar's." In speaking of Jesus, Pew said: "At no time did he countenance civil disobedience or promote political pressure either to correct social evils or to advance his spiritual mission. His highest priority was given to measures for changing the hearts of men and women, knowing full well that changed men and women would in time change society—as indeed they have done all down the ages."[8] This distinction between the ministry of Jesus as spiritual and the work of justice as temporal has been deeply damaging to the witness of the church through the ages. Similar arguments have been used historically to the detriment of all involved. For example, for decades the Bible was used to uphold and justify slavery in the United States.[9]

Pew did not publish the above-mentioned article in isolation. As the president of Sun Oil Company, he held significant power in shaping national Christian perspectives and contributed significant financial resources to conservative Christian organizations of the day. *Christianity Today* depended so significantly on his support that the general editor at the time, Carl Henry, often felt pressure to edit the magazine's theological statements to assuage Pew's philosophy that the church should be disengaged with civil affairs.

In 1967 Richard Mouw went head to head with Pew—though perhaps not intentionally—with an article in *Christianity Today* that insisted that there are times when it is absolutely essential for the church to intervene in social matters to respond to the needs of the world. For example, Mouw said it is the "'church's duty' to address the topic of civil rights" and emphasized that "it is often necessary for the church to take an unequivocal stand against prevailing economic, social, and political conditions, even where it is practically impossible to offer any solution."[10] After Mouw's article went public, Pew called Henry to complain. Henry's response remains germane to our conversation more than fifty years later. In five distinct points, Henry defended Mouw's article:

- The Bible is critically relevant to the whole of modern life and culture—the social-political arena included.

- The institutional church has no mandate, jurisdiction, or competence to endorse political legislation or military tactics or economic specifics in the name of Christ.

- The institutional church is divinely obliged to proclaim God's entire revelation, including the standards or commandments by which men and nations are to be finally judged, and by which they ought to now live and maintain social stability.

- The political achievement of a better society is the task of all citizens, and individual Christians ought to be politically engaged to the limit of their competence and opportunity.

- The Bible limits the proper activity of both government and church for divinely stipulated objectives—the former for the preservation of justice and order, and the latter, for the moral-spiritual task of evangelizing the earth.[11]

Henry still maintained that it was the role of individuals, and not the role of the church, to determine the specific solutions to the ills in society, and he asserted that the church's expertise did not lie in economics or politics. Nonetheless, he was doggedly convinced that evangelicals needed to do a "more effective job of 'enunciating theological and moral principles that bear upon public life.'"[12]

Mouw expanded the discussion by inviting in the thoughts and teachings of others, while also highlighting the importance of Christian organizations "that focus on specific areas of cultural involvement, in order to engage in the kind of communal reflection necessary to develop a Christian mind for the area in question."[13] Ultimately he came to agree with Carl Henry's assertions that there are limits to the church's expertise and contributions. That does not imply, however, that the church and church communities should not be centers of robust conversations about civil discourse and engagement.

The story of Henry and Mouw reminds me of an experience I had when serving as an executive pastor in northern California. During one of our church council meetings, a quite impassioned debate occurred over whether or not there should be a flag in the sanctuary. Some, mostly baby boomers whose parents or relatives had fought during World War II, felt it was imperative that the US flag be at the front of the sanctuary next to the altar, to show loyalty to both God and country. Others, myself included, felt that US nationalism and our allegiance to Christ should not be conflated. The church ended up compromising by displaying the flags of all the countries where we were engaged in missions, including the American flag, in the lobby of the church. According to what was understood to be standard protocol, the American flag hung slightly higher than other flags.

What was at the heart of this conflict about the flag being in the sanctuary? For some, the flag represented loyalty to the United States and support for men and women who have served in the US military. It is important to note that many of the people currently serving in the US military are people of color and people from impoverished backgrounds. For others, support of the flag and the military represents uncritical support of unjust wars the United States has perpetuated in Vietnam, the Middle East, and other parts of the world. The church needs to wrestle with questions of what it means to support men and women who serve our country while also not providing uncritical support of war and violence perpetuated by the military vis-à-vis the US government. This issue is discussed further in chapter thirteen on religious freedom.

I am arguing for a more nuanced approach in the way the church engages in political activism. I believe it's critically important for us to not put US nationalism on parallel with our allegiance to God and the kingdom. US exceptionalism is the idea that God favors the United States, and specifically white Americans, more than people of color within our own borders and people who live in other countries around the world. I believe one can love and support the United States and maintain patriotic ideals, while also being critical of certain US interventions around the world and while simultaneously being critical of the treatment of people of color and minority groups within US borders.

Nationalism, Police Brutality, and the National Football League

In August 2016, Colin Kaepernick, a San Francisco 49ers quarterback at the time, sat on the bench while the national anthem played before their pre-season game. His silent protest sparked controversy when a photographer posted a photo of Kaepernick on the sidelines. In response to the question of why he was not standing during the anthem, he tweeted, "To me, this is something that has to change. When there's a significant change and I feel that flag represents what it's supposed to represent, and this country is representing people the way that it's supposed to, I'll stand."[14]

Later, Kaepernick and fellow player Eric Reid began to kneel instead of sitting down during the anthem, explaining that their goal was never to take a stand against the military or those who have served. Rather, it was to recognize the ways in which the country has neglected to stand with those who are oppressed. Their protests followed a particularly brutal period where the nation was watching police officers shoot and kill unarmed black men. Following Kaepernick, a wave of fellow NFL players and other professional athletes joined in on kneeling during the anthem.

Many people, including President Trump, were upset with the kneeling, still claiming it was disrespectful to the military. On September 23, 2017, Trump tweeted against the protestors, encouraging coaches to fire anyone who knelt during the anthem. Across the NFL, responses to the kneeling were mixed. While some coaches chose to support their players, others spoke out against them. Dallas Cowboys coach Jerry Jones, the first one to threaten to bench players who knelt, stated, "If we are disrespecting the flag, then we won't play. Period. Period. We're going to respect the flag."[15] The NFL officially responded by enacting a national anthem policy that requires athletes to stand during the anthem but also gives them the option to remain in the locker room if they're unwilling. Though the policy passed almost unanimously, there was little player input.[16]

As of 2019, Kaepernick was still a "free agent" in the NFL and hasn't played since the 2016 season because no team had picked him up. This led Kaepernick to believe that the NFL was engaging in collusion. Between 2016 and 2019, Kaepernick and Eric Reid engaged in a lawsuit against the NFL to prove collusion was happening. In February 2019, the case was finally settled, though because of privacy laws, not many specific details have been released. We do know that Kaepernick officially withdrew his case against the NFL, and that he and Reid were both paid restitution. No official amount has been announced but insiders estimate it could be anywhere between sixty and eighty million dollars. Because the NFL opted for the settlement, many believe there was strong evidence against them.

Regardless of one's devotion to the flag, one of the merits of a true democracy is the right to protest. In September 2018, a new Nike ad campaign featuring Kaepernick played into the controversy, offering him support. A celebration of thirty years of the Nike brand, the ad touted the slogan, "Believe in something. Even if it means sacrificing everything."[17] There is hope that the settlement between the NFL and Kaepernick and Reid will make space for those who want to participate in protest without having to lose their jobs.[18]

Inclusive Patriotism

Erwin Lutzer, pastor emeritus of The Moody Church in Chicago, writes, "Can we serve the kingdom of God even when actively involved in the kingdom of man?"[19] Lutzer argues that our loyalty to God must be our highest priority, but at the same time, we cannot "shirk our responsibility to Caesar." He spells out what he means by US Christians constructively engaging in politics by laying out four principles. First, Christians should vote, even though candidates are "sinners at all levels of government." Second, the limitations of government must be acknowledged and the government should not be "naively" assumed to "rescue us from the abyss of moral and spiritual failure." Third, we should ask how God would have each of us be involved, since we are all called to engage differently and to different degrees. Fourth, preachers and teachers of the Word of God should stay out of endorsing candidates but should elevate the gospel above personal political allegiances. Lutzer's encouragement is a good start on making conservative Christian arguments for why people who choose to follow Jesus should engage more constructively in the political sphere. However, I do not think he goes far enough. I agree that the gospel should be *elevated above* politics. The gospel should *also be used to* inform, educate, and equip our understanding of what Christian engagement might look like in the public square. Consider all of the verses in the Scriptures that address what laws and practices a just society might include from Leviticus 25 to Matthew 25 and the hundreds of additional verses about God's call for us to care for the poor and the oppressed.

Since the 2016 controversy surrounding the National Football League and the American flag and anthem, many in media have been talking about "inclusive patriotism": the idea that the United States can be na- tionalistic *and* promote an inclusive society that is not all white and that embraces the diversity of the American landscape. This centrist view wants to allow for nationalism and devotion to the United States while honoring the histories of people of color who have often been oppressed in this country. One person espousing inclusive patriotism said, "We should be the kingdom of God, not the kingdom of the United States." As Berkeley professor Robert Reich writes, "Inclusive patriotism prides itself on giving hope and refuge to those around the world who are desperate—as memorialized in Emma Lazarus' famous lines engraved on the Statue of Liberty: 'Give me your tired, your poor, your huddled masses yearning to breathe free.'"[20] This is in stark contrast to the rhetoric of President Trump and his administration calling for the ban of Muslim immigration, placing limitations on the number of refugees allowed sanctuary in the United States, and espousing xenophobic ideas in an attempt to "Make America Great Again."

Hope over Fear

From what I've read about inclusive patriotism, it seems quite idealistic. Reich says, "Inclusive patriotism instructs us to join together for the common good." My primary concern with the movement is that the ideals it espouses continue to ignore the significant power differentials between people groups of color and whites in the United States. Unless we take a harsh look at the centeredness of whiteness, and the prolific role of white supremacy in the establishment of the United States, we will continue to be "whitewashing" our own history. As Fea writes, "Hope, humility, and a responsible use of American history defined the political engagement and social activism of the civil rights movement."[21] One of the dangers of inclusive patriotism is letting the US political system and structures off the hook for the ways they have systematically oppressed marginalized people groups and communities of color.

In our questions about politics and the gospel, we must be willing to ask how evangelical politics might change if we replace fear with hope, the pursuit of power with the cultivation of humility, and nostalgia with history. In order to be truly patriotic, we must look directly at the ongoing abuses of theological imperialism; broken promises and abuses, including genocide, of indigenous communities across the United States; the commodification of black bodies in the hundreds of years of slavery; and other grave injustices that even in the twenty-first century have yet to be rectified.

For Further Study

Ballor, Jordan J., and Robert Joustra, eds. *The Church's Social Responsibility: Reflections on Evangelicalism and Social Justice.* Grand Rapids: Christian Library Press, 2015.

Boyd, Gregory A. *The Myth of a Christian Nation: How the Quest for Political Power Is Destroying the Church.* Grand Rapids: Zondervan, 2005.

Fea, John. *Believe Me: The Evangelical Road to Donald Trump.* Grand Rapids: Eerdmans, 2018.

Harper, Lisa Sharon, and D. C. Innes. *Left, Right & Christ: Evangelical Faith in Politics.* 2nd ed. Boise: Elevate Faith, 2016.

Leeman, Jonathan. *How the Nations Rage: Rethinking Faith and Politics in a Divided Age.* Nashville: Thomas Nelson, 2018.

Margolis, Michele. *From Politics to the Pews: How Partisanship and the Political Environment Shape Religious Identity.* Chicago Studies in American Politics. Chicago: University of Chicago Press, 2018.

Wallis, Jim. *On God's Side: What Religion Forgets and Politics Hasn't Learned About Serving the Common Good.* Grand Rapids: Brazos, 2013.

Questions for Discussion

- What kind of influence have your parents, upbringing, or culture had on your current political views? Have those views shifted over the course of your life? Why or why not?

- What role do you think politics and nationalism should play for Bible-believing Christians? What do you think the Scriptures have to say about politics? Do you agree with Erwin Lutzer's four principles of Christian engagement in politics? Do you think anything is missing?

- What is the most difficult part of discussing politics with friends or family?

- Do you think your church could become more engaged in politics and, if so, how?

- How can someone engage in constructive conversations regarding differing political opinions?

PART 2

Poverty

3

Global Poverty

The poor will eat and be satisfied;
those who seek the Lord will praise him—
may your hearts live forever!

PSALM 22:26

IN 1985, LIVE AID shows around the world raised $127 million for famine relief in Africa.[1] Gone are the glory days of large benefit concerts, but the extreme poverty they sought to address continues to exist. Current progress and the potential for real change, however, also continues to give hope.

I recently discussed the present state of global poverty with Sidney Muisyo, the senior vice president of global program for Compassion International. We spent more than an hour talking about extreme poverty and the ways children around the world continue to suffer from malnutrition, preventable diseases, slavery, and oppression.

Muisyo described what it was like to grow up in Nairobi, Kenya, with poverty all around him. "Knowing poverty isn't cognitive, but experienced," he told me. In that context, it was common for friends to drop out of school because of the inability to pay for uniforms and other necessary fees. When I asked him what the consequences of being uneducated are, he explained, "You grow old before your time. Not just emotionally, but also physically. . . . People who are poor and seventeen years old often look like they are forty-five years old. One's mind grows old, their physical appearance, as if the expectation of the world is upon their shoulders." The weight of poverty robs children and youth of the possibilities of "what could be" without the opportunity to thrive, grow, explore, he said. An entire stage of a person's life is stolen from children who live in poverty.

At two years old, Muisyo developed polio. To this day, he walks with a limp. Growing up "handicapped" in Kenya was considered a curse. The handicapped were not given the opportunity to go to school but were often hidden in a room where they could not be seen. Even when present, those with disabilities were ignored and "unseen." As a child, not being able to play football (soccer) was only one of the many ways Sidney felt like a social outcast. Children like him, and others with disabilities, were treated without any expectations or hopes for their future. "To not be included and to be unseen, your humanity, your person, your belongingness was all brought into question," Sidney continued. "You become the 'cripple' and nothing else. It wasn't just as if my legs were handicapped, but all of me was considered insufficient and inadequate."

Muisyo's grandfather was God's provision. While he was being cared for by his grandfather, his mother worked hard and tried to make a way for her and her son, going to college to become a secretary in Nairobi. She worked for the government and was able to raise her family up to the middle class. Muisyo credits his success to the hard work and diligence of his grandfather and mother. As an executive at Compassion, Sidney's life's work focuses on "releasing children from poverty in the name of Jesus."[2]

Children with Disabilities and the School of Joy

One of my favorite places in the world is called the School of Joy, located in the Palestinian village of Beit Sahour just outside of Bethlehem. The school is run by Abouna Abu Saada, an Eastern Catholic priest, who loves the four or five dozen children there as his own. With limited resources and support, Father Abu Saada pours all he has into giving the students at the School of Joy an opportunity for education and job skills training.

> Every time I go to Bethlehem, I try to visit the school and meet with a young man named Peter. Peter is mostly deaf and mute but is still quite communicative. During one visit, Peter showed me a picture of the opportunity he had to meet and shake hands with Pope Francis, which seemed to bring Peter great joy and pride. I celebrated the special occasion with him.
>
> Around the world, people with disabilities are often the most overlooked and neglected. In Palestine, for example, children with disabilities have limited options for the future. Programs like the School of Joy give children, youth, and adults like Peter an opportunity to learn job skills and to work for a living in a society where they are more often than not rejected.
>
> Justice and human rights for people with disabilities in the United States and around the world continues to be an issue in the twenty-first century. Communities seeking social justice are starting to push back against *ableism,* the centering and privileging of able-bodied people, and their efforts are gaining traction. Theologian Amos Yong grew up alongside a brother with Down syndrome, and his book *The Bible, Disability, and the Church* is an excellent resource that focuses on what it might mean for Christians in the church to be more inclusive of members with disabilities.

Realities of Global Poverty

Sidney Muisyo explained the paradox of poverty as both oppressive and redemptive. The stark material needs of poverty are oppressive, but also redemptive because of the necessity to trust in God for provision and care. Poverty is something that must be both named and understood. In the naming and defining of poverty, we can begin to deconstruct both its causes and effects, while also working to dismantle its limitations and control.

So what is poverty? Muisyo defined it in its simplest form as the "chronic state of wondering about how you are going to have your most basic needs of food met."[3] In 2005, the World Health Organization defined extreme poverty as when an individual's income goes below $1.25 per day. In 2015, this amount was adjusted to $1.90 a day.[4] In other words, this amount of money has been deemed below what is needed for daily sustenance including food, water, health needs, and the other basic necessities of shelter and care.[5]

We are seeing measurable improvement in some areas of extreme poverty. For example, prior to the turn of the millennium, UNICEF reported that about 29,000 children under the age of five died every day of preventable causes like diarrhea, malaria, neonatal infection, pneumonia, and preterm delivery.[6] In 2018, more than two decades later, this number had decreased to about 15,000 children under five dying a day.[7] The decline of extreme poverty in India from 268 million in 2011 to less than 50 million in 2018 is another illustration of marked progress.[8] There is still much more work to be done.

At the start of 2019 we had reached the lowest percentage of extreme poverty in human history.[9] This progress is to be celebrated. However, as the website Do Something reports in its compilation of facts about poverty, more than one billion people, nearly 15 percent of the world's population, continue to live in abject poverty.[10] And the poverty rates have declined unevenly in different regions, with sub-Saharan Africa still being one of the geographic regions that is most affected by abject poverty.[11] In addition, efforts to eradicate extreme poverty have slowed in recent years because of increasing difficulty reaching the geographic locations where such poverty exists. According to the World Bank, "Access to good schools, health care, electricity, safe water, and other critical services remains elusive for many people, often determined by socioeconomic status, gender, ethnicity, and geography."[12] When poverty is defined more broadly than just monetarily to include consumption, education, and access to basic utilities, the number of people affected increases markedly by approximately 50 percent.[13]

The unequal distribution of wealth (and disproportionate access to opportunities) around the globe remain significant justice issues. About 1 percent of the world's wealthiest people own 45 percent of the world's wealth.[14] Oxfam reports that the wealth divide between the global billionaires and the bottom half of humanity is steadily growing. Between 2009 and 2017, the number of billionaires it took to equal the wealth of the world's poorest 50 percent fell from 380 to 42. The division between rich and poor is among the most extreme in the United States, where

1 percent of the population holds more than 40 percent of the nation's wealth.[15] The wealth gap highlights two primary issues. One is the disproportionate division of wealth, where some people have an overabundance and others are struggling to make ends meet and provide basic necessities for their families. The other issue is that so many of the world's wealthy acquired their wealth at the expense of the poor, who labor under unfair wages and dangerous conditions. These unjust systems and cycles of poverty must be addressed.

Climate Change and Extreme Poverty

Natural disasters have the most severe effects on those living in extreme poverty. Rising temperatures from climate change not only increase natural disasters but also have a negative effect on agriculture. The World Bank confirms that agriculture is among the most important economic sectors in many poor countries. "Unfortunately," they report, "it is also one of the most sensitive to climate change given its dependence on weather conditions, both directly and through climate-dependent stressors (pests, epidemics, and sea level rise)."[16] Climate change's negative effect on agriculture puts many jobs at risk and also affects food prices, malaria rates, water scarcity, and health care costs.

The organization One Day's Wages, founded by evangelical pastor Eugene Cho, looks at five broad ways climate change affects people living in poverty: (1) natural disasters that sink poor communities further into poverty, (2) greater health risks, (3) flooding and coastal erosion, (4) food insecurity, and (5) forced migration.[17] Journalist Gabe Bullard demands a response to the disequilibrium in how the poor are affected by the degradation of the environment: "First, they [those living in poverty] need support for environmentally-sustainable growth around the world. Second, they need wealthier countries to commit to larger cuts in emissions, so there can be room for growth elsewhere."[18] The global development organization Christian Aid, based in the United Kingdom, is one organization addressing the problem head-on by placing significant emphasis on shifting away from the use of fossil fuels and providing aid and humanitarian efforts for countries that have experienced environmental disasters.[19]

Many international development organizations or non-governmental agencies (NGOs) believe the eradication of extreme poverty is a viable possibility. The United Nations made it a goal to eradicate extreme poverty by the year 2030. In addition, the UN and its member state nations committed to reducing by at least half the proportion of men, women, and children of all ages living in poverty in all of its dimensions.[20]

This audacious goal to eradicate extreme poverty began in 2000 when the United Nations released its Millennium Development Goals (MDGs). The eight MDGs included goals primarily focused on health and education equality that was meant to be accomplished by 2015. Though agreed on by all members of the UN, the goals were met with criticism, including that they were too broad and did not involve the local leadership of developing countries (where many of the MDGs efforts were aimed) enough. In addition, the indicators of the MDGs made it difficult to measure whether or not they were being achieved.

Overall, the Millennium Development Goals did get some traction, but it was inconsistent across different countries. In 2015, a new set of United Nations goals were created, called Sustainable Development Goals (SDGs). These goals have a similar emphasis as the MDGs but are focused on sustainability and on using localized leadership to achieve them. The seventeen SDGs, called "The 2030 Agenda for Sustainable Development," have sought to address the criticism that developed nations should also be held accountable for their achievements in response to the gap between the rich and the poor, equal access to education, human rights for all people, and other measurable aspects of development.[21] For example, countries like China, the United States, and India perpetrate some of the greatest abuses to the environment, such as the production of carbon dioxide.[22] Several large, and particularly developed, nations expressed resistance to having development goals about the environment imposed on them. One possible solution for a more effective way to address the production of carbon monoxide would be to observe per capita differences in output and then make worldwide goals to stabilize emissions, with richer nations cutting back to allow developing nations to grow. Some 2016 reports from the

International Energy Agency (IEA) seem to indicate this methodology may be working with carbon emissions decreasing in countries like the United States and China.[23]

However, President Trump's rise to the presidency now puts environmental progress at risk. The United States' resistance to environmental protection became so strong that in 2017, the Trump administration pulled out of the Paris Agreement, in which 185 countries had committed to implementing steps to maintain low levels of global warming, a major focus of the SDGs. As of 2019, the United States produced the second highest amount of carbon dioxide pollution of any other country in the world. The National Resources Defense Council critiqued the Trump administration's decision, saying, "Reflecting the collective belief of nearly every nation on earth that climate change is humanity's war to fight, the Paris Agreement exposes America's climate skeptics— including Trump—as global outliers. In fact, the mobilization of support for climate action across the country and the world provides hope that the Paris Agreement marked a turning point in the fight against climate change."[24]

Many of the SDGs are interrelated and rely on the participation of all countries, not just developing nations. The United States is culpable and should do our part in addressing the realities of climate change and its negative effects on the global poor.

Models of Development

Hundreds of books have been written about the best and most effective methodologies to address extreme poverty and to distribute wealth more equitably among people and nations. Jeffrey Sachs's book *The End of Poverty* is one such book—one that generated a lot of conversation, including a *New York Times* book review titled "Brother, Can You Spare $195 Billion?"[25] In turn, author Nina Munk dedicated an entire book, *Idealist: Jeffrey Sachs and the Quest to End Global Poverty*, to Sachs's ideas about ending poverty, his support of the Millennium Development Goals, and the failure of the Millennium Villages Project.

The Millennium Villages Project (MVP) invested $120 million in an attempt to elevate several African villages out of poverty by infusing massive amounts of targeted assistance. Munk concludes with disillusionment toward Sachs and his ideas. In 2014, prior to the conclusion of the Villages Project, the World Economic Forum said Sachs was both "wrong" and "right" on development: "While some of the Millennium Villages succeeded in helping families improve their health and incomes, the two villages that Munk spent the most time studying—Dertu, Kenya and Ruhiira, Uganda—did not come close to realizing Sachs's vision."[26] Ultimately, Sachs's projects and projected outcomes failed. He did not give enough weight to variables such as political unrest, natural disasters like drought, and other interruptions in his idealistic plan to raise these communities out of poverty. And his model did not include an economic plan that could be sustained once the MDG money ran out.

International Christian development organizations World Vision and Compassion International are both responding to extreme poverty in targeted ways. However, though they have common commitments, their methodologies are very different from each other. While both organizations have programs in child sponsorship, World Vision prides itself on systemic transformational community development, communicating their vision this way: "For every child, life in all its fullness. Our prayer for every heart, the will to make it so."[27] Compassion states its vision as "releasing children from poverty in Jesus' name."[28] World Vision's model asserts that "the most effective way to provide for a child is to address issues at the community level to improve the situation for all children and to reflect God's love" in service.[29] For World Vision, sponsorship monies are invested in development projects that benefit not only the individual sponsored child but the community as a whole through water projects, health programs, educational opportunities, investment in the economic sector and livelihoods, and other aspects of development. In other words, they focus on addressing systemic issues and core causes of poverty. Compassion's child sponsorship model, on the other hand, focuses primarily on directly benefiting an individual child, who will then benefit their community.

As a longtime supporter and former employee of both organizations, I believe there is great merit in both models of development, and both are necessary in the Christian quest to respond to the needs of the poor as Jesus commanded in Matthew 25. Compassion has sometimes been critiqued as being too evangelistically focused. World Vision has sometimes been critiqued as being "not Christian enough" in its systemic approach. Having worked in both contexts, I can say with integrity that each organization is deeply committed to Christian witness and faithfulness in responding to the needs of poor children around the world.

During my interview with Muisyo, I asked him if Compassion's model really works. He responded unabashedly, "Yes, and let me tell you why." In his explanation, he mentioned how the concept of "we" in Latin America, Asia, and Africa is very different from the Western worldview. The prevailing perspective about family and collective identity in these places rests in the African proverb that states, "It takes a village to raise a child." Thus, when one child is uplifted, the entire village is also uplifted. By paying for the school fees of one individual child, later in life that child will be the savings account and support for their many cousins and others within the community. As Muisyo said, "We are the insurance for each other." When there is no medical insurance, the community pulls together and takes care of those in need within their communities. The obligation to offer support and care for the rest of the family and the broader community is inherent in many countries where the most abject poverty exists. He continued, "When you invest in the life of an individual child, you are investing in the insurance policy for that child's entire community."[30]

The University of Chicago did an independent study on the effectiveness of child sponsorships by Compassion International and concluded that child sponsorship does make a difference. Looking at 10,144 children in Compassion's programs over a two-year time period in Bolivia, Guatemala, India, Kenya, the Philippines, and Uganda, the study's authors concluded, "We find large, statistically significant impacts on years of schooling; primary, secondary, and tertiary school completion; and the probability and quality of employment. Early evidence suggests that these impacts are due, in part, to increases in children's aspirations."[31] Because of my years working with World Vision, I already had confidence in the power and efficacy of their transformational community development model. But after meeting with Muisyo and learning more about Compassion's model centered on individual children, I walked away convinced that both approaches are critically important as models of Christian development responding to children living in poverty around the globe.

How the Church Can Respond

What is the role of the Christian church in responding to global poverty? To get engaged! I firmly believe that all of us, as individuals and church communities, are called to respond in some way, shape, or form to the poverty and injustices we experience and to which we are exposed. This is not only a personal conviction, but it is also a biblical mandate found throughout the Scriptures in their admonition to care for the poor, from the Torah through the Prophets and Wisdom Literature, and throughout the teachings of Jesus. Now that we have seen and heard, we cannot just do nothing. Rather we must allow our "hearts to be broken by the things that break the heart of God," as World Vision founder Bob Pierce used to say. Our responses cannot rest in our own strength, but rather in our faithful attempts to be obedient to God's calling to respond to the needs of the least of these. Muisyo, in talking about the realities of being poor, reminded me that wealth creates the "deceit of self-sufficiency." Those who are poor don't suffer from this deceit. Those of us who are wealthy can learn from the poor how to depend on God and not on our own strength.[32]

With the many complexities of global poverty and the vast array of possible solutions, some effective and others not, what then can we do and how should we respond? Here are a few postures and steps that can help. First, money is a necessary reality in addressing global poverty, but as Jeffrey Sachs learned, throwing money at the problem is not a silver bullet. Poverty does not lend itself to simplistic approaches.

Second, the challenge of food must be studied and understood. Providing food to the poor does not create sustainable long-term solutions. A long-term and sustainable economic model must be addressed. Systemic causes of poverty must be adequately addressed.

Finally, we must be willing to honestly look at how we are complicit in contributing to global poverty and to acknowledge our interconnectedness. The poor are no longer distant and far away; our individual daily choices affect those living in poverty around the world. Sustainable purchasing and understanding the way our choices affect the global poor is critical.

We are no longer ignorant of the abuses of sweatshops and forced labor. We cannot ignore the way our consumption affects people in the world around us. In the article "Who Gets to Eat? Consumption, Complicity, and Poverty," Shannon Jung cites the teachings of theologian Kathryn Tanner who asserts, "God gives unconditionally; God gives to all; and that God wills a community of mutual benefit."[33]

Several organizations and ministries provide great places to get started. You can visit https://worldpoverty.io/ to view the World Poverty Clock, which shows the number of people living in extreme poverty around the world in real time as some people escape from it and others enter into it. This program uses public income distribution, production, and consumption data provided by the United Nations, the World Bank, and other international organizations.

One Day's Wages specifically works toward ending extreme poverty around the world by focusing on ten primary issues including slavery, water, women's empowerment and health, teaching job skills, and education. They partner with a number of other organizations, including World Relief and World Vision; you can learn more about their important work and how to get involved at www.onedayswages.org /our-work/.

If you've ever wondered what the connection is between the shoes you wear and slavery, you can go to End Slavery Now's website to see if the products you purchase contribute to the slavery supply chain. The website includes a series of questions about what's on your plate, the size of your home, the car you drive, the electronics you use, and other areas of consumption to identify links to global slavery and forced labor (see www.endslaverynow.org/act/action-library/find-your-slavery-footprint). End Slavery Now also has some valuable tips on how to start shopping more ethically (see www.endslaverynow.org/blog/articles/how-to-start-shopping-ethically). International Justice Mission (IJM) is another organization doing great work to end poverty and oppression, and they provide opportunities for Christians to host a "freedom Sunday" at your church to contribute toward the eradication of modern-day slavery. Visit www.ijm.org to find out more.

Also consider the power of government in provoking change. Consider what type of political advocacy might address the issues. Advocate for policies (local and otherwise) that promote transparency in consumer market chains to help identify areas where people are being exploited. Consider advocacy for just policies around climate policy reform. Partner with organizations like IJM and World Vision to advocate for policies that protect the rights of women and girls and help provide relief for those trapped in human trafficking.

Finally, consider sponsoring a child through World Vision (www.worldvision.org) or Compassion International (www.compassion.com). Both organizations do great work, and an individual child and community could be blessed by your investment in their lives and future.

For Further Study

Banerjee, Abhijit, and Esther Duflo. *Poor Economics: A Radical Rethinking of the Way to Fight Global Poverty*. New York: Public Affairs, 2012.

Bourke, Dale Hanson. *The Skeptic's Guide to Global Poverty*. England: Authentic, 2007.

Matheson Miller, Michael, dir. *Poverty, Inc.* Grand Rapids: Action Institute, 2014. See www.povertyinc.org/.

Thacker, Justin. *Global Poverty: A Theological Guide*. Norwich, UK: SCM Press, 2017.

- Look up several Bible verses on poverty. What do the Scriptures teach about caring for the poor among us? Some popular verses about poverty include Isaiah 58 and Matthew 25 if you need a place to start.

- What do the Hebrew Scriptures tell us about God's love for those who are in slavery? How is justice reflected in those passages?

- Is there a particular aspect of poverty in this chapter that you found moving? Have you come face to face with extreme poverty or someone struggling with a lack of access to resources to make ends meet? What was your experience? How did it affect you?

- Small changes every day can have an effect on the environment or the consumer chain. What are some changes you can make in your life? What small changes do you think your church could do to help?

- In the section about things you can do, did any opportunities particularly strike you? Might you as an individual, or your group, commit to making one change that could contribute toward the eradication of poverty or ending modern-day slavery?

4

Domestic Poverty

He raises the poor from the dust
and lifts the needy from the ash heap;
he seats them with princes
and has them inherit a throne of honor.

1 SAMUEL 2:8

I'LL NEVER FORGET THE NIGHT Anthony, whom we called AJ, came to us. My husband was away on a business trip, but we had been on a waiting list to open our home to an infant or a child in need of short-term care. I had a bit of trepidation about what it might mean to rearrange our lives around the needs of a little one. Then I received a phone call saying that there was a baby about eighteen months old who needed a home. Could we take him that night?

My heart's response was yes from the moment I picked up the phone. A social worker brought him to our home with only a grocery bag of belongings. The bag was full of numerous medications because of his severe allergies and breathing difficulties, and one extra diaper, and virtually nothing else. I was overwhelmed by the poverty in this child's life.

The time we had AJ was the best and hardest of my life. It gave me a firsthand encounter with domestic poverty in the city of Chicago. AJ was a crack baby. While he didn't show signs of cognitive impairment, some of the behaviors he exhibited such as night terrors, mood swings, and acts of aggression (slapping and hitting) indicated he had experienced trauma in his first year of life.

Over the following months, AJ had numerous doctors' appointments and was treated regularly by Lawndale Christian Health Center through the Christian Community Health Fellowship program. The Fellowship program allows for the urban poor to receive excellent medical treatment while only needing to pay what they can afford. When they don't have money, they are invited to contribute in other ways. I was humbled by the care and attentiveness of the doctors and staff. During one visit I met a man who was there for treatment and was sweeping the waiting room. I learned that patients are often given the option of contributing to their medical costs by engaging in tasks and work that helps the clinic in their daily operations. The man seemed proud of his contribution and grateful for the medical care Lawndale provided. Because of unemployment, he would not have been able to pay for his medical care in any other way.

AJ had an older sister who was also born when her mother actively used cocaine, but she was not as lucky. His sister had severe disabilities and required almost around-the-clock care. Only about a year older, she lived with their grandmother, who didn't have the capacity and resources to also take care of AJ. She loved him but was too poor to keep him. And, as a single mother herself, she couldn't take care of her own children and a special needs child, while also working and being attentive to an infant. During AJ's months with us, we had family weekends where we would all get together so that the kids could play and spend time visiting.

The ministry that gave AJ to us for care was similar to a foster care program called Safe Families for Children in Chicago. Safe Families for Children is designed to keep children out of the foster care system and, if possible, with their biological families. It is an alternative to the foster care system, where there are often reports of children and youth getting lost in the system, experiencing abuse, and being isolated from their communities and families of origin. Families served by Safe Families for

Children might be going through unemployment, homelessness, hospitalization, incarceration, substance abuse treatment, or other interruptions in life that could impede the care of a child.[1] Safe Families for Children now has more than one hundred chapters all around the United States that seek to provide circles of support by uniting churches, friends, and families to come alongside parents and families in crisis. Most people living in poverty in the United States do not have infrastructures of support and thus often suffer from cycles of poverty that place unbearable burdens on them and greatly impede their ability to keep their families together in safe and sustainable environments.

With AJ's maternal grandmother's support, we began to pursue the possibility of adopting AJ and having him become a permanent member of our family. The proximity to his grandmother and sister would have allowed for him to still be directly connected to his family of origin, while also benefiting from the resources, ability, and desire our family had to care for him as one of our own. AJ's mother had abandoned him and given up custody, but in the adoption process, we learned his paternal grandparents wanted to raise him. Prior to that, we weren't even sure they knew about AJ. I will never forget the day we said goodbye. AJ screamed as he was carried out of our home and put into the car that would take him to his new home and to his family. I wept with a depth of loss that hit me deep in my gut. Even now, more than a decade later, the thought brings tears to my eyes. I felt like I lost my right arm. I know it was the right thing to do. I don't doubt that his grandparents love him and have cared for him even better than I would have been able to do. They are his flesh and blood. Knowing that they love him provided some comfort to my soul. But saying goodbye was the hardest thing I've ever done.

The Realities of Poverty

Poverty in the United States looks very different from global poverty. The core issues are less often about whether or not adequate food is available, and more about children and families suffering from malnutrition because of diet and unhealthy food options. Major concerns in domestic poverty include limited financial resources to make ends meet. Single parents often have to work multiple jobs and are still unable to make a living wage. This type of poverty often plays out in limited access to education and health care, not receiving an adequate salary, and other limitations of resources that keep individuals from making enough money to flourish and thrive and adequately support their families.

Poverty USA has compiled a list of facts on domestic poverty, and the statistics are stark. In 2019, the US poverty threshold for a family of four was $24,000 per year. And in 2016, the number of Americans living below that threshold totaled 40.6 million people. About 20 percent of children living in families in the United States live below the poverty threshold. What does that mean for the daily life of these men, women, and children? In 2016, just over half of these households, 12.3 percent of Americans, lived with food insecurity and an inability to provide adequate food to meet their family's needs.[2] Limited access to adequate food, health care, and education are three of the primary manifestations of domestic poverty.

People of color and women are among those most vulnerable to domestic poverty in the United States. Single women who are the head of the household with no husband present represent over a third of the poor in America. Young adults without a high school diploma represent about the same percentage of the US poor at 31 percent. Lack of education and poverty have a direct correlation.[3] The majority of the poor in the United States are people of color. Just over 10 percent of white people experience poverty in the United States, but those percentages increase to 23.4 percent for Hispanic people, 26.2 percent for black Americans, and 27.6 percent for Native Americans.[4] Why does poverty seem to so disproportionately affect communities of color in the United States?

Racism, white supremacy, and unjust systems that disproportionately impact communities of color all contribute to the unequal access to wealth between white people and other ethnic groups. Consider the wage and income gaps that exist between white Americans and Americans of color. A report by the Federal Reserve compared a number of factors that contribute to total wealth, and a sample of the numbers included average income. White Americans' median income came in at about $61,000 with black Americans' coming in at around $35,000. Nearly one in five African American families has zero or negative net worth.[5] There are a number of factors that contribute to income differences, like working in different industries, educational attainment, and part-time work status. Unexplained differences that are harder to measure were also included in the Federal Reserve study—things like the quality of schools, employer discrimination, and differences in career opportunities.[6]

When considering domestic poverty, we must acknowledge the effects of numerous historical and current discriminatory policies like President Franklin Delano Roosevelt's GI Bill of Rights. The GI Bill provided loans for homes at very reasonable interest rates for veterans returning from World War II. Because the bill was implemented by individual states, discriminatory practices ensued. Significant capital and resources were invested in white veterans, thus disproportionately benefiting them through the generational impact of financial resources and home ownership. The unintended consequences of the GI Bill were that "black veterans and their families were denied their fair share of the multigenerational, enriching impact of homeownership and economic security that the G.I. Bill conferred on a majority of white veterans, their children, and their grandchildren."[7] Historic racism and injustice contribute to the disparity in economic status we see between white Americans, black Americans, and other communities of color today. A 2016 report by the Institute for Policy Studies titled "The Ever-Growing Gap" says African American and Latino families won't match the income and net worth of whites for centuries unless something changes.[8]

Not only are communities of color particularly vulnerable to the realities of domestic poverty, but various geographic regions in the United

States also have depressed economies, limited jobs, and other factors that contribute to the susceptibility of their communities to poverty. Urban centers have higher rates of unemployment, lower school attendance, and higher crime than rural areas. As a result, childhood poverty is generally higher in urban areas as compared to rural areas.[9] Southern states such as Mississippi, Louisiana, Arkansas, Alabama, and New Mexico have the highest percentages of people living in poverty in the United States.[10] Poor white people often reside in rural communities in the mountainous regions of the east coast and other parts of the country where industrial plants like steel mills and coal mines used to provide steady jobs, but where work over the past decades has been hard to come by. In many of these communities, the poor and middle class, predominantly white, working Americans fueled Donald Trump's ascent to the presidency because of their concerns about job limitations, economic downturns, and American trade being outsourced to the international community.

Prior to the 1900s, most white Americans thought "being poor" reflected one's work ethic, or the lack thereof. With the rise of capitalism in America and increased consumerism, a distinction between the deserving and the undeserving poor flourished. Unless one was disabled, sick, or a child, the thinking went, poverty directly resulted from a person's life choices and was viewed as their fault. The belief for many white Americans was that opportunity for wealth was available to all. During the Great Depression, with the unprecedented speed of job loss, poverty wasn't necessarily viewed as a moral wrong. However, during the Depression, receiving help from the government or aid groups was viewed as degrading, and poverty relief became increasingly criticized. People who needed assistance were viewed as lazy, undeserving, and irresponsible. These presuppositions were especially true when projected toward groups like single mothers, immigrants, and people of color.[11]

In the 1960s, a resurgence on the study of poverty began creating a "culture of poverty" wherein social scientists identified factors outside a lack of employment that contributed to it. James T. Patterson was one of these scientists who recognized some of the same principles that are also associated with systemic poverty. He argues that things like racism and severe economic pressures drove people into inescapable poverty.

Presidencies from Lyndon B. Johnson to Ronald Reagan declared war on poverty. As a part of his Great Society initiatives, Johnson launched a number of programs focused on solving the symptoms of poverty. However, Johnson's programs did not necessarily address the structural problems associated with poverty such as lack of education, poor medical care, and unequal income distribution.[12] By the 1980s, according to Reagan, America had won the war on poverty. Statistics and the realities continuing to affect the urban and rural poor across America tell a different story.

Government programs are only one critical tool that must be employed in attempts to eradicate domestic poverty. We also need holistic solutions that provide charity while responding to symptoms of poverty and that address systemic injustices that cause it. There must, for example, be an awareness of the cycles of poverty, which can affect every area of life: education, employment, income, housing, transportation, spiritual health, physical health, emotional needs, and nutrition.[13] Charities of the past and many charities and services today often only seek to rectify the symptoms of poverty rather than acknowledging the root causes. Differences in education and access to services severely limit the opportunity of the residents in the inner city and rural environments. For example, when students go hungry or get inadequate nutritional resources, they are unable to focus in school. If they are unable to focus in school, they will not perform well on tests and other performance measures. If they don't perform well on academic measurements, their job opportunities will be limited. If they can't earn an adequate income, they will be unable to support themselves and their families in the future. This is just one small glimpse of what cycles of poverty might look like and how families can get caught in them. Many factors do not allow people to simply "work hard" to escape poverty.

Suicide and the Crisis of Despair

Blessed are the poor in spirit,
for theirs is the kingdom of heaven.

MATTHEW 5:3

When writing about tragedy, brokenness, and human struggles, the pain and suffering behind the statistics is very real. People living in challenging situations with limited or nonexistent financial resources, who are vulnerable to other crises and tragic life circumstances, are also vulnerable to despair and hopelessness. However, depression and suicidal thoughts are not limited to those living in economic poverty. People magazine did a feature story in their October 28, 2019 issue highlighting the prevalence of mental health issues including suicide. In 2017, 47,173 people died by suicide; 69.7 percent of them were white men.[14] Suicide and the crisis of despair is another type of domestic poverty.

In November 2018, the *Washington Post* editorial board published an article titled "America Is Losing Ground to Death and Despair," highlighting how "life expectancy overall in the United States fell for the second time in three years in 2017, driven largely by a surge of drug overdoses and suicide."[15] The situation has been deemed an "opioid epidemic," and one of the main variations of drugs contributing to these deaths is illegally manufactured fentanyl. In October 2017, President Trump declared the opioid crisis a national emergency.[16] For the millions caught in the prison of addiction, the existence of this tragedy not only demands a compassionate response but also intervention and accountability in addressing the primary causes of the crisis.

In 2017, more than forty-seven thousand people took their lives in the United States by suicide. An additional 1.4 million people in the United States attempted suicide.[17] Over the past few years, well-known and respected actors and national personalities such as Robin Williams, Anthony Bourdain, and Kate Spade shocked the world with their self-inflicted deaths. Despair and hopelessness are not limited to those with financial difficulties but can affect anyone who has personal struggles.

How are Christians responding? In March 2019, Faithwire published a piece addressing "the reason behind recent surge [*sic*] in suicides and drug-related deaths" and examining "deeper problems that go beyond mental illness."[18] Drawing on the work and research of mental health professional and

Dallas Theological Seminary graduate Carly Graham, the article identified social isolation as one of the leading causes of the despair being experienced across the United States today.

Kimberly McDonald, a social worker cited in the article, lost her father to suicide in 2010. She explains how current American culture often leads people to despair: "We are a society that criticizes and lacks compassion, integrity, and empathy."[19] The author of the piece, Carly Hoilman, concurs and identifies what she sees as most needed: "Hope is the opposite of despair. If anything, the latest data reflect a nation in desperate need, not for escape, but hope."[20] How do Hoilman and others recommend addressing these realities of despair? "Christians find a message of eternal hope in the person of Jesus Christ, and the Bible is filled with verses that describe the hope we have in God," she writes.[21] Entering into a healthy community, being honest about struggles with friends and family, and meeting with professional counselors and mental health professionals are resources for people who are struggling with emotional distress, depression, and feelings of hopelessness or despair.

The American Foundation for Suicide Prevention (AFSP) provides valuable information and resources about suicide, including warning signs and risk factors, statistics, and options for treatment.[22] AFSP reminds us that there is no single cause to suicide: "It most often occurs when stressors exceed current coping abilities of someone suffering from a mental health condition." In many cases, the mental health conditions have not been diagnosed or have not been able to be adequately addressed.

Christians looking for resources about suicide might consider the anthology *Suicide: A Christian Response*. The thirty-plus chapters include reflections from physicians, lawyers, academics, pastors, philosophers, and theologians. It is an important resource in addressing both biblical and theological reflections from a Christian perspective. Another helpful resource is the revised and expanded *Grieving a Suicide* by Al Hsu, which does not shy away from difficult questions about the loss of a loved one by suicide.[23] After his father's death, Hsu experienced anger, deep shock, a sense of betrayal, abandonment, guilt, and frustration with himself. In sharing so honestly about his own loss and grief, Hsu reminds us that even in the deepest pain and loss, "you are not walking this path alone."[24]

TIME magazine's piece "States of Vulnerability" follows photojournalist Matt Black during his 2016–2017 "Geography of Poverty" visits to impoverished communities across the United States. Black's photographs bring to life the growing gap between the rich and the poor and the increasing difficulties that keep those living in cycles of poverty unable to break out of them. The photos are accompanied by an essay from Wes Moore, an author, combat veteran, social entrepreneur, and the CEO of Robin Hood, one of the largest antipoverty organizations in the United States. Moore directly combats the belief that poverty is an affliction that is earned through laziness or indifference and that if you work hard enough, a better life will come your way, explaining, "The promise of America says that if you work hard—if you sacrifice—you, or at least your children, will succeed. But too many Americans today are sacrificing into an empty void, with no returns for generations. At a certain point, it's not sacrifice anymore—it's just suffering." He continues, "We're lied to about how quickly and how drastically our industries are changing, and how people are being left behind. We're told people in poverty should just 'get a job.' We're told poor people in America's heartland should blame poor immigrants in America's border states for their poverty."[25] Rather, there are tens of thousands of people living across the United States who struggle to make ends meet despite working several jobs, whose lives are destroyed with one medical diagnosis, who will never be able to afford college, and whose children will only continue the cycle of poverty no matter how hard they work.

The increasing wealth gap between the rich and the poor and the chains of poverty in the United States cannot continue to be ignored. Despite the United States being the wealthiest country in the world and having higher quality resources than many other countries, including clean water, broad access to health care, and high levels of sanitation, life expectancy is still lower than you would expect, and even lower in places like Appalachia or the Mississippi Delta where severe poverty exists. The daily cost of living, low wages, and a lack of affordable housing have each contributed to the poverty found in communities across all fifty states. These findings do not diminish the need of those who live in abject poverty abroad, but they do remind us that we also have a spiritual obligation to care for the poor living in close proximity to us, sometimes right next door.[26]

The Challenges of Health Care

One of the greatest debates during the Obama administration related to what role the government should play in providing health care to its citizens. Health is strongly related to income, which means people living in poverty not only have higher mortality rates and increased prevalence of disease and acute illness, but they also have more emotional and behavioral problems.[27] Simply put, the wealthier someone is, the longer they will live. In fact, according to a 2011 report, those in the highest income group in the United States live almost seven years longer than those living in the lowest income group.[28] Black babies have twice the infant mortality rate to that of white babies. Diabetes is twice as prevalent in poor adults than in those who are affluent. Children living in poverty are more likely to have unhealthy levels of lead in their blood than other children. These are just some of the indications that show how poverty adversely affects health.

The main goal of the Affordable Care Act (ACA), passed during Obama's presidency, is to provide affordable health insurance for all people, but especially for those living below the poverty line, and to expand Medicaid. ACA does this partly through its aims to make it difficult for insurance companies to drop a patient because of a medical condition and to end discrimination when it comes to people with preexisting conditions. The program requires people to have insurance coverage, as long as it is affordable (less than 8 percent of their income), and provides subsidies for those who meet the income requirement. The mandated requirement of having insurance helps offset the total cost of the program. In other words, both healthy and unhealthy people are required to buy insurance, which, theoretically, should keep costs down. Having previously applied this model during its major health care overhaul, the state of Massachusetts was able to insure two-thirds of the previously uninsured and lower healthcare costs by 50 percent relative to national trends. An argument for this approach is that everyone uses health care services and very few people can avoid the health care system, and one of its strengths is how the individual mandate reduces uncompensated costs (with nearly 57 percent of health care services provided to those without insurance). Some argue that people are more likely to stay uninsured when there are more sources of uncompensated care (like public hospitals).[29]

In an article on the ACA, Reverend Carol McVetty, interim executive minister of the American Baptist Churches of Metro Chicago, talked about how it has affected her community. "The congregation I pastored for many years worked hard to give rides to the doctor when needed. Well-established refugees helped newer ones navigate the medical system and translated at doctor appointments. . . . Hours and hours of volunteer effort," McVetty said. "Church members take meals to the sick and visit in the hospital. We often host or conduct health education events. But prayer, pastoral care, and loving friends can't replace medical care."[30] McVetty and many other clergy argue that the ACA is a necessity in ensuring Americans have access to health care.

On the other side of the equation, arguments against ACA include that it is unconstitutional to require individuals to have health care.[31] In addition, when the act was passed, some people were affected negatively, narrowly missing the requirements for government subsidies. Others, such as those in their fifties and sixties who are self-employed, had to change providers because certain doctors and hospitals were no longer in their network.[32] One of the major arguments against ACA is the cost of the program and the sustainability of its funding. The anticipated total cost of it is $828 billion over ten years (2010–2019). Though there are action items in place to secure this funding, people worry about the effectiveness of the provisions.[33]

Some Christian groups, predominantly white evangelicals, maintain theological and ideological beliefs that oppose the intervention of the government in health care issues. In addition, some Christians view sickness as a means to bring people to Christ. State senator Mark Green from Tennessee told a church group, "Sickness is one of the main avenues that bring people to religion," adding that, in the Gospels, "every person who came to Christ came to Christ with a physical need. It was either hunger or a disease." Green believes that the ACA did a "great injustice" in helping people recover their health, because it "limited the Christian church's role" and will keep sick individuals from having the opportunity "to come to a saving knowledge of who God is." People who got sick, he said, would now look for help from the government instead of from God.[34]

Christ certainly cared for the sick and the poor. However, he did not do so by denying them access to whatever they needed to make them well; rather he gave them direct access to the greatest health care of all by providing personal encounters with himself, the Great Physician, who could respond to both their physical and spiritual needs and make them fully well.

The Christian community has provided alternatives to public health care through health care sharing ministries (HCSMs). Health care sharing programs have been around for years but saw a large spike after 2014.[35] Participants in these programs pay money every month to cover each other's medical bills, and are exempt from paying the uninsured penalty under the ACA while they're enrolled. HCSMs can sometimes result in lower hospital costs because cash (or other) payments are readily available. However, they are much more specific about what kind of medical expenses they will or will not cover, preventative care is not always covered, and they will often not accept those with preexisting conditions. In addition, complaints are not regulated by any state-run insurance board. Providers of healthcare often prefer HCSMs because of the promptness and guarantee of payment, however, clients do not always receive that same guarantee that their medical bills will be covered.[36] Anthony Hopp, spokesperson for Samaritan Ministries, says: "With all the talk of healthcare reform and, 'What do we do? How do we fix this mess?' the solution will not come from regulations and mandates. . . . We're going to have to think biblically."[37] Shared health care opportunities are one alternative option for health care in addition to ACA and other private programs made available in the United States.

Is ACA effective at achieving its stated goals? If the primary goal was to insure as many people as possible, then it could be deemed successful. From 2010 to 2016, the number of uninsured dropped by about twenty million and the percentage of uninsured fell from 16 percent in 2010 to 9 percent in 2016. Due to a 2012 Supreme Court ruling, states are not required to expand their Medicaid program, and nineteen states have opted out of expanding theirs. However, Medicaid's enrollment has exceeded growth expectations, expanding by sixteen million people since 2013. And analyses have shown that in states where Medicaid enrollment has grown, there is a significant decline in the number of uninsured. In some areas, this access to health care has granted patients earlier screenings of diseases and access to medicine and mental health care.[38]

When I think about AJ, his having been born into poverty, and his health challenges, there is not a doubt in my mind that he would not have had adequate health care for his breathing complications and allergies if it were not for government-subsidized programs. His health realities were so severe that his asthma and breathing difficulties could have even led to premature death if untreated.

Education and Poverty

Education, like access to health care, is gravely affected by poverty. Statistics show that the higher a person's education, the greater the likelihood is that they will achieve a stable economic future. For example, high school graduation rates for Hispanic and black students are already 20 percent lower than for other ethnic groups, and poverty rates within those communities greatly exceed national averages.

In many communities around the country, the education systems are funded by property taxes. This builds in an inherent bias toward communities with wealth and resources, as these communities can afford to pay for the best teachers, textbooks, study materials, and technology. Poor communities often rely on their underpaid teachers to provide basic school supplies and even to supplement heat for their classrooms. Lack of education significantly limits upward mobility and keeps children and youth who are born into poverty caught in cycles of deprivation where they have limited opportunities to escape.[39]

A Christian Response to Poverty

With education inequity, health care struggles, drug epidemics, and depression all contributing to problems affecting communities across America, how are followers of Jesus called to respond? A Christian response to poverty demands that followers of Jesus thoughtfully and diligently seek to understand the causes of poverty and why it exists. In 2017, a study highlighted by the *Washington Post* showed that 46 percent of all Christians believe that poverty is due to a lack of effort on the individual's part.[40] This belief is fundamentally not true. Certainly, personal responsibility is a contributing factor and component, but it is by far not the only factor, and perhaps not even the most significant. As discussed above, leading causes of poverty in the United States include, but are not limited to, family systems, inequality, lack of access to education, inadequate health care, conflict, violence, and cycles of poverty.

A Christian response to the poor needs to be more comprehensive and has to begin with remembering that all people are God's creation and deserving of concern, compassion, and care. Often, poverty services fall short of caring for the whole person, giving them only some food and clothes without addressing some of the deeper issues. People living in material poverty and people with great wealth similarly struggle with a lack of hope. Responding holistically to both people's spiritual and material needs is the only way to engage with the poor from a biblical perspective. In responding to material poverty, there needs to be a pursuit of long-term good through the channels of relief (providing food and shelter), rehabilitation (returning to pre-crisis life), and development (improving lives beyond previous experience).

In addition to Christians needing a more holistic understanding of domestic poverty, they must seek to respond materially to the needs of people within their community. Churches and other Christian communities have a critical role to play in local economic development and in empowering communities.[41] The urban poor are increasingly being forced out of cities and into the suburbs because of gentrification and a return of populations to city centers. This means suburban Christians will have increasing numbers of direct encounters with the poor, many of whom may even be their neighbors. When individuals, communities, and churches work together through creative means and active engagement, systemic poverty can be constructively addressed. Churches have the opportunity to offer a great expanse of services to people within their population who are poor; after-school tutoring or childcare, English classes or job-skills training, or help for new mothers are just a few places to get started.[42] Organizations like the Christian Community Development Association (CCDA) provide great resources and materials for what asset-based development might look like within impoverished communities.

In addition to church-based responses to poverty, the government does have an important role to play. Social service programs started and developed significantly by the Roosevelt and Johnson administrations provide critical resources in combatting domestic poverty. The Center for American Progress identified ten steps that could be taken to "cut poverty and grow the middle class," including creating jobs; raising the minimum wage; increasing the earned income tax credit for childless workers; supporting pay equity; providing paid leave and paid sick days; establishing work schedules that work with family needs; investing in affordable, high-quality childcare and early education; expanding Medicaid; reforming the criminal justice system; and finally "doing no harm."[43]

There is much work to be done in responding to the significant gaps in education and income and in increasing the number of opportunities for communities of color and other at-risk communities. As the wealthiest country in the world, may Americans, and particularly Christians in the United States, be compelled to play a greater role in responding to Jesus' commandments regarding the "least of these" (Matt 25:31-46).

For Further Study

Barry, John D. *Jesus' Economy: A Biblical View of Poverty, the Currency of Love, and a Pattern for Lasting Change.* New Kensington, PA: Whitaker House, 2019.

Blank, Rebecca. *Changing Inequality.* Oakland: University of California Press, 2011.

Bradley, Anne, and Art Lindsley, eds. *For the Least of These: A Biblical Answer to Poverty.* Grand Rapids: Zondervan, 2015.

Corbett, Steve, and Brian Fikkert. *When Helping Hurts: How to Alleviate Poverty Without Hurting the Poor . . . and Yourself.* Chicago: Moody Publishers, 2014.

Feliciano, Kathryn. *Love Your Neighbor: Restoring Dignity, Breaking the Cycle of Poverty.* McLean, VA: The Institute for Faith, Work & Economics, 2016.

Lester, Terence. *I See You: How Love Opens Our Eyes to Invisible People.* Downers Grove, IL: InterVarsity Press, 2019.

Sider, Richard J. *Just Generosity: A New Vision for Overcoming Poverty in America.* Grand Rapids: Baker Books, 2007.

Wilson-Hartgrove, Jonathan. *The Awakening of Hope: Why We Practice a Common Faith.* Grand Rapids: Zondervan, 2012.

Questions for Discussion

- What does poverty mean to you? How have you seen poverty affect your life or the life of a person around you? How have you seen poverty affect your community?

- How does your church community engage in authentic fellowship with those who live in poverty?

- What are ways you can engage with changing the systemic challenges currently in place? Are there local laws or policies that create barriers for those in poverty that you can help change or remove?

- There are a number of ways that Jesus engages with the poor in the New Testament. How have you viewed those texts in the past? Do you feel like your understanding of those has changed?

- Were there elements of this chapter that made you uncomfortable about the way the poor are treated? Or aspects of what is written here that you don't agree with? Why or why not?

PART 3

Race

White Supremacy and American Christianity

Then Peter began to speak: "I now realize how true it is that
God does not show favoritism but accepts from every nation
the one who fears him and does what is right. You know
the message God sent to the people of Israel, announcing
the good news of peace through Jesus Christ, who is Lord of all."

ACTS 10:34-36

IN JANUARY 2017, I had the privilege of preaching during Spiritual Renewal Week at John Brown University in Arkansas.[1] When I received the invitation, I thought the school was affiliated with the abolitionist hero John Brown who played an important role in leading antislavery protests during "Bleeding Kansas" before his raid on Harpers Ferry.[2] But that's not the case. Rather, the college is named after John E. Brown, an evangelist, educator, and author "who recognized the need for an academic institution that would prepare young people to serve Christ."[3]

Just prior to this visit, I had been spending time with one of my mentors, Barbara Williams-Skinner. She founded, with her late husband Tom Skinner, the Skinner Leadership Institute, which creates and empowers leaders in the church around the United States. As the first executive director of the Congressional Black Caucus, Barbara advocates for African American interests to be esteemed in DC, while keeping Christ at the center of her vocation and ministry.[4] I have heard Barbara tell many stories of walking the halls of Congress praying for our nation's leaders and have been learning from her leadership since we were first introduced by John Perkins.

When Barbara learned I was going to be preaching at John Brown, she asked, "You are going to talk about white supremacy, aren't you?" Preaching about the legitimacy of Black Lives Matter to a multiethnic community just outside DC is one thing. Talking about white supremacy in a predominantly conservative white context in rural Arkansas is a whole different scenario. I made a commitment to Barbara that I would be bold in my message and address white supremacy, but inside, I was scared to death.

When I arrived in Arkansas, I found the community to be welcoming and wonderfully receptive to ideas about spiritual formation and growing closer to Christ in our Christian journey. The first day, I preached about God's call on my life and how we are each uniquely called and gifted. I then preached a second sermon deeply rooted in Scripture about God's heart for both righteousness and justice. In between messages, I had the opportunity to spend time in classes on campus and get to know the students a little bit. I love that the school is committed to both education and discipleship.

On the last day, I knew it was time to preach the message that God calls us to be reconciled to all people; to lament the sins of racism, sexism, xenophobia, and other injustices; and to be honest about the deeply rooted white supremacy in American society. My heart pounded in my chest, as I sensed that some of the things I was going to talk about would be deeply challenging for the students and faculty present, myself included. John Brown University is predominantly white. The few students of color are mostly international students. And the very small number of domestic students of color face a lot of pressure within the community to "carry the weight" of addressing realities of white privilege and latent racism.

In my message, I began to call out how today's society has been built on unjust systems from which many white Americans continue to benefit today. I talked about how Native Americans were often converted to Christianity so that whites could take their land and confiscate their resources, with many Native people being moved to "prayer towns" where they were taught about God while also giving up access to the land where their communities had lived for centuries. I also talked about slavery and how much of the capital invested in the Southern states during the antebellum period was slave labor.

The chapel was packed. The acknowledgment and truth spoken of past sins toward communities of color seemed to have a palpable effect on the room. And then, seemingly out of nowhere, a student near the front of the room stood up and shouted, "Lies! What you are speaking is all lies!" He went on to say that it was not true that slave labor contributed to the economy of the South and that racism today does not exist. I don't recall exactly how I responded in that moment. But I'm told that I was both calm and firm, essentially asserting that what he was saying is not true but that I was willing to talk to him after the chapel if he wanted to discuss it. During this encounter, it was as if there was a spirit of resistance in the room that had been spoken out loud by this student. But I truly believe the spirit of truth prevailed.

I tell this story because whatever was inside this young white man caused him to have a visceral reaction to hearing about how centering whiteness has caused great oppression and continues to limit the opportunities of people of color. The internal resistance he experienced was so significant that he couldn't remain quiet but rather shouted out in a chapel of a thousand people that white privilege and white supremacy is a lie and doesn't exist. His reaction demonstrates the resistance that many white people experience when we are exposed to the truth of our privilege, the inherent supremacy of whiteness in most of the systems within our society, and the ways white people uniquely benefit.

After the service, several of the students of color lined up to talk to me. They said it was one of the first times the sin of racism had been addressed publicly at the university and thanked me for acknowledging some of the realities they live with every day.

Racism in the United States

Gone are the days of thousands of lynchings, as in the early twentieth
century. And it has been a long time even since the 1981 lynching of
Michael Donald in Mobile, Alabama.[5] But the underlying racist tendencies of these horrors against black bodies continue to exist today.
One of the questions we must ask is why the deaths of black and brown
bodies seem to matter so much less to our society than when white
people are killed.

Standing with a group of leaders led by Bryan Stevenson of Equal
Justice Initiative (EJI) over a hilltop plot of land in Montgomery, Alabama, I learned of the National Memorial for Peace and Justice that
would be built there. Holding hands and praying together, we dedicated
the land in a spirit of both repentance for the sins of racism and remembrance of the thousands of lives that had been lost at the hands of racial
violence and white supremacy. Opened to the public in early 2018, the
memorial is dedicated to the "more than 4,400 African American men,
women, and children who were hanged, burned alive, shot, drowned,
and beaten to death by white mobs between 1877 and 1950." The dedi-
cation of the memorial continues, "Millions more fled the South as
refugees from racial terrorism, profoundly impacting the entire nation.
Until now, there has been no national memorial acknowledging the
victims of racial terror lynchings."[6]

Racism in twenty-first-century America is a reality. Acknowledging
racism means understanding that white people hold social and institutional power over people of color.[7] The growing face of white supremacy,
which seems to have resurfaced in the public square after being less
acknowledged for decades, must be identified and rooted out. I heard
the legendary black preacher and pastor James Forbes say that "racism
is the primary center of all injustice."[8] In our cultural analysis of racism,
however, it is so often seen as something that is peripheral, rather than
a core issue that must be addressed. Eddie S. Glaude Jr., chair of the
Department of African American Studies and the James S. McDonnell
Distinguished University Professor of African American Studies at

Princeton University, responded to Forbes, saying, "We must demand that racism be recentered. . . . [As one] confronts the reality of the racial issue, we are confronting the reality of oneself."[9]

Daniel Hill's *White Awake* summarizes four interlocking facets of racism: (1) "racism reflecting a social construct created for the purposes of consolidating white power," (2) "racism as the extension of the ideology of white supremacy," (3) "a narrative of racial difference was created to support this ideology of white superiority, which measures human value based on proximity to whiteness," and (4) "the narrative of racial difference . . . [that] infects systems and structures, thus perpetuating racial inequality throughout society."[10]

As Hill acknowledges, racism expands more widely than an individual's feelings toward a group of people. There are also structures in place that contribute to people groups failing in society. These can be found in the educational system (for example, poor neighborhoods don't get enough money for education, and poor neighborhoods are generally where people of color live), health care systems, the court system, the job market, and more.

White Privilege

Throughout the world, those with lighter skin tones experience a wide array of privileges that those who have darker skin do not experience. This inherent advantage can be understood as "white privilege." Often these privileges—such as being able to walk into a store without being accused of shoplifting, entering a neighborhood without fear, or receiving a job offer due to having a more common or "white" name—are unnoticed by those experiencing them.

The civil rights movement of the 1960s challenged many of the legally permissible inequalities imposed on people of color. However, there are several areas where white people continue to have advantages and where accessibility for people of color is not equal to that of their white counterparts. Consider, for example, the 2003 field study by the National Bureau of Economic Research that asked the question, "Are

Emily and Greg more employable than Lakisha and Jamal?"[11] The results? According to the report, "The resumes with white-sounding names spurred 50 percent more callbacks than the ones with black-sounding names."[12]

For the church to be able to truly advocate on behalf of justice, white privilege must be recognized and understood.[13]

White Supremacy

White supremacy is the idea that white people are better than, or should be privileged above, non-whites. It is a belief founded in fear—specifically, the fear that non-white people are out to destroy American culture and the country's identity. Though the modern-day movement of various alt-right groups has grown to include fears about feminism, liberal politics, and "social justice warriors," what most white supremacist groups have in common is the belief that root causes of society's problems are directly related to race. White supremacist groups explicitly fear the increasing agency of non-white people in American society.

Hill's book *White Awake* addresses how white supremacy provides the foundation for the ways white people name and treat communities of color. He cites historical examples such as the 1850s US conquest of the Southwest and then–Secretary of State (later the fifteenth president of the United States) James Buchanan identifying the people as a "mongrel race."[14]

White supremacy has had some of its worst manifestations with groups like the Ku Klux Klan (KKK). Following the Civil War, the KKK formed in an effort to maintain white privilege and dominance in society. The group's influence has fluctuated, gaining popularity again around the turn of the century and then again during the civil rights movement of the fifties and sixties. But the KKK did not just target black Americans; they also zeroed in on Jewish and other immigrant populations. It is important to note that many racist organizations like the KKK were founded by Christians, especially around the time of the KKK's second revival, which began as a Protestant nativist movement.[15]

Lest one think white supremacy is an affliction of the past, consider just a few examples of how white supremacist rhetoric continues to cause physical harm and death for vulnerable communities. In 2015, a white man named Dylann Roof entered historic Emanuel African Methodist Episcopal Church in Charleston, South Carolina—one of the oldest black churches in the United States and a center for civil rights issues in the past—and was welcomed to a Bible study session. Toward the end of the meeting, as the twelve others there, all African American, closed their eyes in prayer, Roof took out his pistol and began shooting at them. He shot the nine victims multiple times. Prior to the shooting and in prison after the event, Roof was very clear about his racism in an online "manifesto" and in his journal. The day after the shooting he admitted that he wished to instigate a "race war."[16]

The response of the survivors of the Charleston shooting to forgive Roof's murderous killing spree was profound. After the attack, I published an article that called on Christians to pray, reach out, listen, learn, and host a worship service focused on lamenting the realities of racism and white supremacy. I also encouraged leaders to close their services with this powerful prayer from April 26, 2015, written by the late senior pastor of Emanuel African Methodist Episcopal Church, Reverend Pinckney, who gave his life while ministering the gospel:

> Lord of all the names that we call you, we invite you into this space today. We pray that you would fill this place, Emanuel, with your love. May we remember that the name Emanuel means 'God with Us' and so we invite you and we welcome you into this place. And God we pray that you would make 'Emanuels' of all of us, that we may be filled with your love, for we know that only love can conquer hate, that only love can bring all together in your name.[17]

In another display of white supremacy, an event called Unite the Right was held in 2017 in Charlottesville, Virginia. Those in attendance comprised a variety of groups including Nazi organizations, the Klan, and other self-described "pro-white" groups. They gathered to protest the decision to take down a statue of Robert E. Lee erected during the height of Jim Crow laws in the twentieth century. On Friday, during the group's pre-march torch walk through the town, tension rose and violence began, with clashes between counter-protesters and the rally-goers.

The rally on Saturday was scheduled to start at noon, but even before it began, a state of emergency was declared in Charlottesville. Before the police totally shut down the protest, however, one supposed Nazi-sympathizer drove his car straight into the crowd, killing one woman and injuring nineteen people. Alt-right groups like the ones who gathered in Charlottesville stand in defiance of "political correctness" and "identity politics," focused, as they are, on the idea of losing American identity and on threats to white America. Many cities and organizations struggle with toeing the line between what constitutes free speech and hate speech, shutting down rallies that descend into violence.

In the aftermath of the protest and violence, President Trump received criticism for not explicitly denouncing racism and for instead remarking on the violence that came from "both sides."[18] A follow-up protest one year later, Unite the Right 2, brought only about two dozen people to Charlottesville. There was also a counter-protest in Washington, DC, where about a hundred people gathered to protest white supremacy.

White supremacy doesn't only manifest itself against people of color but against Jews and other minority groups as well. According to the Anti-Defamation League (ADL), anti-Semitic incidents in the United States have been on the rise and were at near historic levels in 2018, and assaults against Jews have more than doubled.[19] One of the worst incidents of anti-Semitism compelled by white supremacy was the Tree of Life shooting in Pennsylvania.

On October 27, 2018, eleven members of the Tree of Life synagogue, located in Pittsburgh, lost their lives after a violent gunman entered their doors. The congregation had gathered for a bris, the ceremony held after the birth of a child, when Roberts Bowers entered with an AR-15-style assault rifle. He shot indiscriminately at the crowd and then walked out the door, only to be faced with the Pittsburgh police. They fired at each other until Bowers surrendered, sustaining some gun wounds, though it is unclear if they came from the officers or himself. On top of the eleven people who died, six others were wounded by the attack, including four police officers.[20] This was among the deadliest attacks toward the Jewish community in the United States. Bowers was a member of the media sharing site Gab, which has become popular among alt-right groups due to the site's lack of "free speech" regulation. Leading up to the day of the attack, Bowers had shared and posted a number of racist and anti-Semitic statements. He lived about twenty-five minutes away from the synagogue in a modest neighborhood and had nearly twenty-one guns registered to his name. Bowers is faced with twenty-nine federal charges and state charges ranging from violent homicide to obstruction of religious freedom.[21]

The organization I lead, Churches for Middle East Peace (CMEP), put out a statement following the attack. It summarizes what our response should be to white supremacist attacks on Jews and others:

> The cry, "This must never happen again," no longer suffices as a response to murderous hate, in this case the hatefulness of anti-Semitism. It has been used far too often, and "it" tragically does happen again and again. It happens when hate and prejudice become mechanisms for permission to see others as lesser beings who can be done away with. It happens when people in leadership enjoy acceptance by being instruments of provocative and divisive language and behavior, making it tolerable to deny the dignity and humanity of others. It happens when others are perceived as threats to a person's or a group's status and authority. It happens when "good people" keep silent while hearing fellow children of God denigrated with mean and hateful language. We call upon President Trump and all in authority to use their words and exercise their deeds, not to encourage acts of violence, but to promote the dignity of all. And, we remind ourselves and others that we are the grassroots agents called to confront hate and prejudice with word and action by affirming that all people are

created in the image of God and we are responsible for confronting hate-fulness and prejudice.[22]

Again, white supremacy is not distant history, and it affects many groups of people in the United States. President Donald Trump frequently perpetuated fears about Hispanic people during his presidential campaign with statements like, "When Mexico sends its people, they're not sending their best. . . . They're bringing drugs. They're bringing crime. They're rapists."[23]

Christianity and Christian institutions have had a long hard history with the idea of white supremacy. As one article on this history states, "Historically, hate groups have used religious, Christian-based rhetoric to perpetuate acrimony, xenophobia, bigotry, and segregation in America. The misuse of Christian themes and evangelical theology to preserve slavery is a particularly poignant example of such malevolent magniloquence."[24] There are also examples of Christians in history who have taken profound stands against systems of injustice, even at great personal cost. Dietrich Bonhoeffer's imprisonment and death at the hand of the Nazis is one example. William Wilberforce's lifelong quest to end the transatlantic slave trade is another. However, Christian institutions have had difficulty taking a definitive stand against racism, and particularly calling out the racist tendencies of specific leaders, such as President Trump. Some nine hundred hate incidents were documented within ten days after the 2016 election, "one-fifth of which were committed by supporters of the newly elected President or done in his name."[25]

As the population of the United States increases with growing numbers of people of color, the relationship between white Americans and other racial and ethnic groups must be brought to the forefront. The Brookings Institute reports that by 2045, the United States will be "minority white."[26] Dr. Glaude concurs, saying, "The browning of America is not in the distant future, but is already happening today, politically."[27] Many white people fear this shifting demographic reality.

Robert Jones
and *The End of White Christian America*

Robert Jones, the head of the Public Religion Research Institute and the author of *The End of White Christian America,* says white Christian America is a "metaphor for the cultural and political edifice, primarily Protestant Christians, setting the tone for American conversation and the American ideal." About a quarter of American Christians are non-white, whereas white Christians make up about 42 percent of the total population. Only 15 percent of the total population falls under the category of "White Evangelical."[28]

While white Christian conservatives played a very significant role in the election of President Trump to the White House, Jones highlights what the data shows: "White American Christians are aging out. White Christians only make up 23% of 18- to 29-year-olds, as compared to 65+ where over half (63%) contribute to that age bracket." According to Jones, "Within the population of Evangelicals 63% are White with the next largest group at 19% being Black Evangelicals."[29]

What are the political implications of these facts and statistics? Political affiliations are significantly divided by race, and we know that white evangelicals are far more likely to support a Republican candidate over a Democratic one. In 2017, 33 percent of Republicans fell into the category of white evangelical Protestant as compared to the Democratic Party, which only had 7 percent (and also a larger portion of black and Hispanic Christian backgrounds). In elections (midterm and general) from 1992 to 2014, over half of the electorate was white (with a pattern of decline).[30]

While "White Evangelicalism" was once considered the "norm" for US Christianity, this percentage of the population is now falling to the wayside. The category of "unaffiliated" is expanding among 18- to 29-year-olds, and the number of nonevangelicals and black and Hispanic evangelicals are growing. In 2016, the majority of kindergarteners in the United States were people of color. According to NPR, "The crosscurrents of demographic and cultural change are upending traditional voting patterns and straining the fabric of what it means to be American."[31] These changes will likely be hard for white evangelicals, who tend toward nostalgia. In 2016, 74 percent of white evangelicals agreed that American culture has mostly changed for the worse. They do not generally think very positively about the future when it comes to demographic changes in the United States.[32]

In a 2019 article on these demographic shifts, Lisa Sharon Harper challenges the narrative of white evangelical conservatives who care about the deaths of fetuses by abortion but not the deaths of black boys at the hands of the police. She also notes that the 2016 presidential election proved that white Christians are still held captive by their whiteness, but that evangelicalism is rapidly becoming less white. Jones, who was also quoted in the article, affirmed this, explaining, "The absolute number of whites in America is declining. But the decline is really turbocharged by young white evangelicals leaving the church."[33]

White Fragility

In order to understand racism, the social construct of the category of "whiteness" must be understood. Michael Eric Dyson describes whiteness as the "means of dominance, the end to which dominance points, and the point of dominance." He reminds readers that whiteness is a "social construct" and an "agreed-on myth," but that its very strength and superiority rest on being a "category of identity that is most useful when its very existence is denied."[34]

What is white fragility? As white antiracist academic and practitioner Robin DiAngelo puts it in her book *White Fragility: Why It's So Hard for White People to Talk About Racism,* white fragility refers to the defensive reaction of white people for "being called to account for how that whiteness has gone under the radar of race for far too long." It is what "registers the hurt feelings, shattered egos, fraught spirits, vexed bodies, and taxed emotions of white folks." She further explains:

> The smallest amount of racial stress is intolerable—the mere suggestion that being white has meaning often triggers a range of defensive responses. These include emotions such as anger, fear, and guilt and behaviors such as argumentation, silence, and withdrawal from the stress-inducing situation. These responses work to reinstate white equilibrium as they repel the challenge, return our racial comfort, and maintain our dominance within the racial hierarchy. I conceptualize this process as *white fragility.*[35]

White people, in large part, are isolated from racial stress and can choose to withdraw or ignore the realities of racism if we want to. I will never forget conversations I had with a friend, a beautiful young black woman, on one of the Evangelical Covenant Church's Sankofa Journeys. During our several days of sitting together on a bus, she told me the story of how, as a child, she used to look in the mirror and scrub her face until it was raw. "I was trying to make it white," she said. She didn't have a choice about being confronted every minute of every day with what it means to be black in America. She lived it. White Americans, however, can choose to ignore racial prejudices and injustice.

All of us are socialized into a system of racism. But, as DiAngelo writes, "The default of our current system is the reproduction of racial inequality; our institutions were designed to reproduce racial inequality and they do so with efficiency."[36] Taking the initiative to learn about the ways we are inherently racist and have internalized aspects of our cultural views toward race is a critically important step in making progress. One of the things I asked of the community at John Brown University was that the white students not impose their ignorance on their (very few) classmates of color. It is not the responsibility of our African American friends, or other communities of color, to educate us about our ignorance.

DiAngelo describes a process by which white people can commit to taking initiative, receiving feedback from people of color openly, and acknowledging when racism is revealed in our interactions. First, we must be aware that we have behaved problematically. This means we may need to find someone to hold us accountable and help us understand the dynamics that transpired. Then we must clearly identify how our comments or behaviors "reinforced" racism, and this must be acknowledged not just internally but also with the person or community we have violated. After owning our racism, we must apologize and admit the ways the "behavior was offensive." We can then invite the person to whom we're apologizing to provide additional feedback. Our apology should be substantiated by a commitment to change behavior. Then we can move forward.[37]

Recently on the Netflix show *Traitors* I saw a profound scene between two African Americans living in Europe after World War II. One man says: "Negroes are uniquely qualified to develop a larger vision for society because we are uniquely invested."[38] Because of the burden and cost of racism on black and other Americans of color, they are often the most equipped to identify when racial injustice occurs and to provide a "broader vision" for an inclusive society of equality, rights, and justice. African American Ron Potter, son-in-law to civil rights activist and founder of the Christian Community Development Association (CCDA) John Perkins, writes, preaches, and teaches about race, theology, and poverty.[39] As a graduate of Wheaton College, he criticizes white evangelical spaces as being particularly limiting to students of color. In the dissertation of Soong-Chan Rah, who writes about Potter's matriculation with the incoming class at Wheaton College in the fall of 1968, Potter asserted this critique of white evangelicalism:

> Christianity, as it is expressed in American society, has been neocolonialist, oppressive, and racist. This has taken its most blatant form on evangelical Christian campuses. We talk a lot about peace on our Christian campuses, we talk a lot about the bringing together of people, black people and white people, on evangelical Christian campuses; yet, many times this has been primarily based upon the norms of white evangelicals. . . . We have associated Biblical Christianity with the norms and mores of evangelical subculture. We have had a wedding between Christianity as expressed in the Bible and cultural evangelicalism and the two have been so closely knit together that one can hardly differentiate them. Therefore, a student in his junior and senior year at these institutions will say, if that is Christianity, I want no part of it.[40]

According to Potter's critique, prior to talking about reconciliation, we must acknowledge the injustices that have occurred and continue to occur against people of color. Don't misunderstand Potter's comment. He didn't leave Christianity. He maintains a profound faith in Christ. His comments are a critique of white evangelicalism, which is often exclusivist and unwilling to face the consequences and cost of entering into the transformative process of awakening that Hill and others talk about and urge white people toward. Potter calls for the application of

the gospel of Christ through justice and reconciliation while disman-
tling the associations between evangelicalism and white culture.

Lament and repentance are necessary precursors to reconciliation.
Too often, particularly within white communities, Scriptures about
being ministers of reconciliation (2 Cor 5) are used as an excuse to
overlook individual and systemic racism. This does not mean that reconciliation should not be pursued. It just means that reconciliation
must always be sought hand in hand with efforts toward justice.

Kevin DeYoung, an American Reformed evangelical theologian and
author, writes that most Christians believe that all people are made in
the image of God but that "we do not agree on what . . . counts as racism
or the degree to which our cultural, civic, and ecclesiastical institutions
are basically race-blind, racialized, or outright racist."[41] Similarly, most
Christians would affirm the statistics that outline the various areas of
life experiences that differ for white and black Americans but disagree
on what brings about these differences. Some Christians emphasize the
role of personal choice and others choose to focus on the implications
and consequences of structural racism. There is also little agreement
between black people and white people, or communities of color and
white people, on how to close this gap. Since the 2001 publication of
Divided by Faith by Michael Emerson and Christian Smith, it often feels
like the divide between white people and people of color has
only widened.

Consider the debate within Southern Baptist circles between white
pastor Randy White and African American theologian and New Testament professor Jarvis J. Williams. Many Christian conservatives agree
with White's response to whether or not racial reconciliation is a
demand of the gospel: "Seems to me that racial reconciliation is a good
thing and is a social issue, not a doctrinal or theological issue, and certainly not a 'gospel demand.' If there is something Biblical that expresses
racial reconciliation as a gospel demand, I've missed it."[42]

White's words were a response to evangelical engagement regarding
racial tensions in Ferguson, Missouri, after the police shooting of

Michael Brown. (Ferguson is discussed more thoroughly in the next chapter.) His argument boiled down to his own personal experience as a white man in his fifties. "I don't think I'm a racist at all," he writes. "I think I'm a responsible citizen with a Biblical worldview. But when I see what the ever-more-left-leaning Evangelicals (like my fellow Southern Baptists) are preaching about the Ferguson fiasco, I am made to feel like I'm a racist."[43]

Williams disagrees with White's views of racial reconciliation in Scripture, asserting that we must understand the difference between diversity and reconciliation:

> Part of the problem is that evangelicals can confuse racial reconciliation with multi-ethnicity or diversity, and so they begin conversations about racial reconciliation with a push for multi-ethnic churches. . . . I agree that gospel-grounded racial reconciliation produces multi-ethnic and diverse churches. But diversity is not the same as gospel-centered racial reconciliation and the goal of gospel-centered racial reconciliation is not simply diversity. An assembly of the United Nations is multi-ethnic and diverse, as is the army, or the local public high school, or so many other groups. Yet such settings hardly enjoy the racial reconciliation of the gospel.[44]

For Williams, racial reconciliation is definitely a gospel issue. "Gospel-grounded racial reconciliation, after all, is supernatural, not natural," Williams claims. He exhorts Christians to "understand what biblical racial reconciliation is and what it means for the church [making reference to Ephesians 2–3]," understand the social construction and history of race, "be honest about our racist past," and hold leaders accountable.[45]

Who is right? I believe Randy White suffers from the blindness that many white people, including myself, living in a privileged society and environment suffer from. This doesn't mean always conceding only to the values, opinions, and perspectives of communities of color, but it does mean that when it comes to race, those of us who are white must acknowledge that our ability to have "eyes to see and ears to hear" is limited, living, as we do, in a dominant white culture with all of its privileges and assumed superiority.

Countering Racial Injustice

What can be done to combat white supremacy and racial injustice? A commitment to learn and understand more, especially about history, is a good place to start for both white people and people of color. The Legacy Museum, run by the Equal Justice Initiative, in Montgomery, Alabama, portrays the history of black bodies in the United States from enslavement to mass incarceration.[46] Several former slave plantations, like Angola in Louisiana, transitioned from being a slave-breeding plantation to being a state penitentiary. If we ever want to understand the realities of racism in this country, we must be willing to look at history and how it affects our systems and structures today. Other museums to consider include the National Museum of African American History and Culture, which opened in 2016 and is part of the Smithsonian Institution in Washington, DC; the Birmingham Civil Rights Institute in Alabama, right across from Kelly Ingram Park and 16th Street Baptist Church, where four little girls were killed by a bomb planted by a white supremacist; and the National Civil Rights Museum at the Lorraine Motel in Memphis, Tennessee, where Martin Luther King Jr. was assassinated.

In June 2019, Iva Carruthers, cofounder of the Samuel DeWitt Proctor Conference, reminded me that the sins of fathers are often passed along for generations. We discussed the rapidly growing field of epigenetics, and how scientific studies at renowned institutions like the National Institutes of Health have begun to show the ways trauma affects our DNA; there is even the possibility that trauma may be inherited.[47] While still contested, epigenetics is a growing field of study that should be considered.[48] At the very least it highlights that healing from injustice must include spiritual, psychological, and physical restoration toward health and reconciliation.

You might also consider joining the Evangelical Covenant Church (ECC) on one of their Sankofa Journeys.[49] *Sankofa* means looking at the past in order to be able to move constructively into the future. These racial reconciliation pilgrimages do not hide the history of racial disparity and abuse but rather seek to bring these horrors to the light so we can repent, repair, and seek to reconcile across racial divides.

The Question of Reparations

Reparations is the idea that there should be some form of payment or compensation to the descendants of those who were held captive in slavery. On the four hundredth anniversary of slaves being brought to Jamestown, a historic conversation was happening on Capitol Hill. In June 2019, for the first time in a decade, the United States Congress considered a bill (HR40) that would "create a commission to develop proposals to address the lingering effects of slavery and consider a 'national apology' for the harm it has caused."[50] Some Republicans at the hearing returned to the historic argument that black people should just "pull themselves up by their bootstraps." Whereas others, like author and journalist Ta-Nehisi Coates, provided a history lesson and concluded: "We recognize our lineage as a generational trust, as inheritance, and the real dilemma posed by reparations is just that: a dilemma of inheritance. . . . It is impossible to imagine America without the inheritance of slavery."[51] Leading up to the 2020 presidential elections, fifteen of the initial twenty Democratic candidates stated they would support the type of study about reparations proposed in HR40.[52] As of November 2019, HR40 still had not been passed by the House of Representatives.[53]

The decentering of whiteness was a key theme of the Evangelicals for Justice (E4J) event in Chicago in September 2019. The title of the event was Liberating Evangelicalism, and workshops addressed topics like white supremacy, decentering whiteness, theologies of liberation rooted in different experiences of communities of color, and numerous other topics on race and justice.[54] Consider attending a future gathering hosted by E4J, the CCDA, or other groups committed to combating systemic racism and injustice.

The article "#Charlottesville: Some Gospel Thinking on White Supremacy" claims that "the acts of white supremacy that took place in Charlottesville, VA should encourage the church to act aggressively to deter racist ideals within her ranks."[55] The authors suggest five steps that pastors and church communities can take to admonish against racism and address white supremacy. First, encourage participation in the festivities, remembrances, awareness events, artistic expressions, and historical displays of the various minority ethnicities within your congregation and the local community. Second, give strong, clear responses to the issues surrounding local and national incidents of racial conflict, especially where racially charged threats, harm, police or judicial action, and/or tragedy has come to the fore. Third, promote regular, active, intentional, personal fellowship of saints across ethnic lines. Such happenings, often involving the sharing of a favorite ethnic meal by the host family, allow for believers within the same congregation to reveal and understand the private, cultural backgrounds experienced by the marginalized. Fourth, avoid denying the reality of racial insensitivity within your own fellowship, regardless of the numerical assessment of the ethnic diversity in your congregation. And finally, in public gatherings and private moments, pray for those who are contending directly with episodes and establishments of racism and white supremacy.[56] In your quest to discern how you can engage, look to groups that address systemic aspects of racial injustice like World Renew, Equal Justice Initiative, Black Lives Matter, and Sojourners for more ideas and encouragement on your journey.

For Further Study

Brown, Austin Channing. *I'm Still Here: Black Dignity in a World Made for Whiteness*. New York: Crown, 2018.

Carter, J. Kameron. *Race: A Theological Account*. New York: Oxford University Press, 2008.

DiAngelo, Robin. *White Fragility: Why It's So Hard for White People to Talk About Racism*. Boston: Beacon, 2018.

Gilbreath, Edward. *Reconciliation Blues: A Black Evangelical's Inside View of White Christianity*. Downers Grove, IL: InterVarsity Press, 2008.

Glaude, Eddie S., Jr. *Democracy in Black: How Race Still Enslaves the American Soul*. New York: Broadway Books, 2017.

Harvey, Jennifer. *Dear White Christians: For Those Still Longing for Racial Reconciliation*. Prophetic Christianity Series. Grand Rapids: Eerdmans, 2014.

Hill, Daniel. *White Awake: An Honest Look at What It Means to Be White*. Downers Grove, IL: InterVarsity Press, 2017.

Hill, Daniel. *White Lies: Nine Ways to Challenge the Racial Systems that Divide Us.* Grand Rapids: Zondervan, 2020.

Jacobs, Harrison. "Former Neo-Nazi: Here's Why There's No Real Difference Between 'Alt-Right,' 'White Nationalism,' and 'White Supremacy.'" *Business Insider,* August 23, 2017.

Jones, Robert. *The End of White Christian America.* New York: Simon & Schuster, 2017.

Lichtman, Allan J. *White Protestant Nation: The Rise of the American Conservative Movement.* New York: Atlantic Monthly Press, 2008.

Matthews, Kenneth, and M. Sydney Park. *The Post-Racial Church: A Biblical Framework for Multiethnic Reconciliation.* Grand Rapids: Kregel Academic & Professional, 2011.

McNeil, Brenda Salter. *Roadmap to Reconciliation: Moving Communities into Unity, Wholeness and Justice.* Downers Grove, IL: InterVarsity Press, 2016.

Smith, Andrea. *Unreconciled: From Racial Reconciliation to Racial Justice in Christian Evangelicalism.* Durham, NC: Duke University Press, 2019.

Questions for Discussion

- How has the recent news media informed your understanding of white supremacy? What are some ways you can engage in fruitful conversation about the topic?

- If there are white people in your group, how did the topics of this chapter make you feel? What are some ways to engage in racial reconciliation? What are some ways your community engages in conversations around race? Do you resonate with or resist what was written about white fragility?

- If there are people who identify as people of color in your group, what are your thoughts about white supremacy? How did this chapter make you feel? What do you wish others who are of a different race most understood about your racial identity and experiences?

- Where do you see racial disparity or racism in your context and environment? Do you think white supremacist ideas have been more freely expressed in society in recent years?

- What do you think the Bible teaches about racial identity and reconciliation?

- What might God be calling you individually and/or your group collectively to do to respond to white centeredness and racism?

Racial Violence, Police Brutality, and the Age of Incarceration

He will take pity on the weak and the needy
and save the needy from death.
He will rescue them from oppression and violence,
for precious is their blood in his sight.

PSALM 72:13-14

IN A MEETING IN CHICAGO just after the election of President Trump, I sat in a room with many men and women leaders of color. One of the women began to weep. I knew many communities of color were distressed and traumatized by the election of Trump because of his racial bigotry and treatment of their communities. I didn't realize the depth of the trauma until I heard firsthand this woman's desperate plea as the mother of a young strong black man. She said, "I worry every day that my son will survive." She shared that when her son was in college, while he was sitting in a neighborhood park on a sunny afternoon, he was approached by two white police officers. The police began to give him a hard time, as if he didn't have a right to be there. When he said who he was, it didn't matter. The police made him get up and leave. What had he done wrong? He was young and black. It didn't matter that he was a college student and a good kid who never got in trouble. It didn't matter that he dressed well, the sun was shining, and the park was open. This mother worried that if her son protested too much, if he resisted the police officers' authority, he would be shot and killed.

In 2014, Tamir Rice was shot twice in a park by Cleveland police rookie Timothy Loehmann. Tamir's mother, Samaria, had moved near the park because it was close to Tamir's school and the recreation center where he and his sister spent so much time. That morning, he and a friend had fixed a pellet gun that had been purchased at Walmart. He spent the afternoon playing with the gun, pointing it at people and things. Since his family lived in the neighborhood, few saw it as a problem.

A man waiting for the bus called 911, uncomfortable with Tamir's behavior. Tamir was a "big kid," standing at five foot seven and nearly two hundred pounds, but he still had a "baby face." The dispatcher had placed the call to police as a category Code One, the highest priority. When Loehmann and officer Frank Garmback arrived, they pulled the squad car up onto the grass, right next to the gazebo that Tamir was in. Nearly two seconds later, Loehmann shot him. They radioed that a black man was down but did not approach him to help as he lay on the ground. Tamir died the next day in the hospital. He was 12 years old.[1]

Timothy Loehmann had only been on the job for six months after nearly being fired from his police job outside Independence and not receiving any offers prior to Cleveland. The 911 caller had reported that the gun was probably fake and that it was probably a juvenile holding it, however, this information was not given to the officers on duty. Both officers reported that they thought Tamir was pulling a gun from his waistband. The grand jury decided not to indict either officer, stating that the whole event was "a perfect storm of human error and not necessarily a criminal act." The January following the incident, the family argued that the city of Cleveland was at fault for their poor hiring procedures, and negligent. The city settled with a six million dollar payment to the Rice family.[2]

Many mothers worry about violence in urban communities and the often prejudicial and brutal response of the police if they are brought in to intervene. Sarah King lived for almost five years in the neighborhood of Germantown, Philadelphia, with her elementary-school-aged son and husband. One night she woke up to people screaming outside. When she looked out the window, she saw two men and a woman in a domestic violence dispute. The fighting and arguing turned physical when one of the men picked up a brick and hit the other man with it. He fell to the ground. She opened her window and said, "Do you need or want me to call the police or the ambulance?" The man was black, and she knew that calling the police is not always a helpful intervention or a "safe bet" for communities of color.[3]

Violence within urban communities has significant effects on the people who live there, even those who are not immediately impacted by traumatic events. King's home was around the corner from an intersection where there were frequent shootings. Located in a predominantly African American community, that particular corner also has historical significance because it was the location where the first anti-slavery protests were held in the United States. In 1688, the Mennonites of Germantown wrote a petition against slavery and sent it to all of their communities within the Society of Friends.[4]

Life in the community looks a lot different today than it did in the seventeenth century. Just a few blocks from King's house in East Germantown, while six-year-old Mahaj "Haji" Brown played in his front yard on a Thursday afternoon in August 2016, gunfire erupted from at least three shooters, spraying bullets across houses and cars and striking four people, including Mahaj. The child was hit ten times by bullets from an AK-47, with at least one hitting his chest.[5] According to Philadelphia news reports, "The assault rifle's bullets tore through Haji's intestine and his colon. They ripped through his left arm and his right leg, his groin, his side, and a finger."[6] Four children, including Mahaj, were shot in Philadelphia that summer. They were all left with "wounds, fears, and nightmares."[7] King didn't want to tell her then-six-year-old son about the realities of death and violence surrounding them. She didn't have to. Mahaj was a friend of her son's best friend; he learned about the shooting at school.

That same summer, a friend of King's drove her kids through the historic intersection near her home. Two gangs started shooting at one another across the rush-hour traffic. Her friend yelled at her kids to duck down in their seats. Just two cars behind her was twenty-five-year-old Alsharay Ford, who had just picked his three-year-old daughter up from daycare. He was shot and killed. This was all just a hundred yards from King's house. Police reported that if the bullet had not struck Ford, it would have hit his daughter: "He probably saved his daughter's life."[8]

During the summer of 2016, at least ten people were shot and killed within a half-mile radius of King's house. She worried that she and her family, particularly her son, could be similarly caught in the crossfire. "It felt like living in a war zone sometimes," she said. She did whatever she could to make sure she always met her son at the bus stop to walk the half-block home. If she was running late, she experienced dread and panic and would run out the door to get to him in time so he would not have to walk by himself.

King says, "I felt like I needed to shield my kid from the reality of things . . . but here [in Philadelphia] death was right in front of us."[9] Throughout the neighborhood, little memorials made of teddy bears and balloons would pop up, commemorating where a shooting death had taken place.

King and her family later moved to Eugene, Oregon, where she now worries more about school shootings, which she never worried about in Philly. She says, "Yeah, [in Philadelphia] the chance of getting caught as a random bystander in a shooting was a little higher, but it's the sub-urban white boys who are bringing guns to school and killing their classmates." King believes all mothers want their child to grow up in an environment where it's not considered "normal" that people are being shot and shooting at one another, and many mothers never have to worry about that. For those who do, she voices a key question, thinking of her own son: "When you spend your most formative years growing up around violence, how does that affect you?"

Now in the suburban Pacific Northwest, her son can ride his bike throughout the neighborhood and go to his friends' houses unescorted. When he's not home right after school, she doesn't worry that something happened to him. Rather, she just assumes he's with friends. She misses the diversity of the community in Philadelphia but not the violence.

King could afford to move, but many in Philadelphia cannot. And Oregon, of course, has problems of its own—a terribly racist past, for one. King says that predominantly white Eugene has "the vein of white supremacy living just under the surface."[10]

The Trauma of Inner-City Violence

Anyone who read Alex Kotlowitz's 1992 book *There Are No Children Here* learned a bit about what life was like for the urban poor living in Chicago's Henry Horner Homes housing project. Kotlowitz's recent 2019 book, *An American Summer,* continues the story, documenting what happened to the two boys featured in the first book and providing several more recent vignettes of life in the inner city.

In Chicago in the summer of 2013, 172 were people killed and 793 wounded. This was not the most violent summer in recent years, however. By 2016, the annual numbers had risen to 785 killed and 4,369 wounded, a 61 percent increase from the preceding year. In one weekend alone during the summer of 2018, 72 people were shot and 13 people killed.[11] The story of six-year-old Mahaj Brown in Philadelphia brings the victims of each one of these shootings to life. Kotlowitz reminds readers that the "death of the wealthy grabs headlines" but the "death of the poor?" Only "silence."[12]

For children and youth growing up in violent communities, rage often masks the pain that has built up over years of abuse, trauma, and insecurity. The individuals and families he writes about are predominantly African American. And in story after story, they are not affected by singular incidences of violence but rather by ongoing traumatic experiences impacted by limited financial resources and poverty, gang violence, and what Kotlowitz calls "complex loss." Domestic poverty is exacerbated by single parents (mostly mothers), drug addictions, despair, and constant loss. These communities don't have post-traumatic stress disorder (PTSD) because there is nothing "post" about their brushes with violence. Rather they experience ongoing and complex repeats of trauma.[13]

Gun Violence in the United States

Gun violence disproportionately affects communities of color. According to the National Council on Family Relations (NCFR), race plays a significant role in the experience of gun violence. In their report on "Gun Violence and the Minority Experience" NCFR asserts: "1) The white experience of gun violence is often vastly different from that of racial/ethnic minorities in urban settings. 2) News and social media, politics, and implicit biases greatly affect our understanding of gun violence.[14] and 3) Family Scientists should acknowledge gun violence in racial/ethnic minority communities as a particular societal problem."[15]

The Second Amendment of the United States Constitution protects the "right to bear arms," particularly for self-defense. Provoked in large part by the desire of colonists to be able to protect themselves against British imperialism during the time of the Revolutionary War, gun control in the United States has a long and complicated history. Unsurprisingly, efforts at reform and debates about it tend to especially spring up after incidents of violence. The Gun Control Act of 1968 followed the assassinations of JFK, Robert Kennedy, and Martin Luther King Jr. The 1993 Brady Handgun Violence Prevention Act and the 1994 Federal Assault Weapons Ban followed the height of inner-city violence in the 1980s and the 1991 Rodney King incident in Los Angeles. Conversation arose again after the 1999 Columbine school shooting in Colorado and subsequent shootings at Virginia Tech (2007) and Fort Hood (2009), and in Aurora and Sandy Hook (both 2012).[16]

One of the most compelling calls for gun control came in 2018 after the deadliest school shooting yet occurred at Marjory Stoneman

Douglas High School in Parkland, Florida, with seventeen people being killed.[17] Students from Stoneman Douglas mobilized after the shooting and started a national campaign called March for Our Lives, which is committed to bringing about change in US gun laws and senseless deaths. "We cannot allow one more person to experience the pain of losing a loved one. We cannot allow one more family to wait for a call or a text that never comes. We cannot allow the normalization of gun violence to continue. We must create a safe and compassionate nation for all of us," their website says.[18] Stoneman Douglas High School student Emma González declared at one of the gun control rallies: "We are going to be the kids you read about in textbooks. Not because we're going to be another statistic about mass shootings in America, but because we are going to be the last mass shooting. Just like *Tinker v. Des Moines,* we are going to change the law."[19] These students and the many who support them are calling for "bold action" to end the gun violence epidemic.

Their efforts have included organizing the largest single-day protest against gun violence in history in cities across the country, including Washington, DC, Los Angeles, and New York City. The slogan of the movement became "Enough is Enough."[20] I arrived in DC the day of the protests and was surrounded at Union Station by young people carrying signs that said things like, "Mother, mother, there are too many of you crying"; "Protect kids, not guns"; and "It's easier to buy a gun than Hamilton tickets in America."[21] It was difficult to not be moved seeing young participants carrying signs saying, "I don't want to die at school."

Gun control laws have changed some as a result of efforts like March for Our Lives and other student advocacy initiatives. Gun rights advocates have a difficult fight when the struggle is against motivated high school students. It is hard to argue against safety for children and youth at school. Federal legislation has progressed, but comprehensive legislation has been harder to come by.[22]

Florida has had the most significant gun law changes after the Parkland shooting. Governor Rick Scott signed into law the Marjory

Stoneman Douglas High School Public Safety Act, which imposed a three-day waiting period for gun purchases and raised the age of eligibility for purchasing a firearm from eighteen to twenty-one years old. The National Rifle Association (NRA) argues this law is unconstitutional.[23]

"Red Flag" laws, which allow for "family members and law enforcement to seek a court order to temporarily restrict a person's access to guns if they're a danger to themselves or others," have also made a difference. Eight states—Delaware, Florida, Illinois, Massachusetts, Maryland, New Jersey, Rhode Island, and Vermont—as well as Washington, DC, have passed Red Flag laws, and they are providing real opportunities to keep guns away from possible perpetrators of gun violence. According to the Associated Press, in 2018, the Red Flag laws were enacted 1,700 times and allowed "guns to be seized for up to a year."[24]

Some communities around the country, however, such as in Colorado, view Red Flag laws as a violation of Second Amendment rights. Protests against these laws were so severe that many Colorado counties declared themselves "Second Amendment Sanctuary Cities." It is unclear what these sanctuary cities will mean other than legal battles in court. Sheriffs in several of the counties have "declared they will ignore the judge's orders to confiscate guns."[25] The term *sanctuary* is also causing debate because of its usage in the protection of immigrants threatened with deportation.

In addition to Red Flag laws, eleven states passed laws to keep guns out of the hands of domestic abusers. The federal administration also imposed a ban on "bump stocks," which allow semi-automatic weapons to fire faster. And in 2018, more than 90 percent of bills supported by gun lobbyists were rejected.[26]

The debate over gun control holds even greater implications for communities of color, due to the disproportionate effects they face from gun use. Consider the 2018 shooting of Emantic Bradford, a black security guard at a local Alabama shopping mall. Just twenty-one years old,

Bradford was a resident of Hoover, a Birmingham suburb with a population of about 85,000 people, 72 percent of them white. He had been generally discharged from the army due to a back injury during training and was at the mall hanging out with friends when an altercation broke out between two men, Erron Brown and Brian Wilson. The two argued, and then Brown shot Wilson in the stomach. Bradford had nothing to do with their argument but, as a licensed gun owner, he had a gun on him and was ready to defend himself and other shoppers, even while he gave bystanders directions to help them escape safely. A police officer who rushed into the scene saw Bradford with the gun and shot him. Bradford died from his wounds.

Philip Smith, president of the National African-American Gun Association, said of the incident, "When you walk up to a situation as an officer, I think a lot of times there's an assumption that the black guy is the issue or the problem. . . . When you have those stereotypes that are ingrained in your mind, it can be a death warrant for a lot of our black men, unfortunately."[27]

The shooting of Bradford calls into question the veracity of a popular slogan among Second Amendment enthusiasts: "The best way to stop a bad guy with a gun is a good guy with a gun." The *Times* reports, "Black people trying to protect themselves or others with a gun may not have gotten the benefit of the doubt in recent heat-of-the-moment situations."[28]

For people of faith, what is an appropriate response to the gun control debate? The majority of American Christians favor stricter gun control laws. But white evangelicals are more likely than the average American to own a gun. According to Pew Research data, 41 percent of white evangelicals own guns, compared to 30 percent of Americans overall.[29] White evangelicals are also more likely to carry their guns and to live in places that allow people to carry them. There is a strong correlation between Christian nationalism and those who believe Second Amendment rights override the risks of having assault weapons out on the streets. An academic study found that, "for the substantial proportion of American society who are Christian nationalists, gun rights are God given and sacred."[30]

The debate among Christians about gun control largely mirrors partisan divides. The vast majority of Democrats support increased gun control, two to one more than Republicans, where 42 percent support bans on assault weapons.[31]

Christian activists like Shane Claiborne and the group Heeding God's Call to End Gun Violence provide opportunities for followers of Christ to join with others in taking action.[32] These activists are changing the face of evangelical and Christian responses to weapons and gun violence. Opportunities to engage include creating "Memorials for the Lost"; hosting Gun Violence Awareness Days; participating in "Souls Shot," which links fine artists with families of victims to create portraits of victims of gun violence; taking action against gun shops; and hosting worship events and vigils on sacred days like Good Friday. You can learn more at their website, www.heedinggodscall.org. Also see Shane Claiborne's book *Executing Grace: How the Death Penalty Killed Jesus and Why It's Killing Us.*

The documentary *The Armor of Light,* directed by Abigail Disney, is also a helpful resource. It follows the story of an evangelical mother who lost her son to a gun shooting and is asking if it's possible to be pro-gun and pro-life. Find out more at www.armoroflightfilm.com.

Guns, the Law, and People of Color

Trayvon Martin was seventeen years old when he was shot and killed in 2012 by a Florida man named George Zimmerman. Martin was not from the area and had been staying with his father's fiancée while he was suspended from school. Zimmerman, the neighborhood watch captain in a gated community, saw him walking and called 911 to report a suspicious person. The dispatcher instructed him to remain in his vehicle and not approach the person, but Zimmerman chose not to obey. When Zimmerman approached Martin, some sort of altercation occurred. Zimmerman had some injuries to his face and head and reportedly shot Martin with a handgun he owned. When the police arrived, Martin was lying face down on the ground. While this was happening, Martin's father, unaware of where his son was, had filed a missing person's report.

Initially the officers believed Zimmerman's claim of self-defense, but he was later charged with second-degree murder and manslaughter. In July 2013, a jury found Zimmerman not guilty.[33] Black churches grieved and lamented the Zimmerman verdict. Lisa Sharon Harper described her response this way: "Shocked. Absolutely shocked. I went to sleep that night feeling numb. I slept hard that night. Then, as soon as I woke up the next morning, I started crying. Weeping. It hit me. The reality of the moment really hit me."

The majority of white evangelical churches viewed the trial from a legal perspective and had a different perspective. Ken Wytsma, the founder of The Justice Conference, said many white evangelicals affirmed the ruling, stating things like, "It was handled according to the rule of law," and "Justice must have run its course." Trusting in the system, white evangelicals believed that justice must have prevailed. But Wytsma, like Harper, believes many white people missed the broader implications about the heart of justice and the deeper issues reflected in this landmark case: "Whites don't have to worry about race; blacks and people of color do."

These differences in worldview highlight the ways that the black community experiences a very different lived experience of the world than white people, generally speaking. According to Harper, oppressive systems and laws affect black people differently than they affect white people; this goes largely unseen by the white church. Meanwhile, white evangelicals generally reap the benefits of systems like the judicial system and police forces that were created to benefit and protect them.[34]

Black Lives Matter and Police Brutality

The death of Trayvon Martin marked a turning point in the national consciousness of many Americans. In response, community organizers

Alicia Garza, Patrisse Khan-Cullors, and Opal Tometi began a movement called Black Lives Matter (BLM), "an ideological and political intervention in a world where Black lives are systematically and intentionally targeted for demise." The organization "is an affirmation of Black folks' humanity, our contributions to this society, and our resilience in the face of deadly oppression."[35] In the United States, black and brown bodies have often been abused and discarded, from the history of the foundations of this country to the current indiscriminate killings of young black men by the hands of those in authority.

In the years following Trayvon Martin's murder, several cases of young black men being killed by the police and law enforcement came to national attention. One of the most significant was the shooting of Michael Brown in Ferguson, Missouri. In August of 2014, eighteen-year-old Brown was shot and killed by a police officer named Darren Wilson. Brown had no prior record and no weapon on him when he was killed. Unreliable eyewitness accounts resulted in an incomplete picture of what happened during the event, but overall Wilson fired twelve shots that night. In November of that year, a grand jury—nine white jurors and three African American jurors—decided that there was not substantial enough evidence to indict Wilson.[36]

Following the failure to indict, protests and nonviolent popular resistance continued for weeks throughout Ferguson and soon spread to other cities across the United States. Many in Ferguson, upset over the bias of the Ferguson police, erupted into protests that led to the shooting of two officers.[37] Later the federal government investigated the justice system in Ferguson. In their report, they declared an entire overhaul was needed for the city's police department and law enforcement and cited many constitutional violations, including that the city used police and courts as money-making ventures and unapologetically engaged in racial profiling. All of this resulted in the police chief stepping down.

Just a month before Brown was shot, Eric Garner was killed by police officer Daniel Pantaleo in Staten Island, which is notorious for a district attorney who is often sympathetic toward the police force, a large portion of whom live in the borough. Garner was being arrested for allegedly selling untaxed cigarettes.[38] Pantaleo brought Garner to the ground and implemented a chokehold that had been banned by the department. The scene was caught on video, and in the video you can clearly hear Garner yelling that he cannot breathe (he was asthmatic). The autopsy of his body confirmed that the cause of death was the chokehold.[39] Following the incident, Pantaleo was suspended but remained on payroll, and the grand jury chose not to indict him. He was fired in 2019.

On April 12, 2015, twenty-five-year-old Freddie Gray was arrested and taken into custody by Baltimore police officers. The officers who arrested him said that they pulled over to the side of the road and made eye contact with him, which prompted him to run. The police got out and chased him down. When they eventually caught Gray, he requested an inhaler. One was not provided.[40] Cellphone footage revealed some evidence that Gray was crying out in pain and limping a bit while being put in the van. The police were instructed to pick up another prisoner, which meant an hour and a half passed before Gray received any medical attention.[41] In the back of the van, handcuffed with his feet shackled together and with no seat belt on, Gray suffered a broken neck and lost consciousness during the transport. He died about a week later.

Following his death, the city of Baltimore erupted into protests, especially after the six officers were each acquitted. In 2017, the Department of Justice decided not to bring any civil rights violation charges against the officers.[42] A University of Maryland School of Medicine School study found that half the mothers living in neighborhoods affected by the unrest following Freddie Grey's death were "so stressed by the circumstances that they suffered from insomnia, loss of appetite and other depressive symptoms."[43]

In July 2016, during a "routine traffic stop," thirty-two-year-old Philando Castile, a cafeteria supervisor at a Montessori school in St. Paul, was pulled over by police officer Jeronimo Yanez because his brake lights weren't working. A video camera from Yanez's car caught some of what transpired, though it doesn't show what was happening in Castile's car at every moment. The first minutes of the interaction were congenial. At one point, Castile can be heard saying, "Sir, I do have to tell you I have a firearm on me." Before Castile is even finished speaking, Yanez says, "Okay, okay . . . don't reach for it though." Castile continues speaking, and Yanez repeats himself. Castile says, "I'm not pulling it out."[44] Then Yanez yells, "Don't pull it out!" A woman screams, "No . . ." Yanez shoots multiple times and the woman screams, "You just killed my boyfriend!" All of this is visible from the dashcam. Subsequent shouts of obscenities from Yanez can be heard, along with "don't move" and the woman screaming, "Oh my God . . ." The video then shows a little girl, later revealed to be Castile's seven-year-old daughter, getting out of the back seat of the car and being taken by the other police officer on the scene.

After the shooting, Castile's girlfriend, Diamond Reynolds, started a Facebook live stream video of the incident, during which she explains what happened. Yanez continues to yell. Reynolds responds to the officer, "Yes, sir . . . I will sir." In the background, Castile can be seen bleeding to death. "Please, Jesus, don't tell me he's gone," she says.

Those who knew Philando said he was an upstanding man who followed the rules. At his school, he was known as the guy who helped students pay for their lunches if they could not afford them. He died at 9:37 p.m., just minutes after arriving at the hospital. A year later, Yanez was acquitted of second-degree manslaughter.[45] When asked why he pulled them over, Yanez stated it was for a broken taillight and also to investigate if the two passengers matched the description of two men who had committed armed robbery a few days earlier. The dashcam footage reveals that just over a minute after stopping them, Yanez fired seven shots. He claims that he was scared for his life at that moment.[46] And he probably was. But do fear and prejudice justify the killing of so many young black men?

Incarceration and the Crisis of Imprisonment

One of my first encounters with the US prison system came when I was serving on staff at Willow Creek in Chicagoland. Our prison ministry team was active in several local detention centers, city and county jails like Cook County in downtown Chicago, and prisons in both Illinois and other states, such as the Louisiana State Penitentiary in Angola. I learned how to preach in the Billy Graham chapel at Angola. Inmates have a tendency to be honest in their critiques and often know the Bible better than many preachers. They were harsh commentators. My preaching improved.

Of my many experiences ministering among men and women behind bars, one of the most impactful was early on in my ministry when I visited a juvenile detention center in the Chicago suburbs. The residents were all young boys, mostly teenagers, but some as young as eleven or twelve years old. Sitting with them over an evening meal, I began to learn about their personal histories and family situations. One young man told me about how he had no other path than to participate in gang activity. His father and brothers, and almost all of the men in his life, were currently incarcerated, had been in and out of jail or prison, or were dead. He said to me something I will never forget: "If you don't use your own gun, one will be used on you." It was clear that he didn't want to break the law or be a "bad kid," but he felt like he didn't have any alternative to survive.

I wept as I left the detention center and kept thinking about that young man and the other boys he was with who don't have role models or environments or alternatives that can provide a different kind of life for them. My own brother, who is white, has been in and out of county jails and the prison system, but because he had a family and access to financial resources to support him, he was given the opportunity to make different choices time and time again. The judges in his cases provided leniency, and the most time he spent behind bars was a few months at a time. My prayer when I had custody of him during a few of his teenage years was that he would not kill himself or be killed. There is not a doubt in my mind that if he were black, he would be in prison or dead.

Dominique Gilliard's excellent book *Rethinking Incarceration: Advocating for Justice That Restores* addresses incarceration theologically, biblically, and sociologically. It is a powerful call to restorative justice and a wake-up call about racial and socioeconomic discrimination in the American justice system. Gilliard also pushes churches to reconsider presuppositions regarding incarcerated people, the social functions of prisons, and theologies that promote an unquestioned allegiance to law and order.[47]

The book addresses five systems that contribute to what is known as the "prison pipeline": the war on drugs, private prisons, the war on immigration, mental health, and the school-to-prison pipeline. "Each of these pipelines is built on a legacy of racist and classist legislation that has paved the way for our present carceral epidemic," Gilliard writes.[48]

The "war on drugs" was a campaign coined by Richard Nixon and then expanded by Ronald Reagan. As part of it, the Drug Enforcement Administration (DEA) was created, law enforcement was able to retain most cash and assets seized after drug raids, and minimum sentencing for drug offenses increased. The ways that the campaign's laws were structured disproportionately affected minorities; through disparities between sentencing in drugs normally used by white Americans versus drugs more commonly used by African Americans, lax sentencing requirements, and the militarization of the police in the 1990s, it created a 1,100 percent drug increase between 1980 and 2006. Though only about 15 percent of drug users were African American, nearly 95 percent of people, when asked to describe a drug user, pictured a black person. And despite the fact that white youth are seven times more likely to use cocaine or heroin than black youth, African Americans make up the vast majority of drug offenders in prison. The view that black and Hispanic men are criminals and will most likely end up doing something to deserve being put behind bars is an ungodly, socialized view that our discipleship should prompt us to interrogate. Gilliard says about these assumptions: "When we dehumanize others, we become less human ourselves."[49]

The United States locks up more people than any other country in the history of the world. Private prisons, facilities operated by a third party contracted by the government, have contributed to the problem, being paid per diem either per inmate or for each available bed, with quotas that dictate the number of prisoners who must occupy the beds. Many quotas range from 70 to 100 percent occupancy rate. Privatizing prisons has created a multimillion-dollar business enterprise that raises moral and ethical difficulties for law enforcement and communities that depend on these institutions. The two largest prison corporations in the United States, the GEO Group and CCA, are classified as incorporated real-estate investment trusts. Because of this status, they are exempt from federal taxation. In 2011, collectively these institutions made 3.3 billion dollars.[50]

Immigration offenses contribute to the filling of these prison beds and quotas. Between 1990 and 2000 there was a 610 percent arrest increase for immigration offenses. Hispanic people represented only 16.3 percent of the population in 2011 but made up nearly 50.2 percent of those incarcerated for felonies. Half the arrests by the federal government in the 2014 fiscal year were for immigration-related offenses. And over the last twenty-four years, NBC News reported, there's been an overall increase in budget, staffing, and border wall construction, while the number of people trying to cross the border has decreased by four-fifths.[51] President Trump's immigration policies have only added to the number of Mexicans and other immigrants being deported and arrested. This issue of immigration is discussed further in the next chapter.

Mental health has always been connected to the prison population. In 2016, 400,000 people in prison had a mental health condition. As the number of individuals admitted to mental health hospitals fell (due to the deinstitutionalization of mental health facilities), the number admitted to prisons increased. Prison has become the new insane asylum.[52] In prison, mental health is ignored, and inmates are vulnerable to abuse, have a higher rate of deterioration, and are disproportionately left in solitary confinement.

The school-to-prison pipeline, the fifth factor Gilliard cites as contributing to mass incarceration, is defined by the ACLU as "the policies and practices that push our nation's school children, especially our most at-risk children, out of the classrooms and into the juvenile and criminal justice systems. This pipeline reflects the prioritization of incarceration over education."[53] Following the shooting at Columbine, zero-tolerance policies and police presence at school have both increased, but they have been proven to contribute very little to school improvement. Each of these five factors identified by Gilliard—the war on drugs, private prisons, the war on immigration, mental health, and the school-to-prison pipeline—as well as systemic racism, have contributed to the growth and sustainability of prison populations. Gilliard offers this response: "We need to see ourselves as connected to people we thought we were once estranged from."[54]

Catherine Hoke (née Rohr) founded one of the most successful prison programs, Prison Entrepreneurship Program (PEP), in the Texas prison systems. Her idea included training and equipping "really good criminals" to be really good businessmen. PEP had some of the lowest recidivism rates and was deemed hugely successful, even being highlighted by the *Economist* and other international news outlets.[55] After a personal resignation scandal, Hoke moved back to New York City and started Defy Ventures, which utilizes a similar model to what she had been doing in Texas.[56] If you or your community would like to partner with organizations doing great work in responding to our nation's incarceration crisis, consider volunteering and supporting efforts such as those of Catherine Hoke through Defy Ventures.

Violence Against Women of Color

The abuse of power of police and other law enforcement authorities doesn't only affect young men of color. African American racial justice advocate and nonviolence practitioner Micky ScottBey Jones tells of how she won't travel in a car without her cellphone fully charged, to be prepared to record the interaction if she is pulled over by the police.[57] Violence against women and sexualized racial violence continue to be realities. Consider a 2016 Department of Justice report that reveals that cops in Baltimore "coerced sex in exchange for immunity from arrest."[58] The officers specifically targeted "members of the vulnerable population," meaning women of color and women with limited financial resources. The Cato Institute, an American public policy research organization, found that after police violence and excessive force, the second most common form of police offenses is sexual misconduct.[59]

Dr. Kimberlé Crenshaw, a professor of law at UCLA and Columbia Law School and a black feminist, developed the theory of intersectionality, which refers to the intersection of race, poverty, and gender; this often has conflating effects on discrimination and injustice. Crenshaw has been a leading advocate for the "Say Her Name" campaign, a "movement that calls attention to police violence against Black women, girls and femmes, and demands that their stories be integrated into calls for justice, policy responses to police violence, and media representations of police brutality."[60] The African American Policy Forum (AAPF) issued a report in July 2015 focused on "resisting police brutality against black women." The report tells the story of the 548 arrests of police officers for sex-related crimes between 2005 and 2007. It also highlights "Say Her Name" victims like Sandra Bland, Rekia Boyd, Kayla Moore, Natasha McKenna, and so many other women who died while in police custody or directly at the hands of law enforcement officers.[61]

Toward Justice

Racial violence, police brutality, access to guns, and our nation's prison system all contribute to a national crisis that is disproportionately affecting individuals and communities of color. NFL quarterback Colin Kaepernick's refusal to stand during the national anthem at the start of football games was meant to call attention to issues like these.

Groups like The Marshall Project, named after Thurgood Marshall, the first black member of the US Supreme Court, collect stories and articles related to law enforcement. Their commitment and goal is to educate Americans by creating "a nonpartisan, nonprofit news organization that seeks to create and sustain a sense of national urgency about the U.S. criminal justice system."[62]

Christian or faith-based groups like Sojourners and Faith in Public Life provide the opportunity for people inspired by their spiritual convictions to engage not only in awareness and education but also activism and advocacy to address many of the harsh and painful phenomena discussed in this chapter. Bryan Stevenson of Equal Justice Initiative leads the way in his efforts to fight poverty and challenge racial discrimination in the criminal justice system.[63] These are just some of the incredible leaders and organizations who do courageous work responding to gun violence, police brutality, and discrimination within the justice system. May we be encouraged and inspired by their work, and motivated to do what we can to make a difference and respond.

For Further Study

Alexander, Michelle. *The New Jim Crow: Mass Incarceration in the Age of Color-blindness*. New York: The New Press, 2010.

Bradley, Anthony. *Ending Overcriminalization and Mass Incarceration: Hope from Civil Society*. Cambridge, UK: Cambridge University Press, 2018.

Claiborne, Shane. *Executing Grace: How the Death Penalty Killed Jesus and Why It's Killing Us*. New York: HarperOne, 2016.

Coogler, Ryan, dir. *Fruitvale Station*. New York: The Weinstein Company, 2013. Film.

Gilliard, Dominique DuBois. *Rethinking Incarceration: Advocating for Justice That Restores*. Downers Grove, IL: InterVarsity Press, 2018.

Hoke, Catherine. *A Second Chance: For You, for Me, and for the Rest of Us*. New York: Defy Ventures, 2018.

Kotlowitz, Alex. *An American Summer: Love and Death in Chicago*. New York: Doubleday, 2019.

Stevenson, Bryan. *Just Mercy: A Story of Justice and Redemption*. New York: Random House, 2015.

Questions for Discussion

- This was a difficult chapter to write. Many of the stories provoked pain, and it was challenging to imagine what life must be like in communities with significant violence. What from this chapter touched or moved you? Did you experience feelings of anger or helplessness? Why or why not?

- Have you or anyone you know had direct encounters with the police or law enforcement? Were those experiences positive or negative? Process as a group the stories that are shared.

- What information about incarceration and the application of discriminatory laws was new to you from this chapter?

- What from this chapter inspired you? Did any of the individuals or stories offer hope or solutions to some of the realities discussed here?

- How might God be calling you to respond to this chapter? Be attentive to provocations or thoughts that might be brought to mind during your discussions and in the days and weeks following. Is there anything you are feeling compelled to do?

Global Immigration and Battles at the Border

You shall also love the stranger,
for you were strangers in the land of Egypt.

DEUTERONOMY 10:19 (NRSV)

ON SEPTEMBER 2, 2015, the photo of a dead child with dark hair wearing a red T-shirt, navy blue shorts, and small little sneakers, his face immersed in the gently rolling oncoming waves, rocked the world. Aylan Kurdi, a three-year-old Kurdish boy, drowned in the Mediterranean Sea as his refugee family fled to Europe seeking safety from their home in war-torn Syria. NPR reported that the photo did more to mobilize people to respond to the humanitarian crisis in Syria than the preceding five years of statistics and death tolls: "Aylan's photo mobilized empathy and concern, soon bringing in record donations to charitable organizations around the world to aid the victims."[1]

The photo of Aylan's lifeless body also forced the world to come face to face with the realities of the global refugee crisis. Children from around the Arab world, particularly from Syria, Iraq, and Yemen, constitute the most vulnerable of those affected by war and conflict. Forcibly displaced, these children and their families feel like they have no alternative but to leave their native homeland and seek refuge in other countries where they often do not speak the same language and are unable to secure legal status to work and begin to rebuild their lives.

Fast forward to November 25, 2018, to the border between the United States and Mexico. Maria Lila Meza Castro, a mother wearing a shirt with the faces of the Disney princesses Elsa and Anna, pulls her twin daughters, both wearing diapers, away from the border wall to avoid them being suffocated or physically injured by the tear-gas canisters being thrown at them by US authorities. One child is barefoot; the other is about to fall. Castro has a look of desperation on her face as she tries to grab them out of harm's way. *Washington Post* reporter Kristine Phillips writes of the image:

> The smoke from the tear-gas canister, the children in diapers, the look of anguish, the wall in the background, that "Frozen" T-shirt—all encapsulated the chaos of that day, and . . . the truth about Central American migrants . . . as they made their way across Mexico and toward the United States to seek asylum.[2]

Immigration in the United States is one of the most hotly contested issues. It covers several different people groups, including refugees, asylum seekers, and "economic refugees" seeking access to a better life and more opportunities. President Trump and many of his followers paint a picture of violent immigrants seeking to enter the United States. In a meeting at the White House with California lawmakers, the president said, "We have people coming into the country or trying to come in, we're stopping a lot of them, but we're taking people out of the country. You wouldn't believe how bad these people are. These aren't people. These are animals."[3] His outlandish comment denies the human dignity of immigrants, and the claim that immigrants commit more violent acts and are detrimental to society remains unfounded. Karen Gonzalez, an immigrant advocate and staff member at World Relief, reminds us, "Research has shown, over and over again, that immigration is associated with lower rates of violent and property crime. Immigrants are actually less likely than the native-born to commit serious crimes or be imprisoned."[4]

Many immigration advocates assert that "welcoming the stranger" is not only a biblical mandate, but that increased immigration is good for the US economy as well. PBS Newshour published a piece in November 2018 debunking the myths that immigrants are a drain on the US economy. In fact, according to PBS, "Immigration has an overall positive impact on the long-run economic growth in the U.S." [5]

Biblical Considerations Regarding Immigration

Two books that contribute significantly to the discourse about biblical considerations of immigration include James K. Hoffmeier's *The Immigration Crisis: Immigrants, Aliens, and the Bible* and M. Daniel Carroll R.'s *Christians at the Border: Immigration, the Church, and the Bible.* It's worth summarizing some of their key arguments here. While both biblical scholars look deeply at what the Scriptures say about questions regarding citizenship, immigration, and the law, they come to very different conclusions about what a faithful Christian response might look like.

I studied Old Testament under Hoffmeier in 2002 at Trinity Evangelical Divinity School. He self-identifies as an immigrant because of the years he lived as a "legal immigrant" in Canada. He says of his experience, "The attitude of my family toward our host nation always was that we were guests and needed to be sensitive to the laws and social mores of the land." Having grown up with missionary parents in Egypt and being married to a Chinese American, he describes how he is "sensitive to the plight of immigrants." [6]

His goals in writing *The Immigration Crisis* were twofold. First, he sought to study and understand the biblical passages relevant to immigration conversations in their "historical and cultural context" through a "lens of Christian ethics and the theological affirmation that immigrants are people made in the image of God." Second, he sought to "look at the role that law plays and the obligation of citizens in general and Christians in particular, not to mention immigrants, to the rule of law." [7]

Hoffmeier makes a few distinct conclusions from his study of the biblical texts. Regarding nation states and governments, he concludes that recognized political bodies have the right to secure borders. He bases this idea on the fact that the Israel of the Bible had the right to "determine who entered their land and under what circumstances, and they could confer resident or alien status to foreigners should it be mutually beneficial." Applying this principle to governments today, he says it is their right to determine who is a citizen and who is allowed to enter and cross borders. At the same time, Hoffmeier asserts, "Biblical law is unambiguous that when people were accepted in Israel, the alien had to be treated fairly in legal and social spheres." For example, Hoffmeier cites Numbers 15:15-16, which demands that Israel's laws be equally applied.[8]

In his reflection about sanctuary cities for undocumented immigrants, Hoffmeier challenges the current notion and application, saying:

> Cities and municipalities who offer sanctuary for illegal aliens do so without the support of biblical law. Because biblical sanctuary was only intended to allow the innocent party to get a fair hearing and trial, and not for the purpose of sheltering lawbreakers from the authorities and agents of the state, cities that provide a safe haven for illegal immigrants, while intending to be a gesture of justice, are in fact violating federal law and are misappropriating biblical law.[9]

While Hoffmeier does believe that undocumented immigrants or "illegal aliens" should be held accountable to the law, he thinks legal immigrants who have honored the legal process should receive social benefits and services, such as public education, access to health care, welfare, job training, and other benefits. He thinks Leviticus 19:34—"the foreigner residing among you must be treated as your native-born"—applied then and applies now to the alien who lives "legally" among another nation.

This distinction between the "legal" and "illegal" alien is one of the most fundamental aspects of Hoffmeier's interpretation of the text. He argues that the Hebrew word *ger* ("alien") refers to the status of a "legal alien," whereas the Hebrew words *nekhar* and *zar* ("foreigner") refer to illegal or undocumented immigrants. In the end, he holds to a legal-based approach to immigration, saying that "it is legally and morally acceptable for a government to deal with those in the country illegally according to the nation's legal provisions."[10] Hoffmeier, and others who hold to a legal-based approach, refer to Paul's teaching in Romans that says, "Let everyone be subject to the governing authorities, for there is no authority except that which God has established. The authorities that exist have been established by God" (Rom 13:1).

Hoffmeier identifies his approach as a compassion-based legal approach, in that he believes laws must be obeyed but also that churches and Christian institutions can play a role in resettling immigrants once they have entered the country through appropriate legal processes. He doesn't think churches should be *sanctuary* churches that protect people from the law but rather should play a constructive role in mediating "between lawbreakers and authorities to help the defendants understand their rights and due process."[11]

Other Christian scholars, like M. Daniel Carroll R., have a different approach to and understanding of what the Bible has to say about immigrants. They rest heavily on the verses from Leviticus 19 that say, "When a foreigner resides among you in your land, do not mistreat them. The foreigner residing among you must be treated as your native-born. Love them as yourself, for you were foreigners in Egypt. I am the LORD your God" (vv. 33-34). Calling for more open immigration policies, these Christians focus less on legality and more on love.

In a review of and response to *The Immigration Crisis*, Carroll praises Hoffmeier for his sections on how Egypt dealt with foreigners. "The Nile River and the fertile land along its banks were a constant lure for outsiders seeking food and shelter in times of drought or famine, so the Egyptians had a long history of dealing with individuals and groups trying to come into their territory," Carroll explains. "Hoffmeier cites several inscriptions and presents reproductions of reliefs that reflect Egypt's attitudes and policies towards these people."[12]

However, he also offers critique of Hoffmeier's argument, citing his "ignorance" regarding the domestic history of immigration, contemporary

US laws governing immigration, the causes of migration and displacement, and the "devastating impact of global market forces on sociopolitical realities." His main critique is that it is incorrect to assume present US laws governing immigration are "fair and coherent."[13] For Carroll, the right a country has to govern its own borders does not justify nor dismiss the injustices and problematic consequences of bad laws and legislation.

Carroll also comes to a different conclusion from Hoffmeier about the meaning of the scriptural texts regarding immigration, believing that Hoffmeier takes too much liberty in differentiating between legal and illegal entry into a territory. He says, "The point is that the verb *gwr* has the broad term meaning 'to reside,' irrespective of legal standing (e.g., Judg. 5:17; Ps. 15:1; Jer. 49:18, 33; 50:4). . . . Methodologically, it will not do to define the terminology so tightly on the basis of several examples."[14] Carroll believes a more appropriate interpretation of these passages is someone entering into Israel both legally and illegally.

In any case, his overall approach does not rest on distinguishing the legality of entry for immigrants. In his book on the topic, *Christians at the Border: Immigration, the Church, and the Bible,* Carroll begins in Genesis and asks what it means to be human. Being created in the image of God, all people deserve to be honored, respected, and valued as persons. He says, "These immigrants and refugees are people above all else, people caught up in the trials, tribulations, and joys of life." Carroll goes so far as to say that a violation against human rights and the dignity of immigrants and migrants is a "violation against God."[15]

This is not to say Carroll doesn't believe nation-states have the right to control their own borders; he does. However, his approach differs significantly from Hoffmeier's because he insists that laws regarding immigration should be just, fair, and good for the benefit of all humanity. In this way, Carroll's approach toward immigration is based on hospitality and community, citing verses throughout the Scriptures that esteem hospitality as a biblically centered ideal. This model considers the plights and trials of the immigrant with compassion, while seeing a justice-oriented response as an obligation of the faithful Christian.

Carroll concludes his call to activism with the following: "An appropriate response to the complicated situation in society will not come from detached, objective analysis, cost-benefit calculations, efficiency quotients, and cultural arguments." Rather, he continues, "Assured with the teachings of the Word, empowerment of the Spirit, the example of Jesus, and the blessing of the Father, Christians can be the light of the Triune God in this national confusion that sometimes can be so dark. Let the journey to reconciliation begin. May the church lead the way."[16] The church has an opportunity to witness to the world about God's love, acceptance, kindness, hospitality, and goodness through the way they welcome the refugee.

Immigration in Context

According to World Relief, the world is in its worst refugee crisis since World War II. The Syrian civil war has created an enormous refugee crisis in the Middle East, with nearly eleven million Syrians having had to flee their home country since March 2011. Carroll provides some context for the issue: "Each major period of immigration to the United States has been a part of larger migrations happening simultaneously around the world and, therefore, has been inseparable from the political, social, and economic conditions of other nations."[17] In 2019, the global refugee population reached about 68.5 million, with children making up just over half of that. Refugees are one of the most vulnerable populations, as they are at greater risk of violence, and children, who are often out of school, are more likely to be exploited.

Historically, many immigrants entered the United States through Ellis Island near the Statue of Liberty. The most recognizable quote on the Statue of Liberty comes from the sonnet "The New Colossus," written by Emma Lazarus, and says, "Give me your tired, your poor, your huddled masses yearning to breathe free."[18] While the United States has long had a reputation as being a country of immigrants, the racial stratification and poor treatment of immigrants of color must be acknowledged as a darker part of that history.

Early immigration policies were very limiting in who they would allow to become a US citizen. The Naturalization Act of 1790 only allowed free white people who had high moral character to become citizens. In 1875, immigration restrictions didn't allow those who were sick or criminals to enter the US and also limited the rising Asian immigrant population, eventually just banning immigration from certain Asian countries. Immigration continued to flow primarily from Europe. The Chinese Exclusion Act of 1882 was the first significant law limiting immigration to the United States by a particular ethnic group. The act put a ten-year moratorium on the immigration of all Chinese laborers.[19] A few years later, the Alien Contract Labor Laws of 1885 and 1887 limited "certain laborers" from entering into the United States. Often limitations were placed on particular ethnic groups and communities of color.[20]

Early twentieth-century laws began capping immigrant population and creating quotas based on nationality. These immigration caps remained in place even through World War II. For example, the United States only took in 132,000 Jewish refugees during the war.[21] Immigration policies then began to loosen slightly, allowing a limited number of Asian immigrants to enter in the 1950s. In 1965, the landmark Immigration and Nationality Act removed the quotas that favored European countries. Since then, immigration into the United States has primarily been from Asian and Latin American countries. The Immigration Reform and Control Act of 1986 granted legal status to immigrants from Latin American countries who met certain requirements.

The September 11, 2001, attacks on the United States prompted many changes in immigration policies. The government created the Department of Homeland Security, whose entire focus is border control, antiterrorism, and immigration and customs. It is currently the third largest department in the executive branch. Other organizations created in the aftermath of September 11 include Immigration and Customs Enforcement (ICE), US Customs and Border Protection, and US Citizenship and Immigration Services. Each of these departments created a more intense immigration system, including fingerprinting, interviews, sharing information with other countries, and entry-exit systems at airports. National security became the primary focus.

Since September 11, 2001, the United States has welcomed about 800,000 refugees, with only three being arrested for terrorist charges. Compared to other countries, however, we welcome a relatively low number of refugees. For example, in 2016, the United States welcomed 85,000 refugees compared to one million in Germany.[22]

Immigration Under the Trump Administration

In January 2017, President Trump signed an executive order that banned citizens of seven Muslim-majority countries from visiting the United States for 90 days, suspended refugees from entering for 120 days, and suspended Syrian refugees from entering at all.[23] Trump's cabinet members at the time stated that the order was not intended to target any particular religious group. However, Acting Attorney General Sally Yates said that it was targeting Muslims and that she would not support the execution of it. Since Christians in the Middle East are viewed as a "persecuted religious minority," Trump said it was fair to give preference to Christians and minority groups living in Muslim-majority countries.[24]

Across the United States, there was significant resistance to this executive order. Lawyers and court systems began working to override it, and a judge from the Department of Justice blocked it. In March 2017, a new, slightly modified version of the same law removed Iraq from the list of banned countries, allowed in green-card holders and those with dual citizenship, and no longer stated a preference for Christians or singled out Syrian refugees.[25] This order was also blocked by the federal courts. The state of Hawaii actually sued Trump, claiming that the president overstepped his constitutional right in barring specific countries from entering the country.[26]

One of Trump's campaign promises was that he would limit incoming immigrants and refugees. He had also implied that had his immigration policies been in place, 9/11 would not have occurred.[27] However, this ban didn't apply to any of the countries who participated in the September 11 attacks, including Egypt, United Arab Emirates, Lebanon, and Saudi Arabia, where most of the attackers came from.[28]

Then, in September 2018, a "caravan" of immigrants from different Central American countries, mostly from Honduras, began to head toward the United States border to seek asylum. Beginning with just under two hundred people in the Honduran city of San Pedro Sula, the group grew to nearly four thousand people as they made their way through Guatemala.

Taking to Twitter, Trump claimed that this caravan held gang members and dangerous people from the Middle East.[29] With little evidence to back those claims, Trump continued to push for the governments of El Salvador, Guatemala, and Mexico to do something to stop the caravan, even threatening to stop all foreign aid if they refused to act.[30] As the caravan continued, Mexico responded, claiming that "migrants with valid documents and visas will be allowed in, but that those who attempt to enter illegally will be detained and deported. Those seeking asylum or some other forms of protection can request it, but will have to wait in a detention center for as many as forty-five days."[31] But the people in the caravan continued north, and President Trump sent 5,600 troops to the Mexico-US border in preparation for the caravan's arrival and ordered them to remain there until early December. The mission, dubbed "Operation Faithful Patriot," is estimated to cost at least $200 million.[32] However, within a month of the deployment, the Pentagon announced the anticipated cost of the border troops at $72 million.[33] Trump also threatened to close ports of entry. It is important to note that the Pentagon quickly changed the name of the operation most likely due to its political undertones.[34]

In November 2018, the caravan started arriving in smaller groups of travelers in Tijuana, Mexico. Mexico had agreed to hold those waiting for legal entry into the United States. As more and more people began to arrive, they were forced to make shelters, find food, and simply wait until their process for seeking asylum could be started. On November 25, a peaceful march was planned to protest these conditions, after weeks of waiting with the situation deteriorating. Marchers approached the border, and more US officials were sent to set up barricades. As the marchers got closer, a group rushed the border. Points of entry were shut down as people were running at the wall. Shortly thereafter, the United States fired tear gas at people.[35]

By December 2018, US Customs and Border Protection was being scrutinized over their treatment of those detained for illegal entry into the United States. That month, two children from Guatemala died under their authority: Jakelin Caal Maquin, a seven-year-old Guatemalan girl, and Felipe Gomez Alonzo, an eight-year-old boy from Guatemala.[36]

The most controversial immigration policy of the Trump administration in late 2017 and throughout 2018 was the decision to separate children from their parents. It was implemented to deter people from crossing illegally into the United States via the Mexico border. As people illegally crossed the border, they were criminally prosecuted and arrested. And because children couldn't remain with their parents in prison, they were separated. This resulted in at least 2,700 children being taken from parents between October 1, 2017, and May 31, 2018.[37] And, being poorly organized, it overwhelmed border security and border state courts. Even families who sought asylum—technically a legal way to enter the United States—were tried as criminals and had their children taken from them. Once separated, the children were under the responsibility of the Office of Refugee Resettlement, which is part of the Department of Health and Human Services.

This policy of removing children from families was also in effect during the Obama administration. However, in 2014, the Obama administration attempted to detain families together or would not criminally prosecute immigrants who had children. Child separations were more often a fluke. The "zero tolerance" policy under the Trump administration aims to prosecute *everyone* who is caught crossing the border illegally. Separations are a key feature and have happened more frequently under the current administration. [38] In June of 2018, President Trump finally signed an executive order ending family separations as part of the "zero tolerance" policy.[39]

In addition to the crisis at the US-Mexico border, immigration from other countries has also been significantly curtailed. In 2018, the United States only welcomed forty-four Syrian refugees, when a year prior we had welcomed six thousand. Even with the promise of protecting persecuted Christians overseas, many of the Trump administration's policies have led to a decline in Christian immigrants from areas like Syria, Iran, Iraq, and others entering the United States.[40] By June 2019, we were on track to welcome our lowest amount of refugees since the 1980s. In the first six months of 2019, the United States only welcomed about 12,155 refugees, less than 50 percent of the stated goal for the year.

In spring 2019, Trump's immigration policies regarding the Mexican border came to a head. For the entirety of his campaign and on into his presidency, he promised to build a wall at the US-Mexico border. He also made numerous claims that he would have Mexico pay for it.[41] In May 2019, the *Washington Post* reported that numbers of migrant arrests along the southern US border were "blowing past a breaking point," reaching over one hundred thousand. Families from Honduras and Guatemala were detained in such large numbers that the holding cells were overcrowded, with little room for people to even lay down. Children, with or without parents, account for about 40 percent of those apprehended in May. US Customs and Border Protection spent most of their time processing and caring for those who had been detained.[42]

Meanwhile, Congress was retaliating against Trump's policies by passing an immigration bill that would protect Obama's "DREAMers." On June 15, 2012, President Obama created a policy known as Deferred Action for Childhood Arrivals (DACA) for young people who had entered the United States illegally before the age of sixteen years old. These children came to be known as "DREAMers," in reference to a separate bill, the Development, Relief and Education for Alien Minors (DREAM) Act, that did not get passed.[43] DACA did not provide a path to citizenship but rather offered temporary protection from deportation, work authorization, and the ability to apply for a social security number.[44] After a couple of years, the Obama administration planned on expanding the DACA program to extend to the parents of the children protected by the policy. However, several states disliked the expansion and sued the US government, preventing it from happening. President Trump has announced his desire to phase out DACA but has not indicated that he has a plan for its replacement.[45]

On June 4, 2019, the House of Representatives passed the American Dream and Promise Act of 2019, a bill that would allow two million children, including those previously covered by DACA, a path to citizenship. Many Christian groups, including the Presbyterian Church (USA), have come out in favor of the legislation. The PC(USA) Office of Public Witness put out a statement saying, "This legislation will be the first step towards positive immigration reform and will provide protection for qualifying DREAMers, and people with Temporary Protected Status and Deferred Enforced Departure—people who have previously been living in uncertainty and fear." They cited the Hebrew Scriptures as a reminder that God "guided the migration of the Hebrew people, and in God's son, Jesus, who was forced to flee his own land and enter another as a refugee." They continued, "We believe that our God continues to watch over immigrant people and calls us to advocate for justice alongside them (cf. Psalm 46:9, Isaiah 1:17)."[46]

The day after the House's passing of the bill, Trump retaliated by canceling English classes, soccer, and legal aid for unaccompanied children migrants in US shelters, explaining in a notice to shelters who were housing these children that the government would no longer pay for services, including schools or recreational activities. Many Democrats and immigrant advocates were horrified by this, given that many of the children are fleeing from violent circumstances, and the average wait time for their placement is forty-eight days. "These are children that are going through tremendous suffering," Florida Representative Debbie Mucarsel-Powell said. "If the Trump administration does cancel these basic necessities like education, exercise and legal services, they are robbing [these children] of their humanity."[47]

Reform and Response

Many Christians across the United States agree that immigration reform is necessary. Conservative pastor and member of the Gospel Coalition David Platt says, "The gospel compels us in our culture to decry any and all forms of oppression, exploitation, bigotry or harassment of immigrants, regardless of their legal status. These are men and women for whom Christ died, and their dignity is no greater or lesser than our own."[48] Groups like Christians for Comprehensive Immigration Reform (CCIR) explain that their engagement in the plight of refugees and immigrants is "driven by common moral and theological principles that compel us to love, care for, and seek justice for all of God's people, including the foreigner and visitors among us."[49]

Other faith traditions also join together in the call for comprehensive immigration reform in the United States. In late 2018, faith leaders from Islam, Judaism, Sikhism, and different branches of Christianity (including evangelical, Quaker, Methodist, and more) all signed a letter voicing their disapproval of Trump's decision to deny asylum as a legitimate way of entering the country. The letter was delivered to Congress in November 2018.[50]

The Evangelical Immigration Table (EIT), a coalition between Christian universities, evangelical associations, denominations, and nonprofit relief groups that believe successful immigration reform is possible, has been a unique place where both Republicans and Democrats come together to discuss, pray, and work toward comprehensive immigration reform. The group has been active in responding to the current crisis with press calls and letters to specific people—including ICE officials, political representatives, and the president himself—calling for reform.[51]

Many conservative and progressive Christians alike mostly agree that Trump's "zero tolerance" policy has detrimental effects and that the government should be protecting the family unit. However, even among this Christian solidarity, there are some, like Franklin Graham and John Daley, who do not directly link the policy of family separation to Trump and have maintained their support of his presidency. Others who denounce family separations have already been outspoken critics of Trump.

Numerous pastors and church leaders have become part of the Sanctuary Movement. Formed in the 1980s, the Sanctuary Movement committed to provide refuge for immigrants and refugees coming to the United States who were fleeing civil unrest in Latin American countries.[52] Several religious centers around the country and the world have dedicated themselves to being a place of sanctuary for immigrants. The number of religious institutions offering sanctuary in 2017 was nearly eight hundred.[53] One of those institutions was a North Carolina church that housed a Mexican man named Samuel Oliver-Bruno for eleven months before ICE authorities detained him. Congregants were heartbroken, singing "Amazing Grace" and attempting (unsuccessfully) to block the deportation van from leaving.[54] Also in 2017, Arch Street Methodist Church in Philadelphia sheltered a Mexican man in the church's basement for six months, while he was separated from his family. A church in Buffalo, New York, had a Honduran family of six. Although their actions are against the law, these Christian communities believe they are doing the right thing, given that the Trump administration has been indiscriminately detaining any illegal immigrants, even those with no criminal record.[55]

Many Christian groups not only provide sanctuary but also meet basic needs like food and water, even though arrests of those assisting and helping people across the border have been on the rise since 2017, and the harboring statute makes it punishable by law to provide any assistance to "certain aliens."[56] The 2004 national bestseller *The Devil's Highway* tells the stories of migrants seeking refuge and what their experience is like. Often it involves crossing the desert for days with limited access to food and water and being taken advantage of by their "coyote" guides who demand more money along the way. When I first read the book, I wept at the stories of immigrants simply seeking a better life and the struggles they have been willing to go through to offer their children and families opportunities for a better future.

National Justice for Our Neighbors (NJFON) has its roots in the United Methodist Church and is another group committed to comprehensive immigration reform and a compassionate response to immigrants. NJFON provides legal assistance to immigrants by offering free or low-cost legal services at eighteen locations across fifteen states. Clinics run by churches and other community groups provide education for the broader community about immigrants living in their midst. Pastor Chris Pierson of Gary United Methodist Church in Wheaton, Illinois, is on the board of NJFON. In telling about his church's engagement, Pastor Pierson said, "Engaging with these clinics provides a transformational experience for the members of our congregation to be able to engage in significant and meaningful ways in response to the crisis facing immigrants in the United States today."[57]

What are other ways US Christians can respond to these issues? Consider volunteering for the United Nations Refugee Agency (UNHCR).[58] Find out if your city is an area with a large refugee population and volunteer with local community centers teaching English. Partner with and support organizations like Border Angels, which focuses specifically on Mexico-US border relations.[59] Based on Jesus' exhortation in Matthew 25 to "care for the least of these," Border Angels provides assistance to those crossing the border. Many branches of the organization need volunteers to help bring items to the border and to leave water along migrant-heavy routes. You can also pray for the many people who have decided to come alongside refugees and offer care and support, wherever they may be on their journey. On World Refugee Day in June 2019, Congress considered a resolution that aimed at continuing to provide funding for refugee resettlement services; helping to alleviate the burden on host countries like Jordan, Ethiopia, and Bangladesh, who have welcomed a majority of refugees; and meeting the challenges of the worst refugee crisis in history.[60] Christians can pay attention to these kinds of resolutions and engage in political advocacy to support US government funding for refugees.

June 20 is World Refugee Day, a day that "acknowledges the courage, strength, and determination of women, men, and children who are forced to flee their homes due to persecution."[61] Many Christian humanitarian and development agencies have specific opportunities around World Refugee Day to host a prayer service or vigil or to engage in activism and advocacy on behalf of refugees. If your family is looking to be more intimately involved, you might consider hosting a refugee through the site Refugees Welcome.[62] Or declare your solidarity with a refugee by sending #LettersofHope through CARE.[63] You could also watch the documentary on Netflix called *White Helmets*, about a group of unarmed rescue workers who rush to the scene when a bomb is deployed in Syria.[64]

World Vision[65] and World Relief[66] are two of the leading Christian humanitarian and development organizations responding to refugees in Syria and the Middle East. Visit their websites to learn more about how you can move beyond hashtag activism and get involved in meaningful and transformative ways.

For Further Study

Amstutz, Mark. *Just Immigration: American Policy in Christian Perspective*. Grand Rapids: Eerdmans, 2017.

Carroll R., M. Daniel. *Christians at the Border: Immigration, the Church, and the Bible*. Grand Rapids: Baker, 2008.

Chang, Alvin. "Watch How Immigration in America Has Changed in the Last 200 Years." Vox, August 3, 2017, www.vox.com/2016/1/4/10709366/immigration-america -200-years.

Gladwell, Malcolm. "General Chapman's Last Stand." In *Revisionist History*. Produced by Pushkin Industries. June 13, 2018. Podcast. http://revisionisthistory.com /episodes/25-general-chapman's-last-stand.

Hoffmeier, James K. *The Immigration Crisis: Immigrants, Aliens, and the Bible*. Wheaton, IL: Crossway, 2009.

Jeung, Russell. *At Home in Exile: Finding Jesus Among My Ancestors and Refugee Neighbors*. Grand Rapids: Zondervan, 2016.

Kaemingk, Matthew. *Christian Hospitality and Muslim Immigration in an Age of Fear*. Grand Rapids: Eerdmans, 2018.

Soerens, Matthew, and Jenny Yang. *Welcoming the Stranger: Compassion & Truth in the Immigration Debate*. Downers Grove, IL: InterVarsity Press, 2018.

Urrea, Luis Alberto. *The Devil's Highway: A True Story*. Boston: Little Brown, 2004.

Questions for Discussion

- Is immigration a complex and controversial topic to talk about in your community? If so, why do you think that is?

- Old Testament laws speak often about how to treat the "stranger" or the "foreigner." Find some of those passages and reflect on how they make you feel. Why do you think God calls us to care for the immigrant?

- What is at the heart of the immigration issue for you? For your church? For your community?

- Spend some time in prayer for the families who have been affected by separations at the border. What are some feelings that come up when reflecting on that situation?

- What are some ways you can create positive change around the issue of immigration?

8

Divisions of Race and Ethnicity Around the World

Do you think I came to bring peace on earth? No, I tell you, but division.
From now on there will be five in one family divided against
each other, three against two and two against three. They will be
divided, father against son and son against father, mother against
daughter and daughter against mother, mother-in-law against
daughter-in-law and daughter-in-law against mother-in-law.

LUKE 12:51-53

NOMINATED FOR THREE OSCARS and numerous awards, the 2004 movie *Hotel Rwanda* brought the horrors of the Rwandan genocide into the homes of millions in the United States and around the world. Featuring Don Cheadle as Paul Rusesabagina, the house manager of a hotel in Kigali, the movie tells the riveting story of his family's struggle to escape the raging mass murders and bloody violence of the conflict between the majority Hutus and the Tutsis. Acting on an arbitrary racial designation imposed by the Belgians, Hutus and Tutsis had been in conflict since the time of colonial rule. Rusesabagina, a Hutu married to a Tutsi—something unacceptable at the height of the violence, given the deeply entrenched hatred of the Hutus and Tutsis toward one another—was even more personally entrenched in the conflict. Because he was working in a context that serves Westerners predominantly, Rusesabagina thought he would be protected by UN peacekeeper forces. But the Western world virtually disappeared in the conflict, evacuating their own and leaving the native Rwandans to suffer genocide.[1]

What transpired in Rwanda is only one example of many of the twentieth- and twenty-first-century divisions that exist in the world today around race and ethnicity. As globalization proliferates and the world is "made small," the historical implications of racial discrimination and injustices continue to affect race relations around the world. Countries that have been historically white, or have at least maintained white dominance in economic power and politics, must come to terms with a new world order that is much more multinational, diverse, and racially complex.

Historians Marilyn Lake and Henry Reynolds's comprehensive work *Drawing the Global Colour Line* expands our scope of understanding about whiteness, helping us see it as a transnational framework that has global implications. They chart the progression of global racial ideologies and conclude by highlighting the many ways the international community has committed to deconstructing racial ideologies and advocating for universal human rights.

The UN has played an important role in this work, the authors note. In 1948, the United Nations General Assembly passed the Universal Declaration of Human Rights with a vote of forty-eight in favor and eight abstentions. The goal of this declaration was that "all peoples and all nations" would be able to promote respect for the enunciated rights and freedoms of all of the member states and people under their jurisdiction.[2] Lake and Reynolds write of the accomplishments of the mid-twentieth century:

> Race had been topped from its eminence. . . . But race was not the only concept under siege. Much of the discrimination within the Western countries and their Empires was premised on the idea of differential development, of peoples being more or less advanced or backward or being more able to exercise the restraint and discipline considered necessary for successful self-government.[3]

In 1963, the UN passed the historic Declaration on the Elimination of All Forms of Racial Discrimination, "shattering the myth that whites were superior to non-whites."[4] This global acknowledgment marked a significant shift in ideology and did contribute to increased decolonization by the United States, Canada, Australia, and the United Kingdom, but in reality the practices of racial violence, discrimination, and injustice continued in national and global contexts.

The relationship between predominantly white countries and the rest of the world is only one aspect of the "global color line." What about the numerous conflicts around the world that include interracial violence and even genocide, such as Myanmar and the Rohingya, the genocide and its aftermath in Rwanda, the conflict between Sudan and South Sudan, the Syrian civil war, and the devastating humanitarian crisis in Yemen? These are the contexts we'll turn our attention to in this chapter.

Myanmar and the Rohingya

The 1995 film *Beyond Rangoon* starring Patricia Arquette captured the world's attention about the Southeast Asian country of Burma (now Myanmar) and what was happening there. It depicted the violence of the country's military rulers in response to the popular pro-democracy protests of 1988, which resulted in massacres and civil unrest. The film also brought global attention to the 1991 Nobel Peace Prize winner Aung San Suu Kyi, who served several years of house arrest during that time.

Today Myanmar continues to be in the news because of the ongoing conflict related to the Muslim Rohingya, one of the ethnic minority groups located in the predominantly Buddhist country. The Myanmar government views the Rohingya as illegal immigrants from neighboring Bangladesh and has denied them citizenship since 1982, which has also denied them the right to vote and to practice certain professions, and excluded them from the 2014 census.

During the era of British colonial rule (1824–1948), the Rohingya people migrated to the land area of Myanmar for labor. Because the British viewed Myanmar as a province of India, this movement was seen as an internal migration. In 1948, however, when Myanmar gained independence, the newly formed country did not recognize the Rohingya as one of their ethnic groups. In 1982, further restrictions were placed on the Rohingya people by making the most basic citizenship level almost impossible to obtain, requiring paperwork proving their families had been there prior to 1948 and necessitating the passing of a basic language test.

In recent years, the United Nations accused Myanmar of ethnic cleansing and genocide.[5] Since 1972, the Rohingya have been migrating back to Bangladesh to escape the persecution they have experienced in Myanmar. Violence escalated in October 2016, when nine border police were killed and the Myanmar government claimed that it was caused by a Rohingya army. Since this incident, brutal attacks have been carried out on the Rohingya people. By August 2017, at least 288 Rohingya villages had been destroyed, and women and children were being brutalized and shot at by government armies.

The Rohingya people constitute one of the fastest growing refugee populations in the world. In the past couple decades, over half a million Rohingya have fled to Bangladesh.[6] The Bangladesh Foreign Minister AH Mahmood Ali said in 2017, "The international community is saying it is a genocide. We also say it is a genocide."[7] However, care for the Rohingya has been minimal in Bangladesh. The refugee camp near the town of Cox's Bazar was relocated to a hilly, rain-prone area, and the majority of refugees have moved out of the official camp, instead occupying surrounding land in makeshift settlements. In November 2017, the Bangladesh and Myanmar governments signed a deal for the return of 650,000 Rohingya refugees, and a camp near the border of Rakhine was set up for arrivals, but the United Nations still reports that conditions are not yet safe or suitable for the Rohingya.[8]

Conflict in South Sudan

The Sudanese civil war in South Sudan has been described in large part as a conflict between different ethnic groups with religious distinctions.

In 2011, South Sudan was formed as an independent nation-state, splitting officially from the country of Sudan, their now neighbors to the north. Before South Sudan was officially a nation, a number of tensions and issues existed that affected the relationship of many ethnic groups throughout South Sudan. Two of the largest are the Dinka and the Nuer. When South Sudan formed, President Salva Kiir, from the Dinka group, elected Riek Machar, from the Nuer tribe, as his vice president, to represent a show of unity between tribes who have a long history of violence. Previously, Machar himself had led a massacre of nearly two thousand Dinka tribe members. The representation and public display of unity did not last long. Machar began publicly criticizing President Kiir. The conflict between the two groups spiraled out of control quickly, with both sides arming themselves and attacking their rivals. In December 2013, violence that started in the capital city resulted in the deaths of a thousand people and the displacement of thousands more in the first few days of fighting.[9]

The civil war in South Sudan is made even more heartbreaking given that the formation of the country came out of a brutal civil war with their neighbors to the north that lasted for over two decades. In 2005, the United States helped create a plan for the predominantly Christian South Sudan to secure independence from the Muslim-majority North. However, after South Sudan's declaration of independence, the international community that had assisted them withdrew, leaving South Sudan to deal with the residual ethnic tensions.

The Dinka and Nuer tribes have fought within South Sudan since December 2013. The shaky treaty that was established in 2015 was quickly forgotten and the fighting has continued. Machar lives in exile in South Africa. It has been difficult to obtain accurate numbers for the conflict because very few humanitarian groups are let in, but many believe the death toll from December 2013 to April 2018 is estimated to be about 383,000.[10] In addition, over a million people have been displaced. A peace treaty was signed in September 2018, but few experts believe that it addresses the root of the conflict.

In 2010 and 2011, I had the privilege of living in Jerusalem during much of what later came to be known as the "Arab Spring," which included largely nonviolent popular resistance against decades-old despotic regimes throughout the Arab world. Leaders like Hosni Mubarak in Egypt, Muammar Gaddafi in Libya, Zine el-Abidine Ben Ali in Tunisia, and Ali Abdullah Saleh in Yemen were ousted as a result of popular uprisings in each of their respective countries.[11] There is much debate about the long-term effects of the Arab Spring, and some have called the ongoing unresolved violence in places like Syria and Yemen the "Arab Winter" to denote the resurgence or continued success of authoritarianism and Islamic extremism.[12]

In 2019, the Syrian Civil War, which began in 2011 when a group of peaceful protestors were shot and killed by the Bashar al-Assad government, continues as a complicated mess of rebel groups, governments, and inconsistent intervention by foreign powers.[13] The group of protestors who were first attacked turned into a rebel group to fight the Assad regime.[14] As the conflict within Syria continued to develop, an ethnic group in the northeast (on the border of Turkey), the Kurds, began organizing to fight a separate battle against the Assad government to establish self-rule. Further complicating the civil war, the extremist group ISIS (Islamic State of Iraq and Syria), also known as *Da'ish*, began attacking both sets of rebel groups in 2014, claiming large portions of land along the way.

Part of what makes the Syrian Civil War so significant is the geopolitics involved because of the support of different countries for different sides of the Syrian conflict. The United States and Saudi Arabia have been the main support and provided funding for different segments of the rebel groups, whereas Iran, Russia, and Lebanon have supported and equipped the government and troops of Assad.[15]

The Syrian Civil War has also had devastating effects on the populations living within and displaced outside of Syria, and in surrounding areas. Turkey hosts more Syrian refugees than any other country (about

3.6 million).[16] There are 935,000 Syrian refugees in Lebanon, 664,000 in Jordan, and 252,000 in Iraq.[17] And about half of all Syrian refugees are children under the age of eighteen. The majority of Syrian refugees do not live in camps but are scattered in urban centers in Lebanon and Jordan, making it more difficult for relief agencies to efficiently help them. Zaatari and Azraq in Jordan, two of the few refugee camps, are home to around 139,000 Syrians total.[18] The civilian population of Syria has felt the brunt of this civil war, though. As of April 2018, there were nearly 5.6 million registered refugees and 6.5 million people displaced inside the country's borders.[19]

US involvement and intervention in the Syrian crisis grew when Assad carried out chemical attacks on his own people on August 21, 2013. Assad's forces released a chemical weapon outside of Damascus in nearly twelve different locations, killing 1,429 people, including 426 children.[20] Following this attack, the Obama administration drew a "red line," indicating that they would no longer tolerate this behavior and threatening a military strike. Obama and his advisers convened political, religious, and other leaders to discuss whether or not they would have the support of different communities if they decided to go to war with Syria. I was on a phone call with the White House with several other religious leaders, the vast majority of whom only expressed being against a US war in Syria. In the end, the administration chose not to intervene with military action. Another chemical attack was carried out by the Assad regime in April 2017. This time the Trump administration chose to deploy cruise missiles to the location where US intelligence believed Assad's forces launched their attack from. The Syrian government denounced this action.[21]

In 2019, as the Syrian conflict entered its ninth year, the United Nations reported that the crisis was "far from over."[22] Though the anti-government uprising that began in 2011 has largely been crushed, three new conflicts continue in Syria. One of the conflicts is in northwest Syria in Idlib, where Turkish forces and allied local groups are fighting against pro-Assad forces. In February 2019 this conflict displaced eighty-six thousand people and killed ninety civilians, half of whom were children.[23] The second area of conflict is in northeast Syria in Hasakah where Syrian Democratic Forces (SDF) (US-backed Kurdish groups) are fighting against foreign insurgents. SDF blames Turkey, but some appear to be the remnants of ISIS, even though ISIS no longer holds territory in Syria. The third region of violence is in southern Syria, which is controlled by the government. Tensions have been building between Syrian government forces and foreign allies such as the Russian military police, Iranian militias, and Hezbollah.[24]

In early October 2019, President Trump announced he was removing US troops from the border between northeastern Syria and Turkey. This marked a shift in US policy vis-à-vis Syria and was criticized by many peace activists and Christian experts on the Middle East. Jeremy Courtney, founder of the Christian nonprofit Preemptive Love based in Iraq, wrote about three unintended consequences of the US pullout. First, Courtney says, "We've told the world you can't trust the US. The United States is proving that, as a matter of foreign policy, we will use our allies when it suits our short-term objectives."[25] Courtney continues and identifies the second unintended consequence is that the removal of US troops would allow for the "return of ISIS" to the battlefield. Finally, the presence of US troops in Syria had prevented Turkish bombing in the Kurdish region of Syria and deterred the exacerbation of the refugee crisis.[26]

The organization I lead, Churches for Middle East Peace (CMEP), represents more than thirty denominations and organizations committed to ending conflict and violence in the region. CMEP provides resources and materials on the geopolitics of the conflict and provides opportunities to engage in political advocacy in Washington, DC. In 2013, we called for the immediate release of the Greek Orthodox and Syriac Orthodox priests kidnapped in Aleppo.[27] In 2017, we condemned the Syrian government's use of chemical weapons and called on the Trump administration to show restraint and not escalate violence in the region.[28]

Yemen

Yemen, the poorest of the Arab countries in the Middle East, is another country that has had ongoing conflict since the Arab Spring. Now called the Yemeni Civil War, it has resulted in what has been called the greatest humanitarian crisis of our time.[29] The Yemeni government backed the 2003 US invasion of Iraq, which led to increased internal sectarian conflicts. The Houthi group, which began as a religious revival of Shiism in northern Yemen, has been fighting against the Yemeni government military since 2004. Prior to the Arab Spring, the president, Ali Abdullah Saleh, had been in power since 1958. In 2011, Abdullah Saleh handed over power to Abdrabbuh Mansour Hadi. Having been unhappy with the rule of Saleh, the Houthi group (and the civilian population) took advantage of the transactional period during the transfer of power and were able to occupy the northern Saada province. After fuel subsidies were lifted in July 2014, angry people took to the streets, calling for the president to step down. In 2014, the Houthis were able to take over the capital city of San'a. President Hadi fled the country in 2015.[30]

Essentially, the Houthis, backed by the Iranian government, are fighting those who are loyal to the Hadi government.[31] The Hadi government, in turn, is backed by a number of countries, including the United States, but particularly Saudi Arabia.

According to Amnesty International, neither the Hadi regime nor the Houthi rebels have been beyond reproach. Rather, both sides have committed serious human rights violations, and civilians are experiencing the brunt of the conflict. Airstrikes from the government have targeted schools, medical facilities, and mosques. Houthi rebels have arrested and harassed journalists, academics, and human rights defenders. On both sides, they are using imprecise weapons in heavily populated areas that result in many civilian casualties. As of 2018, the death toll was up to 6,800, with more than 10,000 casualties.[32]

In addition, as a result of fighting, Yemen has been pushed to the brink of a famine. Of the twenty-eight million people in Yemen, half of the total population face pre-famine conditions and are reliant on external aid for survival.[33] In 2017, nearly fifty thousand children died, though the number is probably much higher. With only about half of the health facilities operating, and many Yemenis too poor to access them, people often die at home and go unreported. Humanitarian assistance has been significantly limited because of the delay of visas and restrictions on imports like equipment and other necessary supplies. As a result, thousands of civilians living in Yemen are going hungry and starvation-related diseases are on the rise, including cholera and the collapse of immune systems.[34]

The issues in Yemen are not just because of a lack of food but also because of the economic turmoil that the Saudi-backed Yemeni government has inflicted on its people. After the Houthi rebels took the capital city of San'a, the government transferred its banking operations to the southern city of Aden. Because the Saudi government dictates the bank policies in this region, civil servants in Houthi locations were no longer paid and money was printed quickly, causing the value of the riyals to plummet and eroding the savings of most of the population.[35] While in some locations in Yemen food is plentiful, many people are unable to afford the soaring costs of food. And both the government and Houthi rebels are doing what they can to undercut the other. The Saudi Arabian Coalition, supported by the United States, bombed bridges and factories, leading many to believe that they were attempting to stop food from reaching Houthi rebel areas. The coalition has also issued a blockade to stop the import of food and supplies, especially in the northern area of Yemen. Meanwhile, Houthi rebels have rerouted relief aid to areas where their families or other rebels live or have used it as a way to make money for themselves. Many workers in the region believe that the key to reducing the famine is to stabilize the economy of Yemen so that people are able to earn incomes again.[36]

Yemeni workers and residents feel the indifference of the West toward their suffering. This is particularly sad given that the United States has played a role in the ongoing civil war in Yemen because of its complicity in and support of the Saudi-led coalition. The United States and Saudi Arabia have had a longstanding alliance since 1933, when the first US business involvement with oil contracts occurred.[37] Saudi Arabia is the world's largest holder of oil reserves, and for many decades the United States was reliant on them for its oil needs.[38] In recent years, the need for Saudi oil has dropped, but they still control a large portion of the world's total oil supply, giving them leverage in the global economy. The Trump administration has had a special interest in Saudi Arabia, with President Trump making it the first country he visited after becoming president and taking a harsh stand against the Iran nuclear deal in support of Saudi Arabia's interest. Following the death of journalist Jamal Khashoggi in October 2018, President Trump did little to criticize the Saudi government—who many believe was instrumental in the death—choosing instead to highlight Saudi Arabia as an important US ally and business partner. And during his 2015 campaign, Trump emphasized his great relationship with Saudi Arabia and the large amount of interaction that his own business has with Saudi powers. Currently, Trump cites the arms deal with Saudi Arabia as something that will bring many jobs to the United States.[39]

In US politics, the relationship with Saudi Arabia and its coalition forces' effects on the Yemeni people have been highly debated. However, in April 2019, both the Senate and House passed historic legislation that would remove all US armed forces currently supporting the Saudi-led coalition's war effort in Yemen. Churches for Middle East Peace (CMEP) praised the bipartisan vote "as a promising step toward addressing the world's worst humanitarian crisis that has left 80 percent of Yemen's 28 million people in need of humanitarian assistance." The press release included this statement by me:

> In the interest of ending U.S. complicity in a conflict, which has claimed the lives of tens of thousands of civilians and displaced over 2.5 million people, we call upon President Trump to sign this resolution into law. The destruction in Yemen neither promotes regional stability nor is in the interest of the United States. Not only does the humanitarian crisis

demand an immediate response, but the U.S. must also stop being a contributory factor in the escalation and continuation of the conflict.[40]

But on April 16, 2019, President Trump vetoed the bipartisan resolution, explaining, "This resolution is an unnecessary, dangerous attempt to weaken my constitutional authorities, endangering the lives of American citizens and brave service members, both today and in the future."[41] The following month, Trump declared a state of emergency in Saudi Arabia and the UAE to justify the sale of arms to Saudi Arabia without going through the process in Congress. Representative Ro Khanna expressed his disappointment to the *New York Times* over the action. "The president had the opportunity to sign a historic War Powers Resolution and stand with a bipartisan coalition, including his allies Rand Paul, Mark Meadows and Matt Gaetz, to stop endless wars," Khanna said. "He failed to uphold the principles of the Constitution that give Congress power over matters of war and peace."[42] The United States continues to defend its support of Saudi Arabia with the argument that they need to stop Iranian forces and their influence of the Houthis. The claim is that if the Houthi rebels are not under control, it will lead to further instability in the Middle East.[43]

Several humanitarian organizations like Oxfam America lead the way in highlighting the reality and effects of war on the civilian population in Yemen.[44] In June 2019, twenty-one Christian churches and denominations, including Bread for the World and CMEP, signed a historic letter addressed to congressional leaders stating:

> We thank you and Congress for playing a key role in pushing for humanitarian relief and ensuring the U.S. government does more to apply pressure to the warring parties, as most recently demonstrated through its unprecedented passage of the Yemen War Powers Resolution. We believe that the President's veto of that Resolution must strengthen the resolve of Congress to ratchet down the fighting and help broker peace.
>
> We therefore urge you, as elected leaders, to exhaust every possible legislative option to end U.S. support for the war in Yemen; hold all warring parties accountable; and help foster peace that people of Yemen

desperately need and deserve. Given the magnitude of human suffering as a result of this war, we call for the immediate end to any policy that continues military support in the form of intelligence, logistical support and through the sale and transfer of weapons. . . . We ask that you take advantage of the political momentum built in Congress to push for an end to the fighting and to help broker peace.[45]

Those who signed the letter included Orthodox, Catholic, mainline Protestant, and historic peace churches, and evangelical denominations, member communions, and organizations. The church is leading a rallying cry to respond to the crisis in Yemen.

Rwanda: The Aftermath of Genocide

The 1994 genocide in Rwanda is one of the many scars across humanity from the late twentieth century. And because just under 90 percent of the Rwandan population is Christian, including Catholics, Protestants, and Seventh-Day Adventists, the church remains culpable. Academic and former staff member with Human Rights Watch (HRW) and International Federation for Human Rights (FIDH) Timothy Longman writes in the first chapter of his book *Christianity and Genocide in Rwanda* that "people came to Mass each day to pray, then they went out to kill." Longman's conclusions are harrowing. He says, "Not only were the vast majority of those who participated in the killings Christians, but the church buildings themselves also served as Rwanda's primary killing fields." It has been difficult to read Longman's research and findings. He continues,

> The involvement of the churches, however, went far beyond the passive use of church buildings as death chambers. In some communities, clergy, catechists, and other church employees used their knowledge of the local population to identify Tutsis for elimination. In other cases, church personnel actively participated in the killing.[46]

For anyone questioning the legitimacy of Longman's claims, he provides hundreds of pages of explanation and examples. Lord, have mercy.

More than a quarter of a century ago now the Rwandan genocide began, with its systematic killing of the Tutsi minority. When Rwanda was still under the control of Belgium and Germany, the people of Rwanda were divided into two categories: the Tutsi and the Hutu. Colonists classified Tutsis as anyone with a "long nose"; they were considered foreigners.[47]

The event that ignited the genocide was the shooting down of a plane carrying the Rwandan and Burundian presidents over the Rwandan capital city, Kigali. This ushered in chaos and violence that particularly affected Tutsi civilians, who were hunted down and killed. In just one hundred days, eight hundred thousand people were killed at the hands of Hutu extremists. The genocide came to an end when the Tutsi-majority rebel group, the Rwandan Patriotic Force (RPF), defeated the Rwandan army and government. While the Tutsi people also killed thousands of Hutu civilians, the amount was hardly comparable to the genocide of the Tutsis at the hands of the Hutus.[48]

The immediate effect of the Rwandan genocide was a crisis in neighboring Zaire (now the Democratic Republic of Congo or DRC), where refugees died of water-borne illnesses and military leaders started two more wars. Other effects included economic destabilization and trauma in Rwanda. When leaders of the genocide fled the country, they took several monetary assets with them, leaving behind no economic structure. In addition, a lack of attention to cash crops and the destruction of any infrastructure made it hard for Rwanda to attract business growth. Those who remained in Rwanda were faced with ruined physical structures as well; many had no place to live. Socially, thousands of children were orphaned, abandoned, or lost. Many women were left pregnant or were infected with STIs as a result of war crimes. The overall population of Rwanda fell by 40 percent due to death or people fleeing the country. The withdrawal of foreign aid in the early 2000s caused the country's service sector to suffer.

The United States, as well as several other Western countries like France, were criticized for how they handled the crisis. France had received information that detailed much of what would eventually occur during the genocide. And yet even with foreknowledge of what would transpire, Western nations did not intervene.

Longman warns of the Rwandan church's enmeshment with governing powers and authorities. He writes,

> The Christian message received in Rwanda was not one of "love and fellowship," but one of obedience, division, and power. Far from exonerating the churches, the resistance that some Christians presented to the genocide—and my own research indicates that a number of people were indeed inspired by their faith to challenge authoritarianism and oppose ethnic violence—demonstrates that the churches potentially *could* have opposed the genocide.[49]

Then he spends the rest of his book seeking to answer the question of why the churches, overall, chose not to stand against authoritarianism and ethnic violence. Both the Rwandan church's complicity and the global church's lack of intervention are questions that Christians around the world must contend with. The church's being in bed with power and authority, informed by political associations, affiliations, and ideological presuppositions, has allowed and even contributed to the murder and death of millions. We aren't just talking about historic Christian depravity such as the Crusades of the twelfth century or uses of the Bible to support slavery in the United States and around the world. The question of Christian culpability in the annihilation of people groups remains a contemporary question—one with which the Rwandan genocide forces us to contend.

For Further Reading About Rwanda

Longman, Timothy. *Christianity and Genocide in Rwanda*. New York: Cambridge University Press, 2010.

Sebarenzi, Joseph, with Laura Ann Mullane. *God Sleeps in Rwanda: A Journey of Transformation*. New York: Atria, 2009.

Temple-Raston, Dina. *Justice on the Grass: Three Rwandan Journalists, Their Trial for War Crimes, and a Nation's Quest for Redemption*. New York: Free Press, 2005.

A Response of Repentance

One of the clearest ways Christians can make a difference in these global crises is by providing money and supporting relief and development agencies that are actively responding to racial violence around the world. InterVarsity Christian Fellowship's triennial Urbana Student Missions Conference (urbana.org) provides a place where Christian college students can gather to learn more about mission agencies and relief and development organizations seeking to both provide assistance and advocate for justice. If you are interested in engaging further with relief and development agencies that are on the ground providing crisis management and humanitarian assistance, look up both Catholic Relief Services (CRS) and Save the Children and the work they are doing to care for Yemeni children.[50] Also consider exploring the work of Islamic Relief USA, which is one of the main development agencies responding to these realities in the Arab world.[51] Finally, if you are interested in supporting one of the leading Christian organizations responding to the violence against the Rohingya people, consider World Relief, which is one of the most active groups working in Myanmar.[52]

Genocides around the world have long been instigated because of assumptions of racial or ethnic superiority. Consider the *Shoah* (Holocaust of the Jewish people), where Hitler and the Nazi regime caused the forced extermination of more than six million Jews, and where millions of the Roma people, Poles, and the handicapped were also targeted.[53] In his book, Longman identifies the problematic reality that Christian ideology and theology is often abused to make genocide possible. Comparing the Rwandan genocide to that of the Jewish people under the Nazis he writes: "Though the Nazi leaders were themselves often hostile to Germany's Christian churches, Christianity nevertheless provided ideological support that made the Holocaust possible." Longman does not claim that the longstanding animosity and hatred toward Jews by Christians was a "sufficient cause for Nazi genocide" but rather that Christianity allowed Nazi commands to be made "comprehensible and tolerable." Other than resistance from a small minority, which included leaders like Dietrich Bonhoeffer and the Confessing Church, the leadership of most of the denominations within Germany supported the Nazi regime, or at a minimum did not oppose it. For example, Christian leaders shared baptismal records that by exclusion helped identify the Jewish members of the community. The 1933 signing of a Concordat with Hitler by Pope Pius XI further shows the lack of resistance within the dominant denominations and most predominant church leaders including the Vatican.[54] While the Holocaust remembrance museum Yad Vashem in Israel includes memorials to the "Righteous Among the Nations," the majority of formal church organizations and leaders were at best silent during the forced extermination of the Jewish people.[55]

One of the only appropriate responses to these realities of brokenness, violence, and evil within the church is to repent. The book I coauthored, *Forgive Us: Confessions of a Compromised Faith,* provides a chapter that focuses on the church's sins against Jews and Muslims. Christian history is fraught with horrific examples of anti-Semitism and hatred toward Jews. From the first century, Jews as a collective whole were blamed for the crucifixion of Christ. Levi Parsons, one of the first US missionaries to the Middle East, exemplifies how many Christians carried that belief well into the nineteenth and twentieth centuries in his description of the Jews as "degenerate children" whose hands were "imbued in the blood of the Son of God."[56] In the twenty-first century, the Anti-Defamation League reports that anti-Semitic incidents reached near historic levels in 2018.[57]

In *Forgive Us*, at the end of the chapter addressing Islamophobia and anti-Semitism, we invite people to pray this closing prayer:

> Be silent . . . Breathe . . . Listen to God's words to you about the real people whose cries God hears every day . . . people who cry out in every corner of the world; whether that corner is peppered with steeples, temples, mosques, or synagogues. Listen to God's heart for them. Listen . . . Can you hear their cries? When you're ready breathe in deeply. As you breathe out, say "Forgive us."[58]

This could be prayed in response to Christian anti-Semitism but also in response to the church's culpability in violence and genocide in places like Rwanda. Lament over the brokenness of the world and repentance as manifested in the simple prayer "Forgive us" are appropriate initial responses. But repentance is not enough. The church must also be committed to never allow these types of atrocities to be committed again in the name of God. What can we learn from Christian complicity in Rwanda? How can the church today respond to racial divisions and violence such as the civil wars in Yemen and Syria? These are questions we must continue to ponder and to which we must respond.

For Further Study

Belz, Mindy. *They Say We Are Infidels: On the Run with Persecuted Christians in the Middle East*. Oxford: Lion Books, 2016.

Elmer, Duane. *Cross-Cultural Conflict: Building Relationships for Effective Ministry*. Downers Grove, IL: InterVarsity Press, 1994.

Katongole, Emmanuel M., and Jonathan Wilson-Hartgrove. *Mirror to the Church: Resurrecting Faith After Genocide in Rwanda*. Grand Rapids: Zondervan, 2009.

Lederach, John Paul. *Reconcile: Conflict Transformation for Ordinary Christians*. Harrisonburg, VA: Herald, 2014.

See, Suzanne. *We Walk Afraid: A Fifty-Two Week Prayer Guide for Yemen*. Scotts Valley, CA: CreateSpace, 2016.

Tizon, Al. *Whole and Reconciled: Gospel, Church, and Mission in a Fractured World*. Grand Rapids: Baker Academic, 2018.

Questions for Discussion

- Why do you think it is important for American Christians to care about conflicts that are happening on the other side of the world? Are there biblical texts that come to mind that speak to global violence and ethnic conflict?

- Why are these international conflicts easy to ignore? Considering the scale of many of these conflicts, why do you think that they're often ignored in the media?

- Were you aware of the ways that the United States is involved with international conflict? What do you think about the way that the United States influences international policy?

- Was there a situation above that especially moved you? How can you pray for Christians in the midst of these conflicts?

PART 4

Gender

9

#MeToo, Women in the Workplace, and Women in the Church

Again I looked and saw all the oppression
that was taking place under the sun:
I saw the tears of the oppressed—
and they have no comforter;
power was on the side of their oppressors—
and they have no comforter.

ECCLESIASTES 4:1

THE "SILENCE BREAKERS" ON the cover of the 2017 Person of the Year issue of *TIME* magazine are credited with having released the story of Harvey Weinstein's sexual misconduct and abuse toward hordes of women in Hollywood.[1] The courage of those first few voices unfurled an almost never-ending list of victims, including movie stars, high profile athletes, church congregation members, and girls and women from all walks of life. According to *TIME*, this was the "great unleashing that turned the #MeToo hashtag into a rallying cry." Coined by social activist Tarana Burke in 2006 to build solidarity, #MeToo is now a national movement.

In June 2018, the *New Yorker* published an article called "Silence Is Not Spiritual: The Evangelical #MeToo Movement," which highlighted how prevalent the abuse of women is in the context of the church.[2]

What lessons need to be learned from these injustices toward women coming to public light?

My ministry began at Willow Creek Community Church. Considered by many to be the founder of the megachurch movement, Willow Creek founder Bill Hybels and his ministry-shaped evangelism helped the church once again became relevant through "seeker services" designed to reach generations of people who had been disheartened and hurt by previous church experiences. The Willow Creek Association expanded and eventually included churches and ministries in 130 countries. My ministry, spiritual life, and relationship with God have been deeply shaped by my years at Willow Creek, and I consider myself a "daughter" of the church. It's not surprising then that people had a hard time making sense of the tidal wave of allegations about Bill Hybels that began to become public in 2018. The *Chicago Tribune* reported that he "had been the subject of inquiries into claims that he ran afoul of church teaching by engaging in inappropriate behavior with women in his congregation—including employees—allegedly spanning decades."[3]

What the public did not know was that behind the scenes over multiple years, leaders within the Willow Creek community, people on the board of the Willow Creek Association, and former pastors and employees had been asking that the multiple allegations from three women related to sexual misconduct on Bill's part be thoroughly investigated. The allegations included a confession from one of the women concerning a fourteen-year sexual affair (this woman later recanted under troublesome circumstances).[4] The *Chicago Tribune* article, and the many articles that followed, were a last resort for these Christian leaders who felt they had no recourse but to go public. Former teaching pastor Nancy Ortberg said this about the experience: "Telling the truth about this has been the most painful decision of my professional career, but it is the right one."[5]

While church elders have apologized, resigned, and sought to take responsibility, it seems Hybels has not. Initially the church elders responded by supporting Hybels in his denial of the allegations against him and accusing those who brought forth their concerns of "collusion."[6] After repeated denials, Hybels did resign from Willow, but without any acknowledgment of guilt regarding the claims brought against him. He did say he wished he'd responded more "humbly" and acknowledged "anger at the accusations." He also conceded a lack of judgment on his part in placing himself "in situations that would have been far wiser to avoid."[7] Within six months, more accusations of wrong behavior and abuse arose. Among those speaking up was Pat Barnowski, who had worked for Hybels and whose story was recounted in a *New York Times* article.[8] Within a few days of this new round of allegations, Willow's copastors, Steve Carter and Heather Larson, and the entire elder board of the church resigned.[9] Later that year an independent investigation was conducted that found that the claims against Hybels were "credible" and that there was evidence he had used "sexually inappropriate words and actions."[10]

The story of what happened at Willow breaks my heart. Willow Creek has been known for its education on leadership. Its Global Leadership Summits have brought in some of the top leaders in the world, including pastors, business leaders, and politicians. However, "leadership" at Willow Creek has always included dysfunctions related to power, where leaders who are "stars" and A-players are the most esteemed, valued, and lauded, seemingly beyond accountability. The abuse of power has also included the mistreatment and abuse of women. Celebrityhood, big screens, and the pressure to perform in front of thousands of attendees every week only adds to dysfunction.

Some believers, citing 1 Corinthians 6 with its exhortation to "not take believers to court," felt that making the allegations against Hybels public was unbiblical. New Testament scholar Scot McKnight, who worked closely with Willow for more than a decade, responded to that sentiment this way:

> At times one has to go public, has to announce things public, has to speak
> the truth to the powers because the powers won't listen. Prophetic action
> is profoundly biblical; it has been the agent of truth-telling, repentance,

and restoration time and time again in the history of the Bible and the history of the church. Prophetic action should never be the first thing someone does; and in this case the Ortbergs and Mellados very biblically waited and waited and waited before they went public. When interpersonal and behind-closed-doors in the church options are worn out and not finding the truth, then public, prophetic action is both warranted and biblical.[11]

Willow Creek is still trying to pick up the pieces. Leadership has sought to follow the recommendations of the advisory group, elect new elders, and keep the congregation informed about the process.[12] Conversations and meetings between some of the people who brought forward the allegations and the new elder board have taken place. The church is working to rebuild, repair, and restore.

My own story at Willow involves a situation where a boss acted inappropriately toward me in a sexual manner, soliciting intimacy and making inappropriate comments. When I did not return his advances and sought to set boundaries, my ministry roles and responsibilities were significantly diminished. I was punished for not welcoming his advances. This transpired over the course of several months.

I soon learned he had made propositions to other women. Together, we went to the elders. An "independent investigation" took place that was found "inconclusive." I was instructed that I needed to be better about "saying no" and letting him know the advances were not welcome. It felt like the elders were telling me that his overtures were my fault. The politics of the situation made firing him difficult, so church leadership decided to move him out of his role supervising our staff team to a different part of the organization. I, and I believe the other women, were forced to sign a "nondisclosure" agreement that we would never tell about what happened. This is the first time I am publicly writing a small piece of my story.

A few years later it was discovered that this senior leader had been involved in an inappropriate sexual relationship with someone outside the context of his marriage, and he was fired. In many ways, I am indebted to this man. He hired me for my first major role in ministry. I learned a lot from him. But his treatment of me—and other women—and the silencing of us by the elders was spiritual (and sexual) abuse. This wrong has never been reconciled. #MeToo.

Gender Violence in Society and the Church

Sexual violence against women and discrimination toward the female sex has a long history within the United States, predating the founding of our country. Native American historian and gender rights activist Andrea Smith writes in her groundbreaking book *Conquest: Sexual Violence and American Indian Genocide* about the intersections of race and gender. She begins by calling for analysis and strategies that address the reality that gender violence is "not simply a tool of patriarchal control, but also serves as a tool of racism and colonialism." In other words, "colonial relationships are themselves gendered and sexualized."[13] Violence against women of color, particularly Native Americans and black women who were enslaved, was a mechanism by which white men could dominate and use their power to control and oppress. In response to these historic abuses, which continued for decades in boarding schools that housed Native American children who were taken away from their families and communities, Smith cofounded an organization called INCITE! Women of Color Against Violence. INCITE! is a national organization of feminists of color that builds coalitions around the intersection of state violence and interpersonal sexual and domestic violence from the perspective of grassroots organizing.[14]

The story of African American women in the United States also rests in the intersection of race and gender. The 2003 book *Shifting: The Double Lives of Black Women in America* celebrates the success of black American women while also acknowledging that, "no matter how intelligent, competent, and dazzling she may be, a Black woman in our country today still cannot count on being understood and embraced by mainstream white America." Based on the African American Women's Voices Project, *Shifting* asserts that "racist and sexist attitudes and discriminatory behavior are still taking a significant toll on Black women."[15] Their analysis concludes:

> Race discrimination against Black women persists. Gender discrimi-nation against Black women is also pervasive. Most Black women "shift" their behavior to accommodate others. Discrimination is experienced most frequently at work. Black women frequently submerge their talents and strengths to support Black men. Sexual abuse and harassment of Black women is all too frequent. There is increasing pressure for Black women to meet conventional beauty standards. Black mothers are acutely aware of having to train their children to cope with discrimi-nation. Black women have a disproportionately high risk for depression. And Black women often feel discriminated against within their churches.[16]

As the #MeToo movement has revealed, discrimination, harassment, and abuse in the workplace, sports, churches, and throughout society has been far too prevalent. Communities of color are often the most vulnerable because of the effects of intersectional injustices and the oppression of racism and white supremacy.

As the #MeToo movement grew, so did rumblings of sexual abuse and discrimination within the church. The #ChurchToo movement was started by two progressives, self-described "ex-vangelicals": Emily Joy, a poet, author, and yoga instructor; and Hannah Paasch, a writer. By November 2017, there were more than two thousand tweets using the hashtag #ChurchToo. *Bustle* published an article called "These 'Church Too' Tweets Are a Powerful Reminder That Sexual Abuse Isn't Limited to Hollywood."[17] In describing the #ChurchToo movement on her website, Joy says, "At the root of #ChurchToo stories are patriarchy, male leadership coupled with female submission, purity culture, evan-gelical personality cult culture, lack of sex-positive and medically ac-curate sex education, homophobia, and white supremacy."[18] Joy and Paasch don't critique just the abuses of women within the context of the church but also conservatism and abuses of church leadership and power.

In an interview with Emily Joy, I learned that her father was a Southern Baptist youth minister when she was born. After graduating from the conservative fundamentalist Moody Bible Institute in Chicago, she began to "move way" from some of the traditions she had been raised in. Slowly and over time, she explained, she started "meeting real people with life experiences" that didn't fit the things she had been taught within the context of conservative evangelicalism, and she came to realize "this thing that I was taught wasn't true." She woke up one day and realized she didn't believe any of it. Today Emily is "sex positive" in every way, shape, and form and now believes in the "complete destruction of purity culture rooted in white supremacy." When I asked Emily how she was received by her family and community back home, she responded, "Not well." She doesn't have a good relationship with most of her family, and the majority of her mentors have unfriended her or abandoned her because of her shifts in perspective about life. As a woman who self-identifies as queer, she described being largely abandoned and ignored by the church. "My skin is pretty thick," she told me.[19]

Another movement, called #SilenceisnotSpiritual, has sought to respond to questions of sexual abuse within the context of the church, particularly within the evangelical community, and has challenged the church "to stop standing by and start standing up for women and girls who experience violence."[20] Launched by a statement with more than 150 initial signatories and facilitated by One Million Thumbprints, Freedom Road, and the Imago Dei Fund, the #SilenceisnotSpiritual community affirmed: "Women are equally called and created with the full potential and capacity to steward the world. All abuse disfigures human dignity and distorts the image of God."[21]

By 2019, the #MeToo, #ChurchToo, and #SilenceIsNotSpiritual movements had swept through the Southern Baptist Convention (SBC), the largest Protestant denomination in the United States, with nearly fifteen million members. On June 12, 2019, PBS put out a report titled "Why Survivors Aren't Surprised by Sexual Abuse Inside Southern Baptist Churches."[22] More than seven hundred victims within the SBC came forward in a "growing wave of survivor stories." The SBC president responded, saying that their churches need to "repent of a culture that has made abuse, cover-ups, and evading accountability far too easy," while also launching a study group to provide resources and recommend policy changes. Numerous leaders within the SBC, including the Southwestern Baptist Theological Seminary President Paige Patterson, lost their jobs over "mishandled allegations or their own misconduct." *Christianity Today* told the stories of several survivors of abuse within the SBC.[23]

How prevalent is sexual violence? According to the National Sexual Violence Resource Center (NSVRC), one in five women and one in seventy-one men will be raped during their lifetime. The victims of rape and sexual assault are 91 percent female and 9 percent male.[24] Forty-four percent of women have experienced some other form of sexual violence, including sexual coercion, unwanted sexual contact, and noncontact unwanted sexual experiences. Among women who have experienced rape, more than 28 percent report that it happened when they were between the ages of eleven and seventeen.[25] And overall childhood sexual abuse in the United States is prolific, with one in four girls and one in six boys being sexually abused before they turn eighteen years of age. [26] Sexual abuse and violence are major problems that affect millions of women, and the church has often perpetuated it or been complicit.

With the rise of #MeToo has come much conversation about false reporting. The 2006 case where an African American student falsely accused three white members of Duke University's lacrosse team of rape also brought questions about reporting to the forefront. The boys were suspended from upcoming lacrosse games, the coach was forced to resign, and the 2006 season was canceled, but when the charges were dropped, the woman faced no consequences.[27] Nonetheless, in a ten-year study on allegations of sexual assault, it was found that only 8 out of 136 cases were false.[28] And when it comes to rape and assault, it is more likely that cases go completely unreported than that they are falsely reported. Indeed, because less than 5 percent of rapes are reported, less than 1 percent of accusations out of all rapes that actually occur are false.[29] The ten-year study also concluded: "Given the intense debates and controversies that mark the public discourse on sexual assault, it is remarkable how little research has been done in the United States on how rape cases are handled in the criminal justice system."[30]

What Does the Bible Have to Say About Women and Abuse?

More than two decades before the #MeToo and #ChurchToo movements hit the scene, academics Catherine Clark Kroeger, then–associate professor of classical and ministry studies, and James R. Beck, a clinical psychologist, coedited the book *Women, Abuse, and the Bible: How Scripture Can Be Used to Hurt or Heal,* which addresses theological, spiritual, and practical implications of abuse and the historic treatment of women within the church. Compiled from papers presented at a Christians for Biblical Equality (CBE) conference, their book dives deeply into what the Scriptures have to say about gender roles, clergy sexual abuse, and pastoral care in response to gender violence, and offers theologies for rebuilding and healing brokenness after abuse has occurred.[31]

At times, the verses in Scripture that talk about the submission of women to men have been used to justify the physical and sexual abuse of women. *Women, Abuse, and the Bible* stands firm in its conviction: "Make no mistake about it—the purpose of God is to deliver believers from the hands of violent men." Citing verses in Scripture where God is the rescuer from oppression, such as Psalm 72:14, the authors call God's people to "go and do likewise."[32]

The book also provides practical, and still relevant, examples of how the church can respond or seek assistance when the presenting troubles may be beyond its capabilities. They assert that, "through prayer, action, study, and planning, we can create an environment within our churches that communicates our repudiation and abhorrence of abuse in any form within the household of God."[33]

The 2019 Annual Meeting of the Southern Baptist Convention sought to address the allegations of hundreds of abuse cases within the church that had been unreported or unpunished.[34] Just prior to the meeting, the convention published a report called "Caring Well: A Report from the SBC Sexual Abuse Advisory Group," which was designed "to educate churches on the sexual abuse crisis, equip churches on how to care well for survivors, and prepare churches to prevent abuse."[35] In acknowledging significant failings of the church in ministering and responding to the victims of abuse, the report says, "We lament the fact that it took a national movement of reckoning for abuse to force us to take this issue seriously in our own convention. . . . It should now be obvious that the problem has been and still is more widespread than anyone has realized, affecting our congregations all over the country, from the smallest church pastored by a bivocational minister to the megachurch with hundreds on staff."[36]

The #ChurchToo movement as a more specific expression of #MeToo has brought to light decades of abuse toward and oppression of women and other minority groups within the context of the church. It is an example of "light shining in darkness," where truth has been revealed because of the persistence of a few courageous voices saying we will be silent no more.

Women in the Workplace

Significant progress has been made in workplace equality for women through the years. For example, according to the International Labor Organization, in 1979 women in the United States earned 62 percent of what their male counterparts earned. In 2010 the number was up to 81 percent.[37] But there is still much work to be done! Equality for working women in the United States continues to be elusive, even in the twenty-first century.

Women's participation in the labor force also continues to be unequal compared to men (though this can be for many reasons, of course, including personal choice, finances, and family life). In 2000, 60 percent of American women participated in the workforce, but by 2010, this number had decreased to 46.7 percent. The great recession of 2007–2010 affected these numbers, because one in five women worked part-time due to the economic depression and the inability to find full-time work. Prior to the recession only one in ten women worked part-time.[38] And while women are attaining jobs in executive leadership and becoming CEOs of companies, it still happens at significantly lower percentages than men. In 2019, only 6.6 percent of Fortune 500 companies were led by female CEOs. And this number was a historic high, with *Fortune* reporting: "As of June 1, [2019], 33 of the companies on the ranking of highest-grossing firms will be led by female CEOs for the first time ever."[39]

Sexual harassment in the workplace also continues to create real challenges for working women. According to the Equal Employment Opportunity Commission, 25 to 85 percent of women in the workforce report that they have experienced sexual harassment.[40] What's more, 75 percent of harassment victims experience retaliation when they speak up, and 95 percent of reported incidents go unpunished.[41] Author Peggy Orenstein aptly captured part of the problem when she wrote: "Women can't lead fuller lives until men are equal partners in the home, but men can't be true partners at home until there's further change in the workplace."[42]

What does it mean for things to change in the workplace? One area that needs reform is the way connections and relationships are built in many companies. Often, informal connections and opportunities arise through social gatherings, such as hanging out at a bar after work or playing a few rounds on the golf course. There is a more natural male camaraderie that happens from these after-hour connections, and the settings themselves limit women from being part of the "inner circle" where decisions get made. How can these types of realities be addressed? The intentional creation of social spaces that are open to men and women is just one way to expand the inner circle of decision-making.

In addition, consider how the "Billy Graham rule" limits opportunities for women. The rule, according to writer Karen Swallow Prior, is "basically a guideline that says men and women should not meet alone, whether in offices, or cars, or other places in order to avoid illicit temptations or appearances of impropriety." While honoring the marriages and boundaries of her male colleagues, Prior calls leaders to an ethical response to the women they work with, rather than rule-driven behavior that could limit their opportunities: "Virtue ethics is better than the Billy Graham rule. Virtue ethics relies on moral character that is developed through good habits rather than rules or consequences for the governing of behavior."[43] She also exhorts leaders to practice prudence and moderation "for the good of all." Reflections like Prior's can help create respectful spaces for male and female colleagues to collaborate and do their best work together.

A few years ago, Sheryl Sandberg, author of the 2013 book *Lean In,* became one of the most well-known voices regarding women in the workplace. Based on her experience as COO of Facebook, her book offers inspirational advice and practical wisdom about how women can be more successful in corporate environments and addresses some of the internal and external obstacles to success that women experience. I love that Sandberg places significant emphasis on personal responsibility and on helping women make the best of their circumstances and overcome challenges. However, my critique is that she also at times seems to place the burden of change on women rather than addressing real systemic challenges that women often face in corporate and business environments. Others agreed. In December 2018, the *Washington Post* published a piece titled "The End of Leaning In: How Sheryl Sandberg's Message of Empowerment Fully Unraveled." And former First Lady Michelle Obama said about *Lean In:* "I tell women, that whole 'you can have it all'—nope, not at the same time; that's a lie. . . . It's not always enough to lean in, because that s— doesn't work all the time."[44] Sandberg's message was critiqued not because of its "can do" attitude but because we must acknowledge that women—regardless of life circumstances—continue to face real challenges and limitations because of our gender.

Leadership in the Church

Gender roles are particularly challenging within Christian communities because of long-standing biblical interpretations of verses like Ephesians 5:22, which says, "Wives submit to your own husbands." Church leaders, pastors, and others often completely ignore the preceding verse: "Submit to one another out of reverence to Christ."

When I was on staff at Willow Creek, a couple came to me for marriage counseling. Over the course of the weeks we were meeting together, when we talked about what Scriptures they wanted read during their ceremony, they insisted that they only wanted Ephesians 5:22. I let them know my perspective that the isolation of verse 22 without the context of the entire passage and its call for mutual submission was inaccurate. However, the husband-to-be was recalcitrant about having Ephesians 5:21 included in the ceremony. I was firm and said that the proceeding verses also needed to be read or I would not be able to perform the ceremony. As we talked about the multifaceted implications of mutual submission, it was not my goal to convert this young couple to become egalitarian and agree with my personal convictions. Rather, I simply found it terribly problematic that the groom had predetermined that only his future bride was called to submission in marriage. The couple did not get married at Willow.

Our cultural background, ethnic background, and upbringing can also all contribute to our understanding of gender roles and expectations. In the book *More Than Serving Tea*, the coauthors, all Christians, recount some of their experiences growing up as Japanese, Chinese, Korean, Malaysian, and South Asian women in the United States. One author, Kathy Khang, writes in her chapter on sexuality about the presumed inferiority of girls in Asian culture, evidenced by the thousands of forced gender selections, the selling of young girls into slavery, and the expectations placed on girls and young women about their appearance and behavior. The epilogue, written by Tracey Gee, closes with a poem that says, "May you know that your identity is triply blessed. / May you walk with a new name that God gives—daughter, chosen, beloved—in place of shame. . . . / May you lead with confidence. / May we experience all of what / God intended for us when he created us / as Asian American women."[45]

The church has many opinions on gender roles. I have been mentored by New Testament theologian Gilbert Bilezikian (known better as "Dr. B"), who was the inspiration behind Bill Hybels's planting of Willow

Creek. Dr. B is known as a staunch advocate of egalitarianism and of the right of women to have all of their gifts used within the context of the church. First published in the 1980s, his *Beyond Sex Roles: What the Bible Says About a Woman's Place in the Church and Family* has been a seminal resource for the liberation of women and their gifts within the context of the church. And thankfully, denominations like the Evangelical Covenant Church (ECC), in which I am ordained, welcome and value women as pastors, ministers, and leaders. But there are still many Christian faith traditions where this is not the case.

I recently heard a story of a woman who served as a chaplain in a Catholic hospital. Even though she was a Protestant minister, she was asked to wear a collar, which is not all that unusual. But during one of her evening rounds in February, when a surgeon joined her in the elevator, he asked in a condescending and critical tone, "What is this, Halloween?" Another time at the same hospital, a doctor made a joke and asked if he should address the minister as "Father." Still another hospital staff person suggested that she should quit her job and "go home to have children" where her gifts would be better utilized.

A friend recently shared her experience of asking a leader in the church for advice on pursuing leadership opportunities. She was told that if she was good at her job, opportunities would find her. This may be true for men, but it is frequently not true for women, particularly in conservative Christian communities. Often, women are not invited to the table, regardless of how accomplished or experienced they are.

In many conservative fundamentalist or evangelical churches, women are allowed to serve in any capacity as missionaries, and are often permitted, if not encouraged, to teach the Bible as missionaries or evangelists externally. But in the local church context, these same women are often blocked from holding mantles of leadership. It is common for women to be given roles in worship or called as directors of children's ministries or care ministries (two areas where women's stereotypical strengths may be showcased), but they are often unable to rise to other positions of authority.

Many churches believe that a woman can only be in positions of power if a man has authority over her. This is not only harmful for women, but it hinders our ability to worship and minister to our communities at our fullest potential. Romans 12:6-8 says: "We have different gifts, according to the grace given to each of us. If your gift is prophesying, then prophesy in accordance with your faith; if it is serving, then serve; if it is teaching, then teach; if it is to encourage, then give encouragement; if it is giving, then give generously; if it is to lead, do it diligently; if it is to show mercy, do it cheerfully." This passage is clear that when people are blessed with the gifts of leadership, they are called—regardless of gender—to lead diligently. By limiting the roles of women in the church, we are dismissing this beautiful diversity of God's creation and missing out on experiencing the blessings that comes from that diversity.[46]

Many books have been written about the exegetical arguments for and against women in leadership in the church. Some say women can lead and preach as long as there is a male senior pastor in ultimate authority over them. Others, like Wayne Grudem and John Piper, claim that the Bible teaches very clear roles for women, including that they should not have any authority over a male once he comes of age. I will not parse all of the arguments and viewpoints here.

My own understanding of the topic has grown greatly through the years. I was baptized in a Presbyterian Church in America (PCA) church that adhered to Reformed theology and conservative views on women. Among other things, this meant that I went to seminary thinking I could only be a "minister of the gospel" in foreign lands, because it was permissible for women to "preach" to brown people in those places but not in their own home context. But it used to drive me crazy that Elisabeth Elliot would stand up in front of thousands of male and female students at Urbana conferences and teach us that women can't teach men. The inconsistencies in her "preaching the gospel" but calling it "ministry" or "evangelism" used to provoke me greatly. Now I see quite clearly the inherent contradiction and racial ideology undergirding the belief that women can be missionaries but not preachers!

While I was at North Park Theological Seminary, I had the opportunity to study under some of the country's foremost egalitarians. And in our Greek exegesis and New Testament theology classes, I came to understand that the gifts of the Spirit discussed in Corinthians and other passages are not limited in their distribution based on gender. Some of the best resources I encountered include *Discovering Biblical Equality: Complementarity Without Hierarchy*, edited by Ronald Pierce and Rebecca Merrill Groothuis with Gordon D. Fee serving as a contributing editor, and Linda Belleville's *Women Leaders and the Church: 3 Crucial Questions.* You might also check out *How I Changed My Mind About Women in Leadership: Compelling Stories from Prominent Evangelicals*, edited by Alan Johnson, as well as the excellent resource *Emboldened: A Vision for Empowering Women in Ministry* by Tara Beth Leach.

Advocating for Women

In light of #MeToo and #ChurchToo, what does it mean for Christians to be advocates of women during these times? Certainly engaging with others' stories, offering encouragement and solidarity online, and joining in conversations around social media can and do make a difference. According to a LifeWay Research survey among Protestant pastors familiar with #MeToo, 40 percent say it has helped them better understand issues of sexual and domestic violence, and 41 percent say they are more inclined to preach on the topic as a result.[47] Hashtag activism such as these two movements can be powerful and effective and, as has been seen, can change the course of history in calling for accountability and change.

Within the local church, small and large, we must be attentive to unrealistic expectations placed on pastors who are often overly esteemed and in the spotlight. Pastors, especially men, have often not been trained and equipped on how to handle situations of sexual harassment and abuse within the church. In addition, the celebrity culture and idol worship of famous people and famous institutions set up individuals for failure and also do not honor the community of Christ we are called to be as the church. Within relationships and institutions, power dynamics must be understood and deconstructed. It is wrong for a woman who has experienced discrimination or abuse to be told to "be silent" or to not be believed or, worse yet, to have the burden of fixing the problem placed on her. We must put Jesus back on his proper place on the throne, where Christ is at the center rather than human celebrities.

In December 2018, Sally Schwer Channing and Tammy Schultz, professors of psychology and counseling, respectively, at Wheaton College, wrote an article for *Christianity Today* titled "What We Long for the Church to Face About Sexual Violence." In calling for "sustained" and "significant" efforts, Channing and Schultz offered four strategies for the church in moving forward. First, while they acknowledge that addressing painful realities like abuse and sexual violence is not only uncomfortable but can also cause "distress," they are firm in their belief that "there is no way to respond to these experiences with justice and accountability without encountering profound disruptions and palpable distress. Avoidance and minimization may temporarily reestablish a sense of comfort and cohesion, but will do far greater damage to victims, and result in congregations and communities that are less safe and whole in the long run." Second, they acknowledge that though lack of evidence can sometimes make judgment calls difficult and though evidence is nice, it is an unfair expectation on the victim. Third, they point out that an accused person will often deny the charges because of vocation, perceived action, and self-preservation, and that this must be acknowledged as a limitation in addressing circumstances. Finally, they assert that offenders are difficult to recognize because many acts of violence are carried out by those in positions of power and authority who have a loyal following.[48]

In late 2018, in response to the rising reports about abuse within the evangelical church, including Willow Creek, Wheaton College hosted a one-day gathering called the GC2 (Great Commandment + Great Commission) Summit to respond to and address the atrocities of sexual harassment, abuse, and violence within the church.[49] With the first half of the conference focused on the victims of abuse and the second half on the unhealthy power structures in play at several churches, the event represented the largest interdenominational response to sexual abuse since #MeToo took off. Speakers at the event were pastors, counselors, and advocates and included former Willow Creek teaching pastor Nancy Beach, one of the nine women who spoke up about harassment by Bill Hybels, along with one of the most famous female evangelical teachers and Southern Baptist favorite, Beth Moore. Beach highlighted the dangers of "unchecked power" in church hierarchy and how that dynamic can foster conditions that allow continued abuse to go unaddressed. Beach also warned against creating more rules that support the division of genders. #ChurchToo founder Emily Joy commented that the event did little to call out the dangers of purity culture and critiqued the organizers for not calling in outside experts. However, these types of events can serve as markers and help move conversations forward about individual and community healing in response to publicly raised incidents of abuse.

Many of the messages at the conference emphasized the need to bring things out of the darkness and acknowledge that for too long churches were unsafe places for girls, women, boys, and men who were victims of abuse. It also focused on encouraging pastors to take responsibility and not ignore the women and other victims of abuse within their congregations. Speakers like Ed Stetzer acknowledged that pastors have had less accountability with their power or do not recognize the power and influence they might have in someone's life. In addition, several of the leaders present revealed that they too had been the victims of sexual abuse or harassment. This included the last speaker of the day, Max Lucado, who said, "My name is also on the list of those who have been sexually abused. . . . As a young man, in my boyhood, not by a church member or a family member but by a community leader." This was the first time the Texas pastor had ever revealed this publicly.[50]

The progressive evangelical periodical *Sojourners* also published a piece laying out four ways churches can respond to the #MeToo movement. These include ministers and church leaders openly addressing sexual violence on a regular basis, pastors and churches not neglecting biblical passages that describe sexual violence, churches bringing more women into upper levels of leadership and positions of decision-making authority, and church leaders refusing to be party to conspiracies of silence.[51] Only when the church is able to have these hard conversations and honestly address these realities will there be opportunities for healing, reconciliation, and justice.

In addition to these ideas and steps, there are Christian organizations committed to responding to the needs of women and others who have been victims of sexual abuse. For example, GRACE (Godly Response to Abuse in the Christian Environment) is an organization that does advocacy in local communities and on Capitol Hill in response to abuse within the church.[52] Lisa Sharon Harper's organization, Freedom Road, hosted a podcast about #SilenceIsNotSpiritual and emphasized what a global conversation protecting the rights of women might look like. Nikki Toyama-Szeto, executive director of Evangelicals for Social Action, is highlighted in the podcast and talks about Asian women's experiences with abuse and violence.[53]

Yes, we need to make these wrongs right. And yes, we need to create a new reality for young women growing up in the context of the church (and the world). We have to do better. As we seek to respond to violence against women, may we start our quest with a cry to the Lord saying, "Christ, have mercy."

For Further Study

Allender, Dan B. *The Wounded Heart: Hope for Adult Victims of Childhood Sexual Abuse.* Colorado Springs: NavPress, 2018.

Belleville, Linda L. *Women Leaders and the Church: 3 Crucial Questions.* Grand Rapids: Baker, 2000.

Everhart, Ruth. *The #MeToo Reckoning: Facing the Church's Complicity in Sexual Abuse and Misconduct.* Downers Grove, IL: InterVarsity Press, 2020.

Fee, Gordon D., and Rebecca Merrill Groothuis, eds. *Discovering Biblical Equality: Complementarity Without Hierarchy.* Downers Grove, IL: InterVarsity Press, 2012.

Gay, Roxanne. *Hunger: A Memoir of (My) Body.* New York: Perennial, 2017.

James, Carolyn Custis. *Half the Church: Recapturing God's Global Vision for Women.* Grand Rapids: Zondervan, 2011.

Johnson, Alan, ed. *How I Changed My Mind About Women in Leadership: Compelling Stories from Prominent Evangelicals.* Grand Rapids: Zondervan, 2010.

Jones, Charisse, and Kumea Shorter-Gooden. *Shifting: The Double Lives of Black Women in America.* New York: Perennial, 2003.

Kroeger, Catherine Clark, and James R. Beck, eds. *Women, Abuse, and the Bible.* Grand Rapids: Baker, 1996.

Leach, Tara Beth. *Emboldened: A Vision for Empowering Women in Ministry.* Downers Grove, IL: InterVarsity Press, 2017.

Miles, Autumn. *I Am Rahab: Touched by God, Fully Restored.* Nashville: Worthy, 2018.

Orenstein, Peggy. *Flux: Women on Sex, Work, Love, Kids, and Life in a Half-Changed World.* New York: Anchor Books, 2000.

Smith, Andrea. *Conquest: Sexual Violence and American Indian Genocide.* Cambridge, MA: South End, 2005.

Storkey, Elaine. *Scars Across Humanity: Understanding and Overcoming Violence Against Women.* London: SPCK, 2015.

Toyama, Nikki, and Tracey Gee, eds. *More Than Serving Tea: Asian American Women on Expectations, Relationships, Leadership and Faith.* Downers Grove, IL: InterVarsity Press, 2006.

Yancey, Philip. *Disappointment with God: Three Questions No One Asks Aloud.* Grand Rapids: Zondervan, 1988.

Questions for Discussion

- For women in your group, have you had experiences with the Billy Graham rule? How did you respond? Have you had times in your work or personal life when you felt excluded because of your gender?

- For men in your group, did you learn anything in this chapter? What content or stories struck you? Why?

- How do you believe God has called men and women to honor one another in relationships in light of the prudence and virtues that Karen Swallow Prior discussed?

- Has there been brokenness in your community in terms of pastoral abuses of power or sexual misconduct? How did that affect you personally and as a community? Do you feel like those involved have sought to address biblical accountability and reconciliation (if possible)?

10

The Liberation of Women Around the World

Many women were there, watching from a distance.
They had followed Jesus from Galilee to care for his needs.

MATTHEW 27:55

MY HUSBAND WORKS FOR a Christian international development organization that seeks to respond to the needs of children in poverty around the world in Jesus' name. In October 2018, he took a trip with some other executive leaders to West Africa to visit projects in Ghana and Togo. Over the week of his travels, he called to tell me about the exorbitant differences in wealth he experienced in the two countries. In Togo, he witnessed deep poverty—he called it "crushing" and "unnecessary"—and was disturbed by the disproportionate effects poverty has on young girls. For example, if a family is poor, often the girls are the last ones to be able to go to school—if they are able to go at all. Many times the uniforms, books, and other necessary education fees are too costly. He said that what he saw in Togo made neighboring Ghana look like a prosperous nation.

Togo is a small country on a narrow strip of land on the west coast of Africa. The more than seven million people who live in Togo continue to depend significantly on international aid and assistance for development and economic opportunities.[1] In 2000, the United Nations reported that close to 12 percent of the girls in Togo were subjected to female genital mutilation (FGM).[2] As of 2011, 74 percent of the male population in Togo could read, whereas only 48 percent of girls over the age of fifteen could read and write.[3] In 2016, Togo was near the bottom of the list at 166th of 187 in the UN Women's Gender Inequality Index, with countries such as Yemen and Rwanda scoring better. These statistics reflect the inequality between women and men in reproductive health, political power, educational attainment, and labor market participation.[4] Almost a quarter of women in Togolese society get married before the age of eighteen, while 22 percent of women aged fifteen to forty-nine have experienced intimate partner physical or sexual violence at least once in their lives.[5]

After my husband's trip to Africa he stopped in Barcelona, where our then four-month-old granddaughter lived. After a lovely afternoon with his son and family reading *Goodnight Moon* to his granddaughter (and miserably failing in his attempts to do so in Spanish), he called me to say goodnight. It was clear in listening to the tone of his voice that he continued to be deeply disturbed by the poverty he had witnessed in Togo and West Africa. But more specifically, he was moved by the plight of the young girls and women there who had such limited opportunities— so different from our granddaughter, who, as he said, "will always have a warm home, be surrounded by family who loves her, and . . . have every opportunity in the world. That's not the case for the young girls whom I was just with in Togo."

Challenges Facing Women Globally

The achievement of gender equality and the empowerment of all girls is one of the seventeen main Sustainable Development Goals (SDGs) of the United Nations.[6] It's an incredibly important goal, and an ambitious one, as women and girls around the world are subject to unique challenges such as FGM, child marriages, the effects of HIV/AIDS, limited opportunities to go to school, and a lack of economic opportunities.

FGM is defined as "all procedures involving partial or total removal of the female external genitalia or other injuries to the female genital organs for non-medical reasons."[7] As of February 2018, according to UNICEF, the total number who have undergone this surgery is estimated to be nearly two hundred million girls and women in thirty countries around the world. In the last three decades, the practice has become less common and is losing support from men and women alike, but it is still a prevalent practice. The highest levels of support for FGM can be found in Mali, Sierra Leone, Guinea, The Gambia, Somalia, and Egypt. In these countries, more than half of the female population think the practice should continue. In the thirty countries where data is available, about one in three girls have the surgery (compared to one in two in the 1980s).[8] FGM is often practiced with the goal of tightening the girl's vaginal area to make intercourse more pleasurable for their male sexual partners.

Child marriages continue to be another problem that affects young girls in developing countries. Overall, the rate of child marriages (under eighteen) has decreased around the world, especially in areas in South Asia where rates have dropped from 50 to 30 percent, but it is still very common, particularly for girls, and particularly in areas of sub-Saharan and West/Central Africa. Child marriage is most common in sub-Saharan Africa, where four in ten young women are married before the age of eighteen, and in the least developed countries 12 percent were married before the age of fifteen. About twelve million girls are married in childhood per year.[9] Child marriages are often driven by poverty; girls are "married off" so that they can be fed and taken care of by their husbands. Child marriages increase risks for girls in many areas, including sexually transmitted diseases, cervical cancer, malaria, death during childbirth, and obstetric fistulas. In addition, girls' offspring are at increased risk for premature birth and death as neonates, infants, or children.[10]

While the HIV/AIDS crisis has been in steady decline, it continues to affect hundreds of thousands of people around the world. Because of progress in drugs and other treatments, HIV/AIDS is not the epidemic it was more than a decade ago, but it still affects poor communities around the world, with women often paying the greatest price. In 2018, 770,000 people died of complications related to HIV/AIDS. One of the differences from past decades is that now 62 percent of adults and 52 percent of children who have HIV receive antiretroviral therapy (ART). And 80 percent of women who are pregnant and breastfeeding and have HIV receive ART therapy.[11] But it is still a pandemic in areas of sub-Saharan Africa. About two-thirds of the total number of people infected are located there, and the women are often the most affected by the crisis. A wide variety of factors contribute to this, including poor access to health services, biological factors that make women more susceptible to infection, and several cultural practices that are, in general, harmful to women's health. Discrimination against women and those with HIV is extremely common.[12]

Access to work and sustainable jobs continues to be a challenge for women around the world. A lack of gender equality in many countries means 2.7 billion women are legally restricted from having the same choices regarding jobs as men. The World Bank's "Women, Business and the Law" report found that 104 economies, specifically, prevent women from working in certain jobs. In addition, fifty-nine economies have no laws about sexual harassment in the workplace, and in eighteen economies, "husbands can legally prevent their wives from working." Over the last couple years, governments in sixty-five economies passed eighty-seven legal reforms with the goal of providing more economic opportunities for women. And the recently launched Women Entrepreneurs Finance Initiative—a collaboration between banks, governments, and other stakeholders—is hoping to provide over $1.6 billion for women entrepreneurs in developing countries to help close the gap between working men and women.[13]

The United Nations is also creating opportunities for women around the world. The year 2020 will mark twenty-five years since the UN's historic gathering in Beijing for the Fourth World Conference on Women. Commemorating the quarter century and what has been accomplished since then, the United Nations launched a program called "Generation Equality: Realizing Women's Rights for an Equal Future."[14] The Beijing platform identified twelve critical areas of concern related specifically to their effects on women: poverty, education and training, health, violence, armed conflict, economy, power and decision-making, institutional mechanisms, human rights, media, environment, and the girl child. The United Nations is seeking to increase the participation of women in political processes and peacebuilding, work on the economic empowerment of women, and end violence against women who are disproportionately affected by violence and abuse.[15]

Violence Against Women

Women are the most vulnerable community when it comes to physical and sexual violence. Elaine Storkey's *Scars Across Humanity: Understanding and Overcoming Violence Against Women* is one of the most impactful books I've seen about this issue. It received a *Christianity Today* Book Award in 2019 in the category of politics and public life.[16] Storkey's work addresses the broad-sweeping manifestations of patriarchy in Christian history, internalized gender discrimination, the justification of abuse in societies around the world, and the church's inadequacy in productively responding to these violations and injustices. She also highlights the astonishing reality that acts of violence against women who are between the ages of fifteen and forty-five across the globe have caused more "deaths, disability, and mutilation" than cancer, malaria, and traffic accidents combined.

Storkey wrestles with the question of whether or not inequality between genders is entrenched within the Scriptures and Christian tradition. Pastors and church communities who are inadequately equipped to respond to abuse frequently tell women to "stay in abuse" because of Christian obligations to "take up the cross" and remain committed in marriage and fidelity. Generally, the Christian community has been unsuccessful in providing the support, nurturing, and safety women need after they have experienced abuse and gender-based violence. However, Storkey does highlight some incredible organizations around the globe that are making a profound difference in the lives of women and girls as they work to both prevent abuse and restore and heal victims.

SOLD: Sex Trafficking and Preventative Measures

The sale of young girls (and boys) into sex trafficking and prostitution is a reality for many families who cannot afford to feed their children. According to the International Labour Organization, close to twenty-five million people around the world are "trapped in forced labor," and an additional sixteen million are exploited "in the private sector" for domestic work, construction, or agriculture. Nearly five million people are caught in sex trafficking or forced sexual exploitation.[17]

Working predominantly in northern Thailand, The SOLD Project, led by Rachel Goble, provides education and opportunities for young girls *before* they are sold into prostitution. By providing scholarships that allow young girls to stay in school, The SOLD Project helps prevent the recruitment of girls by older women who are addicted to drugs.[18] Over time the programs run by Rachel and her team have expanded to include The FREEDOM Project, which has four components: (1) scholarships, (2) a mentor for each sponsored child, (3) a community resource center, and (4) school programs, starting with sixth-graders, that make children aware of the realities of human trafficking and prostitution.[19]

Another activist who is doing similar work and who partnered with Goble and others to produce the documentary *The SOLD Project: Thailand,* featuring short stories of children who have been forced into prostitution, is Nikole Lim. Her organization, Freely in Hope, is committed to "see an end to the cycle of sexual violence." Working predominantly in Kenya and Zambia, Freely in Hope focuses on education, leadership development, and storytelling "for young women who are survivors of or vulnerable to sexual violence through academic scholarships, health care, safe housing, and trauma-based counseling."[20] The hope is that scholars in the program will be compelled to transform their communities into violence-free places. The work of fierce female leaders like Lim and Goble is changing the face of how Christians and others around the world can contribute to the end of slavery and sex trafficking.

When Goble was asked what inspires her in her work, she said, "Each person should work on the passions of their own heart. . . . Pay attention to what's in front of you. There are so many ways to help—tutor a child or help a homeless man." Quoting Mother Teresa, she added, "If you can't feed a hundred people, then feed just one."

Violence against women is not limited to certain places and countries but rather is present all over the world in all kinds of circumstances and settings. In 2014, when Nadia Murad was twenty-one, Islamic militants from *Da'ish* attacked her village in northern Iraq, killing hundreds of men and capturing the women. Murad was one of them. During her three-month capture, she was subject to physical and sexual abuse as she was bought and sold several times. Murad and her family are Yazidi people, a distinct ethno-religious minority of the region, but under capture, she was forced to convert to Islam. Her mother and brothers all refused, which led to their death. Murad was able to escape one night and received help from a Muslim family who brought her to a refugee camp. Eventually she escaped to Germany, where she now lives. In 2017 she published her memoir, called *The Last Girl*, and in 2018 she was awarded the Nobel Peace Prize for her courageous endurance while captured.[21] Murad also began a non-profit called Nadia's Initiative that seeks to help women who are rape victims.[22]

Dr. Denis Mukwege is another recent Nobel Peace Prize recipient who is doing powerful work on behalf of women. A gynecologist working in the Democratic Republic of Congo (DRC), Dr. Mukwege has been serving girls and women who have been victims of war-based rape crimes since 1995. Rape being used as a weapon has been widely reported in the DRC. Though numbers are difficult to gather, the UN estimates more than two hundred thousand women are rape survivors. "I absolutely have to tell the world, show the world, that there is a collective responsibility to act in DRC," he says. "We share the same humanity and we cannot continue to allow economic wars to be fought on women's bodies."[23] Congolese women have experienced horrific violence at the hands of soldiers as well as ordinary citizens since the political conflict broke out in 1995. As recently as 2012, men have been entering villages and raping women and children indiscriminately. In a two-day stay in the town of Minova, for example, soldiers in the Congolese army raped hundreds of women as well as looted and destroyed large areas of the town.[24]

The fortitude and inspirational stories of Murad and Dr. Mukwege remind us that hope, persistence, and resistance can make a difference. While horrors and violations against young girls and women continue, women are also making significant progress around the world.

Imago Dei: Body Image and the Image of God

Women around the world have long struggled from personal infliction and the expectations of others in terms of the way we should look. And the definition of beauty changes often throughout the ages. Ancient Greece esteemed women with plump bodies and full figures. The Han dynasty desired women with slim waists, pale skin, and tiny feet (even to the point of butchering them by binding them). During the Italian Renaissance, full-bodied women with an ample bosom, rounded stomachs, and full hips were most valued, whereas during the Roaring Twenties in the United States, women who had boyish figures and flat chests were the most sought-after. In the twenty-first century, according to The Science of People, the body type of Kim Kardashian is the most revered, with a big and shapely bosom and a big bottom, but a flat stomach and small waist.[25]

The expectations of women and their appearance also differs from culture to culture, but around the world, women are judged for what they look like and objectified. Kathy Khang writes about the expectations of Asian women to look a certain way: "Asian women around the world continue to magnify Satan's whispers by willingly cutting and reconstructing their faces and bodies to achieve beauty." She describes "Asian eyelid surgery" that is performed so women can have the perfect crease, and how women known as the *muu-dari* or *daikon-ashi* with "radish shaped calves" can have the nerve behind their knee severed in order to target a portion of the calf muscle which results in the "thinning out of the thickest part of the calf."[26]

The pressures make young women, in particular, some of the most vulnerable to eating disorders like bulimia and anorexia, which involve either bingeing and vomiting or self-imposed starvation in attempts to achieve a certain body type. In the era of the stick-thin supermodel Twiggy, famous and incredibly talented musician Karen Carpenter died of heart failure related to her years-long struggle with anorexia.[27] The 1989 TV movie *The Karen Carpenter Story* implies that her anorexia began after a fan criticized her for being "chubby."

African American writer Roxane Gay writes about her struggles, pain, depression, and anxiety that came from expectations being placed on her by society. A deeply painful and profound story, her book *Hunger: A Memoir of (My) Body* tells of abuse, self-loathing, and other struggles she experienced on the journey to self-acceptance. She writes, "On bad days, . . . I forget how to separate my personality, the heart of who I am, from my body. I forget how to shield myself from the cruelties of the world."[28]

In Christian circles, some conservatives seem to believe that being overweight is a sin against God. The undergirding theology is that size is a direct consequence of the sin of gluttony or overindulgence. J. Nicole Morgan takes on these false beliefs directly in her book *Fat and Faithful: Learning to Love Our Bodies, Our Neighbors, and Ourselves.* As a part of the body and fat acceptance movement, Morgan is an important voice in helping us understand what it means that the image of God is not found only in skinny bodies.

Women and Reproductive Rights

Reproductive rights are a human rights issue that greatly affects women. According to the Global Fund for Women, 214 million women in the world "want, but lack access to contraception." Why is this a basic issue of human rights? Because women, many of whom are young girls, are forced to have sex against their will and cannot control whether or not it will result in childbearing. More than eight hundred women die every day from "preventable causes related to pregnancy and childbirth."[29] Some of the barriers to sexual and reproductive health include "discrimination, stigma, restrictive laws and policies, and entrenched traditions." [30] Condoms and other forms of contraception can provide women with valuable choices in protecting their own bodies.

In preparation for the 2010 World Cup that was held in South Africa, Dr. Sonnet Ehlers, a blood technician and medical researcher, designed a condom literally "with teeth" to try to deter rapes during the event. She acknowledged that the device, called Rape-aXe wouldn't prevent rape, but once penetration occurred, the condom would attach to the man's penis and then could only be removed by a doctor. Ehlers said, "It hurts, he cannot pee and walk when it's on. . . . If he tries to remove it, it will clasp even tighter . . . however, it doesn't break the skin, and there's no danger of fluid exposure."[31]

Ehlers designed the device with the prevalence of rape in South Africa at the forefront of her mind. According to the website Jezebel, a 2006 study showed that a woman in South Africa is raped every seventeen seconds, and, as reported by Amnesty International in 2009, only 8 percent of twenty thousand reported rapes led to a conviction. In addition, "a quarter of South African men have admitted to rape, half of whom admitted to multiple rapes. Rape is used as a bonding experience for men and a way to 'cure' lesbians. Although rape is a problem around the globe, for South African women, it is a far more impending threat."[32]

In 2013, CNN posted a news piece titled "Could Condoms Change the World?" Often viewed as controversial by Christian conservatives because of the fear of promoting promiscuity, condoms play a critical role in the prevention of pregnancy and the spread of sexually transmitted diseases, thus promoting the overall health of communities. CNN reported, "While data on the direct effect of free condoms in developing nations is limited, past campaigns in Uganda, Thailand, and Brazil have shown that making condoms readily available can significantly reduce the transmission of HIV."[33]

What about the question of how abortion relates to reproductive rights? The Center for Reproductive Lives (CRL) monitors the world's abortion laws and believes they are an inherent human right, stating:

> The right to safe and legal abortion is a fundamental human right protected under numerous international and regional human rights treaties and national-level constitutions around the world. These instruments ground safe abortion in a constellation of rights, including the rights to life; liberty; privacy; equality and non-discrimination and freedom from cruel, inhuman and degrading treatment. Human rights bodies have repeatedly condemned restrictive abortion laws as being incompatible with human rights norms.[34]

However, many Christians, myself included, disagree. In my first master's degree, I studied bioethics with an emphasis on reproductive rights.

Throughout the course of my study, I came to affirm that embryos also have the inherent right to life. I do not believe that an embryo or an in-utero fetus (unborn child) has the same rights as a human being who is already living and breathing. However, I do believe that the potential life form has the right to life and to being protected, particularly once a heartbeat is determined. Sam Brownback, during his tenure as a senator from Kansas from 1996 to 2011, was one of the leading members of Congress calling for the protection of the human embryo.[35]

Hillary Clinton was ardently pro-choice in her run for president during the 2016 election. However, she was also fervently committed to decreasing the number of abortions. Christian author Rachel Held Evans wrote an article for Vox about why she supported Clinton. She began the article, "I'm pro-life. Or, put another way, as a Christian, I believe the sacred personhood of an individual begins before birth and continues throughout life, and I believe that sacred personhood is worth protecting, whether it's tucked inside a womb, waiting on death row, fleeing Syria in search of a home, or playing beneath the shadow of an American drone." Evans continued, "In the eight years since we've had a pro-choice president, the abortion rate in the US has dropped to its lowest since 1973. I believe the best way to keep this trend going is not to simply make it harder for women to terminate unwanted pregnancies but to create a culture with fewer unwanted pregnancies to begin with."[36] In other words, pro-choice candidates can also strategically work to decrease abortions, which is very much in alignment with the goals of those with a pro-life agenda.

Some Christian groups go so far to protect the human embryo that they have created adoption agencies for embryos that have been left behind and not utilized during in vitro fertilization (IVF) and other procedures that address fertilization. Snowflakes is one such embryo adoption program, allowing families to "gift" their embryos to other families who might be struggling to have children.[37]

Abortion rights activists do not emphasize the rights that belong to the potential life form that is being developed from an embryo to a fetus and eventually to a child, emphasizing instead the rights of women. The American Civil Liberties Union (ACLU) and many other groups identify abortion rights as a fundamental right of women to control their own body.[38] And in fact, many conservatives agree with women's rights and thus allow for abortion in cases where the mother's life is at risk or if the child was conceived by rape.[39]

What is the significance of the human embryo and why is it so controversial? Embryos and the umbilical cord that gives a fetus nutrients are considered valuable because of the existence of embryonic stem cells. Stem cells are specialized cells that can develop into many other types of cells. They renew themselves by dividing, even after they've been inactive, which makes them incredibly valuable to scientific research; they can be used to create healthy cells that could be used in the curing of diseased cells.[40] People have long debated whether or not embryos should be allowed to be used for research. Numerous embryos created for usage during IVF or for other techniques to address infertility issues are frozen and then later discarded if they are not needed for reproductive purposes.[41] Many scientists believe that these embryos should be allowed to be used for scientific research to learn more about embryonic stem cells. A new technique may help in the debate though. Umbilical cord storage allows the blood and stem cells from the cord to be saved and utilized and does not harm the baby, nor embryos, in any way.[42] I wholly support this viable alternative. The quest to cure horrible diseases is a noble one, but not at the expense of embryonic life forms.

Progress for Women

It is important to underscore again that progress *is* being made in the quest for equal rights for women around the world. Women's participation in government and their placement in significant positions of influence and leadership have increased. For example, in 2018, Spain appointed a majority female cabinet (eleven of seventeen) and now has the highest female cabinet representation (beating France and Sweden). In the United States, many young and diverse women broke records during the midterm elections in 2018. And even in places where opportunities for females are limited, small steps are being taken. Saudi Arabia, for example, made international news with its announcement of the intent to repeal the ban on women drivers.[43] And for the first time in forty years, the women of Iran were (temporarily) able to watch a male soccer game in the stadium along with men.[44] These points of progress should encourage us to keep doing what we can to see more equality established for women around the world.

Toward a Better Future

Nicholas Kristof and Sheryl WuDunn's book *Half the Sky: Turning Oppression into Opportunity for Women Worldwide* tells the stories of women and girls who are suffering under horrific circumstances. But they do not leave the reader hopeless. Instead they inspire us with a courageous vision of what a world without gender inequality and misogyny might look like. The book concludes with four steps that can be taken immediately to empower women around the globe. The first is giving money directly to women who are struggling via websites like www.globalgiving.org. The second is sponsoring a girl through a program like those offered by Compassion International or World Vision. The third is signing up to receive direct and regular communication about the treatment of women and girls around the world from organizations such as www.womensenew.org. And the last one is joining the CARE action network at www.can.care.org to take political and social action against injustices that affect women.[45]

Carolyn Custis James, a writer and speaker, was deeply inspired and challenged by *Half the Sky*. Her book *Half the Church: Recapturing God's Global Vision for Women* directly responded to *Half the Sky* from the lens of the church. She writes, "When half the church holds back—whether by choice or because we have no choice—everybody loses and our mission suffers setbacks."[46]

Inspired by the story of missionary Amy Carmichael in India, who experienced an inner conviction that she could not know the horrors of what was happening in places and do nothing, James encourages women to follow in her footsteps.[47] And today there are so many organizations already doing great work in response to sex trafficking, slavery, and violence against girls, so it is easy to get involved. We should pray, seek, discern, learn, and act. Consider organizations already mentioned such as The SOLD Project or Freely in Hope. Or check out the organization A21 (www.a21.org), which considers itself a group of "modern abolitionists" and is committed to ending slavery around the world. There are more than enough opportunities to make a difference.

In the words of James, "In light of God's global vision for his daughters, we owe it to ourselves, to the church, and to the world to stop and reflect. Now is the time to ask ourselves—both individually and collectively—where we are on track with God's vision both for us and for his world, where we've lost our way, and how we need to change and correct course."[48] Like James encourages, may we join the efforts of so many around the world and not only pray "Thy kingdom come" but also join with God in his work in the world by pursuing peace, advocating for justice, and being ardent activists for a better future for girls.

For Further Study

Filemoni-Tofaeono, Joan, and Lydia Johnson. *Reweaving the Relational Mat: A Christian Response to Violence Against Women from Oceania*. London: Routledge, 2016.

Gay, Roxanne. *Hunger: A Memoir of (My) Body*. New York: Perennial, 2017.

James, Carolyn Custis. *Half the Church: Recapturing God's Global Vision for Women*. Grand Rapids: Zondervan, 2011.

Kristof, Nicholas, and Sheryl WuDunn. *Half the Sky: Turning Oppression into Opportunity for Women Worldwide*. New York: Random House, 2009.

Lim, Nikole. *Liberation Is Here: Women Uncovering Hope in a Broken World*. Downers Grove, IL: InterVarsity Press, 2020.

Martin, Phyllis. *Catholic Women of Congo-Brazzaville: Mothers and Sisters in Troubled Times*. Bloomington: Indiana University Press, 2009.

Morgan, Nicole. *Fat and Faithful: Learning to Love Our Bodies, Our Neighbors, and Ourselves*. Minneapolis: Fortress, 2018.

Walker, Daniel. *God in a Brothel: An Undercover Journey into Sex Trafficking and Rescue*. Downers Grove, IL: InterVarsity Press, 2011.

West, Traci. *Solidarity and Defiant Spirituality: Africana Lessons on Religion, Racism, and Ending Gender Violence*. New York: New York University Press, 2019.

- How do you think women around the world are in need of liberation?

- What do you see in the text of the Bible that speaks to the idea of women being created in the image of God? How is that perspective distorted in our society in the United States and around the world today?

- Has anyone in your group had direct encounters with women living in poverty in the developing world? What did they see and learn and come to understand?

- Are there any particular geographic locations where your church or community focuses on responding to the needs of women and girls? What is that ministry about and how does it seek to respond to the issues discussed in this chapter?

- Reflect on the idea that girls hold up "half the sky." What does that imagery provoke for you? Are there places in the world where you have seen women making a difference and changing their societies? Share those stories.

- How might God be calling you individually and your community to be an advocate for women and girls around the world?

PART 5

Twenty-
First-
Century
Divides

11

Marriage and Sexuality

Marriage should be honored by all,
and the marriage bed kept pure, for God will judge
the adulterer and all the sexually immoral.

HEBREWS 13:4

THERE IS PERHAPS NO GREATER SPLIT in the church in the United States today than the divisions around marriage and sexuality. Many denominations and member communities are debating the question about whether or not same-sex marriage is permissible in the context of the church; some churches and denominations have already split over the issue. For example, in 2010, A Covenant Order of Evangelical Presbyterians (ECO) broke off from the Presbyterian Church (USA). The ECO website provides the following explanation for the division: "they worried that growing denominational disputes over theology and bureaucracy stole focus from their pastoral calling of sharing the gospel of Jesus Christ and equipping a new generation to lead."[1] Most, however, understand ECO to have left the PC(USA) predominantly (or at least significantly) over the question of LGBTQ+ inclusion in congregational life and ministry.

In 2019, the United Methodist Church, the second largest Protestant denomination in the United States, voted to strengthen their ban on lesbian and gay clergy and their stance against same-sex marriages by increasing the consequences for clergy who go outside the regulations in place. Members of the denomination assembled in St. Louis in February and spent three days discussing the issues before a vote of laypeople and clergy began. The measure passed 53 percent to 47 percent, and was backed by a coalition of churches in Africa and the Philippines as well as American and European evangelicals. In January 2020, the denomination announced they will split over the issue that will ultimately divide their twelve million worldwide members.[2] In addition, as the demographic of the churches increases in age, many worry that the vote will only make it more difficult to attract young people to the church. The Reverend Susan Henry-Crowe called the plan "punitive" and said that the conference had brought "unbearable pain" to the denomination. "The wound may one day be healed by the grace of God," she said, "but the scar left behind will be visible forever."[3]

The Evangelical Covenant Church (ECC), in which I am an ordained minister, finds itself in a similar place as the United Methodists. During our June 2019 Annual Conference, the ECC debated the question of whether or not First Covenant Church of Minneapolis (FCCM) should be "involuntarily dismissed" from membership in the denomination because of the church's being "out of harmony" in five areas:

1. The ECC's standard of marriage by eliminating its heterosexual nature;
2. The ECC's prohibition of clergy officiating and participating at same-sex weddings; 3. The ECC's requirement that clergy adhere to a personal behavioral standard of celibacy in singleness and faithfulness in heterosexual marriage; 4. The Covenant's guideline and expectation that congregations refrain from hosting same-sex weddings and related events; and 5. The determination of the Board of Ordered Ministries by locally credentialing a pastor whose ECC credentials were removed for cause.[4]

FCCM disputed the findings of the ECC executive board, but denominational leaders and pastors alike worry about what this division will do to the future of the denomination, which has often prided itself on "walking hand in hand while not seeing eye to eye."

These denominational divisions are only one aspect of the ways the church is being torn apart because of theological divisions and differences in practice. How do these questions affect the lives of clergy, especially those who self-identify as LGBTQ+? The life and ministry of Matthew Nightingale, once an ECC ordained minister, highlights some of the struggle and pain for members of that community.

Matthew Nightingale knew he was attracted to males when he was ten years old, but he couldn't bring himself to admit it to anyone until he was in adulthood. He first told a close friend. And then, when the exhaustion of keeping his secret had welled up inside him so intensely that he could no longer hold it in, he decided to tell his wife of eight years, Luanne. At that point, Matt was serving as the music minister at Peninsula Covenant Church in the Bay Area outside San Francisco. He knew that his declaration would change his life forever.[5] He sought help from his community and told the leadership at the church and of the ECC. At their encouragement and with personal commitment, he pursued numerous resources that aimed to help him "overcome" same-sex attraction. Matt and Luanne both believed that with enough work and prayer, "this feeling could be fixed." However, throughout this process, nothing seemed to work. Matt and Luanne remained faithful to each other, believing this was the best route for them and committed to doing what was best for their family. They each clung desperately to hope, but Matt felt so frustrated that his feelings of attraction to men remained. The guilt of not loving his wife the way Matt thought she deserved to be loved also weighed heavily on his heart, fostering depression and anxiety.

By the summer of 2015, continuing to live the life he had been living did not seem possible to Matt. The frustration of never being himself and the lack of intimacy and total trust seemed inescapable. Entrenched in darkness, he became convinced that the only way out was to embrace the risk of uncertainty and live as a gay Christian man. In February 2016, Matt told Luanne that he wanted to leave their marriage. By November of the same year, they had divorced. Even so, they chose a posture of gratitude instead of regret, being thankful for the things their life together has brought and remaining hopeful for the future. In a TED talk where Matt and Luanne tell their story about choosing gratitude and hope, they close with this message: "But in the end, somehow it will be worth it, and the truth does set us free and love does win."[6]

The Complexities of Sexuality

Much of the guidance for this chapter came from Amanda Olson, the lead pastor of Grace Evangelical Covenant Church in Chicago. Her doctor of ministry thesis from Duke Divinity School is titled "Out of the Church's Closet: Hope for Evangelicals and Sexual Minorities in the Local Congregation," so she has done a lot of thinking and studying in this area.[7]

Open discussions about sexuality and the Bible have historically been uncommon in the context of conservative evangelical Christianity in the United States. Deeply informed by "purity culture" and long-standing traditions of propriety, churches and Christian communities often don't talk openly about sexual intimacy in a heterosexual context, let alone in terms of what the Bible has to say about same-sex relationships. One of the main critiques from progressive "ex-vangelicals" like Emily Joy, cofounder of the #ChurchToo movement, is the overdependency on and the lack of questioning of purity culture. Joy says:

> We have to question things even when it is hard and when we might lose things. When we understand that our previous understanding of God was incorrect. It's scary, but it has to be done. It is scary, but that's the only way we make progress toward justice. We have to take down our golden calves. We can't have anything that is sacrosanct and too immobile to be questioned.[8]

I don't necessarily agree with Joy's conclusions, but I believe her questioning and challenging the church to question are critically important.

This chapter provides an overview of key passages of Scripture and what they have to say about sexuality, and it wrestles with how churches make decisions about practice. This is by no means the end of the story on these questions, but my hope and prayer is that God would provide wisdom, guidance, grace, and clarity as we seek to honor God's commandments and teachings and to be witnesses of the love and mercy of Christ in the world.

Sexuality in the Bible

Many of the stories about sex in the Bible seem to be negative ones that are full of brokenness and attempts to manipulate the promises and commitments of God. Consider the sexual dysfunction in the family of Abraham. God had promised to Abraham (father of the multitude) that he and his wife Sarah, although "long past the age of having children," would bear a son (Gen 18:10-11). Sarah was so astounded by this proclamation that she laughed (Gen 18:12). At this point, Abraham had already taken the slave Hagar as his wife (Gen 16:3). Overcome with jealousy once Hagar was pregnant, Sarah "mistreated" her and Hagar fled (Gen 16:6). This history of the relationship between the descendants of Hagar and Sarah, Ishmael and Isaac, is one that many books have been written about.[9] For our purposes, suffice it to say that sexual dysfunction was present at the very core of Abraham's home life.

Sexual depravity and the manipulation of relationships are common in Scripture as well. Consider Lot getting drunk and having sex with his daughters (Gen 19:33); David's infidelity with Bathsheba and the murdering of her husband (2 Sam 11); Tamar, the daughter of King David, being raped by her half-brother Amnon (2 Sam 13); and many other stories. We would be remiss to not acknowledge that the fruit of some of these unholy alliances contributed to the lineage of Jesus including Lot's daughter, the mother of Moab, and Bathsheba, the mother of Solomon.[10]

The Song of Solomon, on the other hand, is a tribute to a beautiful love affair and is full of imagery about love and sexuality. In praising his new bride, Solomon writes of her incredible attributes:

How beautiful are your sandaled feet, princess!
The curves of your thighs are like jewelry,
the handiwork of a master.
Your navel is a rounded bowl;
it never lacks mixed wine.
Your waist is a mound of wheat
surrounded by lilies.
Your breasts are like two fawns,
twins of a gazelle. (Song 7:1-3 HCSB)

I remember reading some of these Scriptures as a teenager and being embarrassed by the vivid imagery of the sexual encounter between Solomon and his new wife. This was certainly not a passage that we studied in Sunday school. Again, it's beautiful—but it is also difficult to translate into principles of marriage and sexual ethics. Often it seems like the evangelical emphasis on sexual purity ignores the complexity of sexuality in the Scriptures, while overlooking the clearly visible redemption of God at play in the broken sexuality of the Messianic storyline.

Marriage and Divorce

Biblical narratives on marriage and divorce are more diverse and complex than the Western church typically acknowledges them to be. Many American Christian traditions have held up a 1950s American ideal of marriage and read that Western sociological context and expectation into Scripture.

Genesis 2:24 is a foundational verse on biblical marriage. After the creation of the woman, Adam said: "'This is now bone of my bones / and flesh of my flesh; / she shall be called "woman," / for she was taken out of man.' That is why a man leaves his father and mother and is united to his wife, and they become one flesh" (Gen 2:23-24). But after the fall of Adam and Eve (Gen 3), numerous stories of couples throughout the Scriptures highlight dysfunction in relationships between men and women, as I mentioned in the previous section. Solomon had seven hundred wives and three hundred concubines (1 Kings 11:3). Hosea was commanded by God to marry a prostitute as a symbol of Israel's unfaithfulness (Hos 1:2). In the New Testament, the married couple Ananias and Sapphira each "fell down and died" after collaborating in lying to Peter and the apostles about the price for the sale of a piece of land (Acts 5:1-11).

On the other hand, we also have examples of key figures living in singleness in the New Testament—Jesus and Paul being two of them. First Corinthians 7 speaks to singleness—that it is better to stay unmarried (v. 8). It also speaks to sex within the context of marriage ("do not deprive each other except perhaps by mutual consent" [v. 5]).

The original intent of a man and woman being united in a committed relationship comes from Genesis 2:18 where God says, "It is not good for the man to be alone." God thus creates an *ezer* (helper) suitable for him. New Testament scholar Gilbert Bilezikian notes that the term *ezer* appears twenty times in the Old Testament, often referring to God as the "helper" of man. The Hebrew language, according to Bilezikian, has four other terms that could have been used to mean "helper" that all include notions of subordination. Since none of those are used in Genesis 2, Bilezikian and other egalitarian scholars assert that this passage is not about subordination.[11] Rather, the point seems to be that man and woman were created for companionship and for the stewardship of creation (Gen 1:28).

Marriage is sometimes inappropriately idolized within Christian contexts. Too often men and women are told to stay in broken marriages that are emotionally abusive and damaging to the body and soul because it is ordained by God and because divorce is not permitted. The church and people in positions of pastoral leadership and authority need to do a better job of weighing the difference between staying in healthy marriages and constructively working through conflict while honoring biblical mandates and expectations, and staying in broken marriages where there is contempt, unfaithfulness, and other behaviors that can damage the mind, body, and soul.

This account is from a pastor who wishes to remain anonymous:

> Marriage is an idol. I believe it is a sacrament, but that our earthly commitments should not be elevated over our allegiance to God and the principles of his teaching. In my first marriage, my husband was chronically unfaithful. His first "affair" was during our first few years of marriage. After going to the church and hearing it was God's best for us to try to work it out (even though I had a biblical justification for divorce), we went to Christian counselors. The counselor told me that my husband was straying because I was too independent and not being attentive enough. I look back now and think about all the young women like me who waste years of their lives being in a relationship that is not only dishonoring to self, but also dishonoring to God. There is much I

need to own in my own contributions to our broken marriage; but my husband's lack of faithfulness is not one of them. If I had the courage, I would write the book *When God Is More Honored When We Let Our Marriages Die*. My fear is that it would be misconstrued. I believe marriage is good, beautiful, and sacred. I believe God abhors divorce. I also believe that my greatest sin was staying in a marriage that was abusive and a lie. I trusted the institution more than I trusted God. And the church failed to be a place of deliverance, but rather instructed me to be "faithful" and stay in the captivity of a relationship that crushed my spirit and soul. What does our society, particularly within our churches, teach young women about their worth and value? Certainly the expectation that women "submit to their husbands" when such submission results in their mistreatment, and at times even abuse, would not be according to the will of God.

What are the biblical grounds for divorce? Some conservative theologians and pastors teach that a spouse is permitted to "separate" but not divorce if their life is in physical danger. The victim of potential violence then is required to stay in the marriage relationship until the abusive partner repents or dies.[12] David Instone-Brewer looks more closely at Paul's teachings in the New Testament and argues that there are four legitimate grounds for divorce. The first three are types of neglect and the fourth is adultery (because Jesus allowed for this). Exodus 21:10 reads: "If he marries another woman, he must not deprive the first one of her food, clothing and marital rights." According to Instone-Brewer, the listing of these three specific provisions was aimed at men who sometimes tried to get out of their obligations to provide food, shelter, clothing, and "conjugal love."[13]

Christianity Today published an article in 2016 that sought to answer the question, "When does the Bible allow divorce?"[14] The general perception within American Protestantism in response to this question is that there are two scenarios of divorce that are biblically permissible—when adultery occurs and when there is abuse. The article includes a dialogue between Dr. Andreas Köstenberger, senior research professor of New Testament and biblical theology at Southeastern Baptist

Theological Seminary, and Dr. Craig Keener, professor of biblical studies at Asbury Theological Seminary, about this question.

Köstenberger highlights the passages in Ephesians 5 that emphasize marriage—two becoming one—as an expression of the "spiritual union between Christ and the church" (v. 32). Keener responds and says, "Jesus reminds us that in the beginning God joined man and woman together. 'One flesh' often refers to one's relatives or kin, so the husband and wife becoming 'one flesh' should be a family unit no less permanent than our families of origin should be."[15]

According to both Köstenberger and Keener, sexual immorality does make divorce permissible (Mt 19:9), and there is little debate among theologians in general over this point. However, Köstenberger capitulates, "In such a case, . . . divorce is not mandated or even encouraged—forgiveness and reconciliation should be extended and pursued if at all possible. But divorce is allowed, especially in cases where the sinning spouse persists in an adulterous relationship."[16]

Interestingly, both Köstenberger and Keener seemed resistant to clearly identifying abuse as a legitimate means for divorce. While conceding that abuse can justify divorce, Keener continued:

> Now, I don't want to let that be an excuse for people to opt out of their marriages—someone saying, she abuses me (because she doesn't laugh at my jokes) or he abuses me (because we had an argument). . . . But there does come a point where discretion is the better part of valor. Some people are too ready to grasp for that point; others wait much longer than they should. Jesus told those persecuted for his name to flee from one city to another to escape persecution (Matthew 10:23), and sometimes the apostles did so (Acts 14:5-6). It is heartless to make someone remain in an abusive situation.[17]

Köstenberger presents a different perspective that identifies value in remaining in situations of suffering and even abuse:

> The Bible displays a pervasive concern for justice and is concerned with protecting the vulnerable, [but] it also teaches that believers can glorify God by bearing up under unjust suffering. This calls for wisdom and

balance: Certainly we should do everything we can to protect victims of abuse while at the same time respecting the marriage bond and not dissolving it lightly.[18]

The perspectives of Köstenberger and Keener represent just a small glimpse of some of the more nuanced perspectives about what the Scriptures teach about marriage and divorce.

Biblical Sexuality

So what does the Bible have to say about same-sex attraction and intimacy? Few who hold to a conservative interpretation of the Scriptures would argue that the Old Testament Hebrew Scriptures clearly say that homosexual (or same-sex) acts are not sinful, although the number of evangelical leaders with this perspective is growing. In conversations about what the Bible has to say about same-sex relationships, typically six primary passages are discussed. They are each briefly reviewed here: Genesis 1–2, Genesis 19, Leviticus 18–20, Romans 1:26-27, 1 Corinthians 6, and 1 Timothy 1:8-11.

Genesis 1–2. This is often the starting point for discussions about God's intention for the relationship between a man and a woman, and it's a good one. God made male and female (1:27) and commanded them to "be fruitful and increase in number" (1:28). Interestingly, traditional teachings of the church only allowed for sexual intimacy between a man and a woman for the purpose of procreation. In a more progressive interpretation of historical Catholic teaching, St. Luke the Evangelist Catholic Church in Houston, Texas, wrote the following after wrestling with the traditional viewpoint: "Of course God's command to 'be fruitful and multiply . . .' does not mean that a couple must have conception in mind every time they make love. But it does mean that an essential dimension of married genital sex is openness to new life. In fact the Catholic church will not bless a marriage if a couple deliberately chooses to exclude children from their marriage."[19] The United Church of Christ (UCC) wrestled with the same question about the purpose of sex in marriage and concluded that "the Bible does not prohibit sexual relations within marriage purely for pleasure. Indeed, it encourages such union."[20] Most Christian traditions hold that sex, within the right context according to their theological understanding (which is where much of the debate resides), is good and glorifying to God. The Gospel Coalition says this about sex: "Sex is about pursuing physical, emotional, sexual and ontological union. It is about submission, exploration, discovery, and delight. Done right, under blessing, it often results in children, but it isn't ultimately for that. It is for the glory of God and the comfort of mankind."[21]

Genesis 19. This chapter from Genesis tells the story of the destruction of Sodom and Gomorrah. It starts with Lot welcoming two angels to the city and greeting them with hospitality. A mob of men arrives and threatens Lot, demanding he bring out the two men so that the men of the village could "have sex with them" (v. 5). Lot does not comply, but offers his two virgin daughters instead (v. 8). The angels intervene, pulling Lot back inside and striking the men at the door with blindness. They then foretell the destruction of the city, explaining to Lot that "the outcry to the LORD against its people is so great" (v. 13). Most scholars agree that this passage is not primarily about homosexuality but rather is about hospitality and the welcoming of the stranger.

Ethicist David Gushee calls the passage a "text of terror" and says: "In part it's a story about the contrast between the character of a holy God and wayward humanity at its worst." The main critique of Sodom, according to Gushee, is not the attempted gang rape of men by men. Rather, "a host of sins are named but [they are] mainly related to abuses of public justice," including adultery, pride, overindulgence in food, and lack of care for the poor (Is 1:9-23; Jer 23:14; Ezek 16:49). Not once is same-sex interest or behavior explicitly stated as the main sin of Sodom.[22]

Robert Gagnon, a professor of theology at Houston Baptist University, agrees that Genesis 19 should not be used to universally shape a sexual ethic in response to same-sex interactions, but he believes that the passage does have implications for it. What is so depraved about the actions of the men of Sodom, Gagnon argues, is precisely that they pursued "homosexual rape." He does not speak to how the sins of Sodom relate to the proposed gang rape of Lot's daughters, other than mentioning the "devaluation of women in ancient culture."[23] Gushee asserts that the rape of men would have been a worse violation than that of women because of the esteemed position of men within society: "The men of Sodom want gang rape. They are more interested in men than in Lot's daughters because in a patriarchal society men held greater worth, and thus their violation was viewed as a greater offense than violating a woman."[24] Gagnon, on the other hand, sees the cause for the greater offense and sin against God as being "the act of penetrating a male as if he were a female, an act that is by its very nature demeaning regardless of how well it is done."[25]

Leviticus 18–20. Leviticus 18 is the clearest prohibition in Scripture against same-sex encounters. It includes the description of numerous other prohibitions regarding sexual relations, including constraints against sex with close relatives, mothers, your father's wife, your sisters, a woman on her period, your neighbor's wife, and animals, and states: "Do not have sexual relations with a man as one does with a woman; that is detestable" (Lev 18:22). The NRSV uses the word "abomination" instead of "detestable" in its translation. Leviticus 20:13 also says, "If a man has sexual relations with a man as one does with a woman, both of them have done what is detestable. They are to be put to death; their blood will be on their own heads." The Hebrew term for "abomination" (in adjective form) or "detestable" (in noun form) is *toevah,* though, it's also used in prohibitions against certain foods, including pork, rabbit, shellfish, and animals that are already dead (Deut 14:3-21). Gushee points out that the Leviticus laws were "rendered obsolete for Jews themselves centuries ago by the destruction of the last Jewish Temple" and continues with a detailed explanation of how different scholars interpret these passages—some from the frame of God setting boundaries between the Israelites and their Canaanite and Egyptian neighbors, and others from the frame of God rejecting same-sex relationships because of God's design in creation. He asserts that if Christians take the prohibitions against same-sex actions literally in the laws of Leviticus, then every prohibition must be similarly applied. We cannot cherry-pick among the Levitical laws.[26] What about the Levitical prohibition against tattoos (19:28)? What about the other prohibitions regarding eating fat (3:17), failing to testify against a wrongdoing (5:1), carelessly making an oath (5:4), letting your hair become unkempt (10:6), drinking alcohol in holy places (10:9), mixing fabric in clothing (19:19), and dozens of other restrictions that are ignored entirely today?[27]

Robert Gagnon argues that the laws in Leviticus 18 and 20 prohibiting same-sex relations between men are unqualified and absolute. As a part of the Holiness Code, the penalty for violation of this law was extreme—death (20:13). Middle Assyrian laws of the time, by contrast, required castration, not the death penalty. Gagnon and other traditionalists view these Leviticus prohibitions as evidence in "the distinctive holiness of the people of God" rather than the "contemporary trend of Jewish and Christian communities to accommodate to the prevailing cultural approbation of homosexuality."[28]

Gushee and Gagnon differ significantly in their interpretations of the relevance of these Levitical legal requirements. Gagnon clearly articulates the belief that these prohibitions are "carried over into the New Testament" and thus apply to the new covenant and God's expectations of his people.[29] Gushee, on the other hand, asserts, "It is a fair summary to say that once Jesus comes along, and the Church is founded, neither 2,000 years ago nor today has it been as simple as just quoting a passage from Leviticus to settle a matter of Christian morality."[30]

Romans 1:26-27. These verses are considered by many to be two of the most significant in the discussion about LGBTQ+ sexuality and the Bible, and they are the most substantial in addressing both male and female same-sex relations. They state: "Because of this, God gave them over to shameful lusts. Even their women exchanged natural sexual relations for unnatural ones. In the same way the men also abandoned natural relations with women and were inflamed with lust for one another. Men committed shameful acts with other men, and received in themselves the due penalty for their error." Gagnon spends six pages on these verses in *The Bible and Homosexual Practice,* translating, parsing the text, and providing commentary. The prohibition of same-sex intercourse, he claims, is based on the declaration that it is "contrary to nature," or, in other words, against the "anatomical and procreative complementarity of male and female." Gagnon continues (excuse the graphic nature of this explanation): "by fittedness I mean not only the glove-like physical fit of the penis and vagina but also clues to complementarity. . . . These clues make clear that neither the anus, the orifice for excreting waste products, nor the mouth, the orifice for taking in food, are complementary orifices for the male member." Based on these verses in Romans, he concludes that "both idolatry and same-sex intercourse are singled out by Paul as particularly clear and revolting examples of the suppression of truth about God accessible to pagans in creation and nature."[31]

Other scholars read these verses in Romans differently. Presbyterian pastor and theologian Mark Achtemeier wrote in *The Bible's Yes to Same-Sex Marriage* about the prohibitions in Romans 1, and its context of pagan worshipers having "substitute[d] idols for the true God." In agreement with Paul's prohibitions, Achtemeier writes, "Paul's point is that these idol worshipers have made the same substitution in their sexual lives as they have in their worship; they have exchanged the or-dering will and intentions of the one true God for the chaos of crea-turely passions run amok." The sexual practices of the day, according to Achtemeier, were "violent and sacrilegious or exploitative; they arose out of huge power imbalances or unbridled lusts." In other words, for Achtemeier, the prohibitions are less about the same-sex sexual acts and encounters and more about the idolatrous acts of abandon where God was not at the center. He continues, "Out-of-control passions have no ability to foster the mutual, loving gift of one's whole self to another person in accordance with God's intentions. Paul was right; these be-haviors, which his hearers associated with pagan idol worshippers, were completely at odds with God's intended purposes for love, marriage, and sexuality."[32]

1 Corinthians 6 and 1 Timothy 1:8-11. These two passages both include what are known as "vice lists": lists that include types of behaviors that are prohibited and incompatible with the inheritance of the kingdom of God (1 Cor 6:9). They also both include two Greek words that remain quite controversial among scholars. The term *malakoi arsenokoitai* has been translated as "men who have sex with men" or "homosexuals."[33] Some New Testament scholars, including Gilbert Bilezikian, believe an acceptable translation would allow for these terms to be primarily about the injustices of an unequal relationship and a power dynamic between the strong and the weak. These power differentials could be regarding age, social strata, class, wealth, or in sexual relationships.[34] According to New Testament scholar Dale Martin, the few uses of the word *arsenokoitēs* in Greek texts outside of the Scriptures include translations referring to economic exploitations and abuses of power, and perhaps even exploitation and power in the sex trade industry.[35] Achtemeier speaks into this debate about whether or not these terms refer to a pederasty (a sexual relationship between an older and younger male), to male prostitutes and their customers, or to "same-sex behaviors at all." His bottom line is that the specific definition is less important, because clearly the verses are referring "to behaviors that do not look like a marriage relationship" and the way God intended intimate sexual partnerships to be expressed.[36] Gagnon, on the other hand, is resolute in his translations of these terms, saying, "They define homosexual sex as vice or sin that cannot be practiced by those who wish to inherit God's kingdom."[37] Some conservative Christian groups like Focus on the Family claim "same sex-attraction is not a sin" but also say obedience to a Christian sexual ethic demands abstinence.[38]

This is a brief overview of some of the key questions in biblical hermeneutics and the discussion of whether or not, or to what degree, the Scriptures clearly prohibit sexual practice between same-sex couples. Well-meaning, intelligent, and godly men and women disagree strongly about the question of whether or not same-sex monogamous relationships are biblical. I cannot provide a resolution to this debate between scholars. I do believe in the power of the Scriptures as inspired by God (2 Tim 3:16). And I believe they can be used to build up or to tear down (Eph 4:29). Regardless of what we each conclude as individuals and as the community of Christ, I believe the study of the Word of God and the wrestling with the possible interpretations and relevant implications is critical work that must be done within the body of Christ.

Christian Perspectives on Gender Identity

What does Christian practice look like as it relates to what has come to be understood as the gender spectrum and gender identity? Mark Yarhouse, the Rech Chair in Psychology at Wheaton College and founder of the Sexual and Gender Identity Institute, offers three lenses through which we can view gender: integrity, disability, and diversity.[39]

Yarhouse identifies the integrity lens as one that focuses on "the sacred integrity of maleness or femaleness stamped on one's body." This viewpoint emphasizes the complementarity idea that God created man and woman—in other words, that "essential maleness and essential femaleness" is created by God and primarily related to anatomical and biological differences.[40] From the vantage point of this lens, anything outside of this viewpoint is seen as an attack on the integrity of God's creation.[41]

The second lens by which Christians might view gender identity is through a disability lens, which sees gender "abnormality" or differences as not being "God's best," but rather the result of broken humanity and creation. In other words, in this view, gender differences are not necessarily someone's fault; the creative order simply has abnormalities that are viewed as disabilities (or deficits).[42] In contrast to the integrity lens, this lens emphasizes a nonmoral reality that occurs from time to time (though rarely) and should be dealt with by compassion. The Fall (Gen 3) is generally referenced as the cause of gender dysphoria.[43]

The third lens is one that views gender differences through a diversity lens and allows for committed relationships within the context of genders across the spectrum.[44] From this vantage point, God celebrates his creativity and goodness and can create people however he wants to in terms of their gender identity. In other words, God can create people outside of the Genesis narrative. From the lens of diversity, gender spectrum and sexual diversity should be celebrated, and monogamous same-sex relationships are permissible and can be honoring to God in the lives of faithful Christians.[45]

When asked how Christians should respond to people who self-identify as being both gay and Christian, Yarhouse responded that in most cases, "the church is called to rise above those wars and present a witness to redemption." He concluded, "Christians believe that God holds that person and each and every chapter in his hands, until that person arrives at their true end, when gender and soul are made well in the presence of God."[46]

Global Injustices Relating to Sexuality

In the United States, marital rights and legal unions for same-sex couples ceased to be a legal question on June 26, 2015, when the US Supreme Court ruled in *Obergefell v. Hodges* to strike "down all state bans on same-sex marriage."[47] As of May 2019, two dozen countries around the world allowed for same-sex marriage; many others still have laws and practices that discriminate against and even allow for the abuse and mistreatment of gay and lesbian people.[48] For example, "same-sex relationships between consenting adults are . . . illegal in seventy-six countries globally."[49] Same-sex intercourse can result in criminalization in some places, and in eight countries, many in the Middle East, it is punishable by death. According to Amnesty International, even where homosexuality has been decriminalized, "LGBTI people can still face violence, arbitrary arrest, [and] imprisonment and torture."[50] However, the World Economic Forum issued a 2018 report citing some changes in how gender and sexuality are being understood around the world, including the fact that the World Health Organization (WHO) no longer considers transgender people "mentally ill";

they have instead been categorized as "gender incongruent."[51] Regardless of one's viewpoint on biblical teachings regarding sexuality, most Christians agree that members of the LGBTQ+ community should be afforded basic protections and human rights.

Loving Our Neighbors

This chapter has been a terribly difficult chapter to write. Questions about sexuality cause great conflict, tension, and numerous unresolved issues about church unity and mission. In addition, the stories of individuals like Matt Nightingale show glimpses of deep suffering experienced by members of the LGBTQ+ community and their families. How should the church respond? And what is the appropriate posture for us as individuals who seek to honor the Word of God and follow Jesus? Here are a few suggestions inspired from reading, experience, and reflection on various perspectives in response to the theological and missiological questions.

First, let's be humble as we seek answers to these questions. Our discussions and studying will continue to have profound repercussions on the future of the church and members of the communities most directly affected. May we enter into our learning and study with the posture of "God show me," not presuming to have the answers but rather being willing to repent and release our own baggage, sin, and presuppositions—regardless of what perspective we are coming from.

Second, regardless of our individual views about the theological permissibility of same-sex relationships, we all should agree that the way the church has responded to the LGBTQ+ community has been abhorrent. Pastor Fred Phelps of Westboro Baptist might be viewed as an outlier and extremist on one side of the issue, but his church's "God hates fags" signs still cause irreparable harm to those receiving the epithets. The hateful actions of the Westboro Baptist community and those like them certainly do not exemplify what Jesus taught about "loving your neighbor," let alone your enemy.[52] Unfortunately, hatred toward the gay, lesbian, bisexual, queer, and transgender community is far too common in the Christian community.

Third, an appropriate response is lament at the brokenness of ourselves and the world. Far too often, even with the best of intentions, Christians, pastors, and leaders cause harm and fail to constructively address challenging issues and concerns in ways that are loving and accepting of all people. This does not preclude a conservative viewpoint that the Scriptures teach that marriage is to be only between a man and a woman. I believe, as Ravi Zacharias teaches, it is possible to maintain that traditional theological perspective and still be in loving relationships with the LGBTQ+ community.[53]

Not only should we pursue personal relationships with members of the LGBTQ+ community, we should also be in relationship with people with whom we disagree theologically. And we should enter these relationships with good faith—not out of a desire to change someone's mind or convert someone to our way of thinking, but rather to learn, be in fellowship, and allow the Holy Spirit to act in transformative ways in our own lives and in the lives of others. This process is messy but necessary for the body of Christ to appropriately move forward in pursuit of both faithfulness and unity.

Consider volunteering or engaging with a ministry that walks alongside members of the LGBTQ+ community who have been displaced or discarded. One example is Larkin Street Youth Services in San Francisco, an organization that provides much-needed care—including shelter, health care, employment, and education services—to youth who have become homeless, often because their families have kicked them out due to their sexual orientation.[54] Larkin Street does not operate out of a faith-based perspective, but it does provide desperately needed services to those who would be considered the "least of these" in our society.

As Gushee writes, "Regardless of your stance on the sexual ethics issues . . . I hope you will agree that all Christians ought to be eager to offer well-informed understanding and hospitality to people of non-heterosexual orientation and identity in our families and churches. Anything short of that is not consistent with the requirements of the Gospel."[55]

For Further Study

Achtemeier, Mark. *The Bible's Yes to Same-Sex Marriage: An Evangelical's Change of Heart*. Louisville, KY: Westminster John Knox, 2014.

Brownson, James V. *Bible, Gender, Sexuality: Reframing the Church's Debate on Same-Sex Relationships*. Grand Rapids: Eerdmans, 2013.

Collins, Travis. *What Does It Mean to Be Welcoming? Navigating LGBT Questions in Your Church*. Downers Grove, IL: InterVarsity Press, 2018.

Ganon, Robert, and Dan Via. *Homosexuality and the Bible: Two Views*. Minneapolis: Fortress, 2003.

Grenz, Stanley J. *Welcoming but Not Affirming: An Evangelical Response to Homosexuality*. Louisville, KY: Westminster John Knox, 1998.

Gushee, David P. *Changing Our Mind*. Canton, MI: David Crumm Media, 2014.

Harper, Ben. *Space at the Table: Conversations Between an Evangelical Theologian and His Gay Son*. Portland: Zeal Books, 2016.

Hill, Wesley. *Washed and Waiting: Reflections on Christian Faithfulness and Homosexuality*. Grand Rapids: Zondervan, 2016.

Lee, Justin. *Torn: Rescuing the Gospel from the Gays-vs.-Christians Debate*. Nashville: FaithWords, 2012.

Martin, Colby. *UnClobber: Rethinking Our Misuse of the Bible on Homosexuality*. Louisville, KY: Westminster John Knox, 2016.

Paris, Jenell Williams. *The End of Sexual Identity: Why Sex Is Too Important to Define Who We Are*. Downers Grove, IL: InterVarsity Press, 2011.

Sprinkle, Preston. *People to Be Loved: Why Homosexuality Is Not Just an Issue*. Grand Rapids: Zondervan, 2015.

Vines, Matthew. *God and the Gay Christian: The Biblical Case in Support of Same-Sex Relationships*. New York: Convergent Books, 2014.

Yarhouse, Mark A. *Listening to Sexual Minorities: A Study of Faith and Sexual Identity on Christian College Campuses*. Downers Grove, IL: InterVarsity Press, 2018.

Questions for Discussion

- In general, the church has done a poor job talking about sexuality and what the Bible teaches about relationships between men, women, and the broader community. What sermons or Bible studies have you heard or been in regarding the questions around sexuality, marriage, and orientation?

- What materials and resources have you found helpful in your own understanding of what the Bible teaches about sexuality? What did you learn or value from those perspectives? Who have you read or studied of those with whom you disagree?

- Regarding human sexuality, what are the things you personally or your community needs to lament, grieve, and even repent of? Be reminded, we are completely dependent on God's grace through the life, death, and resurrection of Jesus.

- How do you understand what the Bible teaches about family? And what role do you see family playing in the Scriptures? Can you provide some positive examples of healthy family dynamics? What about broken family stories that are told in the Word of God?

- How have your church and community responded to questions around divorce and remarriage? Divorced people used to experience great stigma and often be excluded from ministry. Has that changed? What do you think about what is written in this chapter about divorce?

- After studying this chapter, are there any relationships in your life that need to be reconciled? How might you better experience and express the love of God in your pursuit of those relationships? Share your thoughts with your small group and ask them for prayer and encouragement in your next steps.

The Middle East, Israel, and Palestine

Pray for the peace of Jerusalem:
"May those who love you be secure.
May there be peace within your walls
and security within your citadels."
For the sake of my brothers and friends,
I will say, "Peace be within you."
For the sake of the house of the Lord our God,
I will seek your prosperity.

PSALM 122:6-9 (1984 NIV)

I TOOK MY FIRST TRIP to the Holy Land as a spiritual pilgrimage to see where Jesus lived, breathed, and did ministry. From the time I was a little girl, I couldn't wait to travel to Israel. I wanted to see the places we'd learned about in Sunday school, to visit the holy sites of Jesus' miracles, from the feeding of the five thousand to his walking on the water of the Sea of Galilee. I wanted to see the land of *Exodus*, which Paul Newman had so bravely conquered as a Zionist soldier seeking to establish a place for Jewish safety in their historic homeland.

After high school and into my college years, whenever I wanted to travel to Israel, a major life circumstance somehow intervened, including family illness and escalations of wars in the Middle East. Finally, while serving as a pastor in Northern California, I had the opportunity to take the trip that I had dreamt of for so long. At that point in my life, in addition to my primary vocational calling as a pastor, I was also a doctoral student at the University of California studying American history. My first book, *Social Justice Handbook,* was on the way to the press and I thought I knew a thing or two about the world. Until I went to Israel.

Traveling into the country from the Jordanian border after a few days in Petra, I led the team through the various checkpoints and border patrol processes at the Allenby Bridge. I had never been to the region before but knew our guide would be meeting us on the other side of the Jordan River. Since I was the tour leader, I was stopped for questions. "Will you be traveling to the West Bank?" they asked. For someone well informed about the Israeli-Palestinian conflict, or even someone who knows the basic geography of the region, this would have been a simple question. I was already in the West Bank (territory that has been under Israeli military occupation since 1967 and is designated as land belonging to the Palestinians for an eventual state). However, when asked the question, I answered, "No." Why? Because I didn't know where the West Bank was!

Other than my geographic ignorance, over the course of two weeks of travel, I had several provocative experiences. Yes, I saw the holy sites and the sacred city of Jerusalem. As I ran my fingers along the stone walls of the Old City, I heard the verses that talk about Jesus' triumphal entry into Jerusalem: if the people hadn't called out to worship him, the stones would have cried out (Lk 19:40). Being in the very land where our faith began was deeply moving and spiritually transformative.

Something else happened in the midst of our travels. I began to see things that I didn't understand. For example, one day when riding on the bus, I saw protesters and a sign that said "Free Palestine." I thought Palestine was just a map in the backs of our Bibles! Then I had the opportunity to hear Bishara Awad, the founder of Bethlehem Bible College, tell his family's story. As an Arab Christian, he had grown up in the area surrounding Jerusalem. But in 1948, around the time the state of Israel was established, his father was killed and he became a refugee. I learned about the resulting refugee population of more than 750,000 Arabs who were displaced from their homes in 1948. What the Israelis consider their year of independence and freedom, the Palestinians call the *Nakba* or catastrophe. As Bishara told his story, I began to weep. My heart had long been moved by the historic and present suffering of the Jewish people, and that did not change. But my heart also expanded as I came to understand my own ignorance and the many ways Americans and our government so often contribute in destructive ways to the ongoing conflict between Israelis and Palestinians.

In the more than ten years since that first trip, I have developed deep friendships with both Israelis and Palestinians. Many of those friends have become closer than family. Often I am asked "why" I engage in peacebuilding and advocacy work in the Middle East. My response? Because of the people there whom I love. One of my closest friends is Shireen Hilal Awwad, director of community and development outreach at Bethlehem Bible College (BBC). Spending time in the chaos of her four children growing up, sitting down and doing homework alongside them, and learning about their daily realities has deeply impacted me. Her six-year-old daughter is called "Mae"—and her energy, determination, and childlike love and acceptance motivates me more than anything else to work for peace and justice for all children living under occupation in Palestine, and all the while to also advocate for peace for their Israeli neighbors.

Palestinian Christians

Christians have lived in the historic land of Palestine and Jerusalem since the time of Christ. Arab-speaking peoples were present in Jerusalem on the day of Pentecost and experienced conversion alongside many other people groups (Acts 2:11). Today Christians in the West Bank are thought to make up at most 2.5 percent of the population—about seventy-six thousand people. Most of them live in the Old City of Jerusalem, Bethlehem, and the neighboring villages of Beit Sahour and Beit Jala. North of Jerusalem, the city of Ramallah is also home to a small Christian community. Reports today indicate that only about one thousand Christians remain in the Gaza Strip, which is more than 99 percent Muslim. All together these three populations, from Gaza, the West Bank, and the Galilee region, make up the Palestinian Christian community—a community that can trace its roots in Israel/Palestine back to the time of Pentecost (Acts 2:11).[1] While European missionaries bringing Protestant and Catholic forms of Christianity arrived only within the last couple of hundred years in the Middle East, Palestinian Christians truly have ancient ties to the Holy Land. (Christianity in the Middle East is discussed further in the next chapter on religious freedom.)

Many forms of Christianity owe a great deal to the pioneering contributions of Middle Eastern Christians—including Palestinians—to both Christian theology and practice. Our most basic beliefs about the Trinity and about who Jesus is were all hammered out by Christians living in the ancient Middle East 1,700 years ago. The creeds that form a part of many Christian statements of faith today all have their roots in those ancient debates among Christians in the Middle East. Middle East Christians have also passed along to us the traditions of baptism, Communion, and monasticism. Truly, Palestinian Christians are the caretakers of an ancient faith that gives us insights into the life of the early church.

Palestinian Christians today feel largely ignored by the church around the world. Because of political allegiances to Israel, American Christians often support one side of the conflict over another. When Palestinian Christians are asked what they would most like for American Christians to know about them, the first thing they say is not about the realities of living under military occupation or details of the conflict. The first thing Palestinian Christians say they want American Christians to know is that they exist.

Contemporary Realities and Life Under Occupation

Palestinian Christians, and their Muslim neighbors in East Jerusalem, the West Bank, and Gaza, have been living under military occupation since 1967. *Occupation* is an international legal term that refers to areas under a country's military control as a result of war. Occupying powers have specific obligations toward civilians of occupied territories as defined by the Geneva Conventions. When we speak of the "occupied territories" in the context of the Palestinian-Israeli conflict, we are referring to the areas that Israel gained control over as a result of the 1967 Arab-Israeli War. For a time, that included the Sinai Peninsula, but Israel gradually withdrew from there after signing a peace agreement with Egypt in 1979. However, that still left Israel as the occupier of the Gaza Strip, the West Bank—including East Jerusalem—and the Golan Heights. Occupation is normally a temporary situation that lasts between the outbreak of hostilities and the conclusion of a peace agreement. Israel's occupation, however, has now lasted over fifty years.[2]

The territory between the west bank of the Jordan River and the Green Line (the armistice line from the 1948 war) is known as the West Bank, or as some Israelis call it, Judea and Samaria. It is the largest of the occupied territories, with an area of 2,263 square miles and a population of 2.75 million. Between 1949 and 1967 the West Bank was ruled by Jordan, even though it was part of the proposed Palestinian State according to the 1947 UN partition plan. After 1967 and the Six Day War, Israel maintained control of the occupied Palestinian territories (oPt), including the West Bank. Jordan gave up its claims to the West Bank in a treaty with Israel in 1994. Since the Oslo Accords in 1995, the West Bank has been divided into Areas A, B, and C. The Palestinian Authority (PA) is responsible for the civil administration and security of Area A, which comprises 18 percent of the West Bank and the majority of its Palestinian population. Area B is under the civil authority of the PA while Israeli forces retain control over security. Area C remains entirely under Israeli military control and comprises 61 percent of the West Bank's area. This administrative restructuring was intended as a five-year transitional phase, but it has become a lasting part of Israel's occupation. And it is important to note that, despite these designations, all of the Palestinian territories are ultimately under Israeli military control.[3]

Prior to 1967, the Gaza Strip (a small strip of land along the Mediterranean Sea that borders Egypt) was controlled by Egypt, even though it was promised to the Palestinians in the 1947 UN partition plan. Gaza is one of the most densely populated areas on the planet, with a population now of more than two million people living within 139 square miles, which comes out to about 14,000 people per square mile. Since the 1995 Oslo Accords, Gaza has come under the jurisdiction of the Palestinian Authority. However, Israel still had settlements in Gaza until its unilateral disengagement in 2005. And while Israel removed all of its soldiers and settlers from Gaza, it still retains complete control over all air, sea, and land access to Gaza. This blockade, which Israel maintains with cooperation from Egypt, has severely restricted the movement of people and goods into and out of Gaza since 2007. Hamas is an Islamic Palestinian militant group and political organization deemed by the United States government as a terrorist group. Hamas took control of Gaza after winning the 2006 elections. Since 2015, Hamas has fired over ten thousand rockets into Israel, killing thirty-three people. On three separate occasions since Hamas's rise to power, Israel has conducted large-scale military operations in Gaza (in 2008–2009, 2012, and 2014) resulting in more than 3,500 Palestinian deaths.[4]

Over fifty years of occupation have transformed Israeli society. Security remains a preoccupying concern, and both the military and the police are extremely prominent within Israeli society today. Military service is compulsory for all Jewish Israelis with the exception of the ultra-orthodox and Palestinian citizens of Israel. As Israeli politicians debate the future of the occupied territories, the fate of Israel's political system hangs in the balance.[5]

The United States government under the Trump administration has also significantly shifted historic US policy vis-à-vis Israel.

Israel's first prime minister, David Ben-Gurion, once described the dilemma facing Israeli society this way: Israelis want three things, he said. They want a democracy, that is also a Jewish state, and for that Jewish democracy to control all of historic Palestine.[6] The problem with that, he said, is that at any given time, Israelis can only have two of those three things. This dilemma helps explain the dangers of the occupation for Israeli society. At present, Israel appears on the path to becoming a Jewish state that controls all of the land. But controlling all of the land would give Israel a larger Palestinian population than Jewish population; the only way to remain a Jewish state in such a scenario would be to deny citizenship or full equal rights to the Palestinian population. In other words, democracy is incompatible with a Jewish state that controls all of the land. Alternatively, if Israelis wish to live in a democratic Jewish state, Palestinians must be allowed a sovereign state and minorities in Israel must be given equal rights. By giving up the West Bank and Gaza, Israel would retain the Jewish majority needed to be both a democracy and a Jewish state. Or, Israel could keep control over all of the land and grant citizenship to all Palestinians. In this case, Israel would be a democracy, but it would cease to be a Jewish state. For people who care about justice for both Palestinians and Israelis, ending the occupation through a negotiated peace settlement is the only viable option.[7]

One of the other major issues that has arisen over the decades of the Israeli-Palestinian conflict is the number of Palestinian refugees. The more than 750,000 refugees displaced in 1948 has grown to 5.15 million Palestinian refugees eligible to receive UNRWA (UN Relief and Works Agency) services. In 2018, 515,260 Palestinian refugee children attended UNRWA schools in refugee camps throughout the Middle East, and 3.1 million Palestinian refugees relied on UNRWA health services.[8] Prior to 2018, the United States provided approximately a third of the funding toward UNRWA. However, the Trump administration decided to completely eliminate the contribution of US funds to the refugee organization, which means that the United States has significantly shifted its role and potential as a broker of Middle East peace.[9]

Human Rights Concerns

Today, numerous human rights concerns are a direct outcome of the military occupation of the Palestinian territories, including the effects of settlements, the separation barrier, and limited access to water.

Settlements are communities Israelis have built on land designated for the Palestinians. As of 2018, the Congressional Research Service reported that there are 130 government-sanctioned settlements in the West Bank, excluding East Jerusalem, in addition to at least one hundred unauthorized outposts.[10] Settlements are problematic for several reasons. Not only are they on land designated by the Oslo Accords to be a future Palestinian state, but settlers also frequently confiscate resources and private land from the Palestinian community. Locations of settlements are most often the places where increased tension and skirmishes between Jewish settlers and Palestinian farmers occur. The Israeli military (in addition to private security forces) protects the settlers and often will not intervene when there are incidents of settler violence against Palestinians. One of the Palestinian villages where this happens the most frequently is Nabi Saleh. Palestinian villagers often gather on Fridays in popular resistance against the confiscation of their land and settlement encroachment.

The separation barrier, called the Security Fence by the Israelis and the Apartheid Wall by Palestinians, began to be built during the second intifada in the early 2000s. The wall has been deemed illegal according to international law since more than 80 percent of it is built on land designated for the Palestinians. According to the Israeli human rights organization B'Tselem, if the wall becomes a future boundary between Israel and Palestine, it would annex 9.4 percent of the West Bank's land to Israel.[11] The wall is also deeply problematic because of where it is built, in many places separating Palestinians from their land and Palestinian communities from their Palestinian neighbors. The Just Vision film *Budrus* shows the effect of the wall on a small Palestinian village in the West Bank. Palestinian farmers often have limited access to their own fields. And communities in Bethlehem are surrounded by the barrier. The stated purpose of the wall is security, but its route tells a different story as it snakes in and out of prime real estate and keeps assets like Rachel's Tomb on the Israeli side.

Even after the Oslo Accords in 1995, Israel remains in complete control over the West Bank. Area C—60 percent of the West Bank's land—is still entirely ruled by the Israeli military. Israeli settlements dot the landscape, which now has a settler population of nearly six hundred thousand (including East Jerusalem). Israel maintains control over Area C through a maze of Israeli-only roads, security checkpoints, and the separation barrier. Because Areas A and B are islands amid the surrounding Area C, Palestinians who wish to travel from one Palestinian Authority (PA)–administered area to the next can only do so by navigating Israel's security matrix.[12]

Limited access to and control of resources is another major problem for Palestinians. Water is one of the greatest needs. In 2016, the per capita daily water consumption for Palestinians in the West Bank was 82.3 liters of water per day. The World Health Organization (WHO) recommends one hundred liters of water per day as the minimum for hygiene and other necessary uses.[13] The average consumption of water per day for Israelis is about 220 liters. (For comparison, the average Californian consumes about five hundred liters of water per day.)[14] In 2016, more than thirty thousand Palestinians in the West Bank did not have running water. One representative of a human rights organization said: "It is clear . . . that the water resources of the West Bank are a strategic asset for Israel and the placement of the settlements is also strategic—to ensure control over not just water, but other vital resources in the West Bank."[15]

The Humanitarian Crisis in Gaza

I wrote an article for *Sojourners* magazine about a 2017 trip I took to Gaza. Near the start of the piece I wrote these words:

> The Gaza Strip is now a small territory to the southwest of Israel, bordered on the west by the Mediterranean Sea, with 1.8 million people living in only 140 square miles. During my visit there earlier this year, I was overwhelmed by the place's incredible beauty; at the same time, the lack of functional sewage treatment plants, limited electricity, and other broken infrastructure result in Gazans experiencing a severe humanitarian crisis. Beautiful and tragic.[16]

Gaza's humanitarian crisis is so severe that the territory is "de-developing" even faster than expected.[17] According to Ron Piper, the UN coordinator for humanitarian aid and development activities in the oPt, "In a nutshell, Gaza continues to de-develop in front of our eyes," Piper adds. "From health care, to unemployment, to energy, to access to water, across all of these fields, Gaza's 2 million people are seeing faster and faster decline in their living conditions."[18] More than 96 percent of the water in Gaza is undrinkable. The average amount of electricity at any given point is three-to-five hours per day.[19] According to B'Tselem, there are more than one hundred thousand Gazans without running water, and the daily water usage is 58.7 liters of water per person per day. The infrastructure is so poor that 40 percent of the water pumped through the system is lost due to leaks.[20]

In addition, unemployment in Gaza is so severe that almost half the working-age population (49 percent) was unemployed in 1998. Unemployment among youth reached 65 percent in that same year. And 70 percent of the population of Gaza is dependent on foreign aid.[21]

In 2018–2019, many residents of Gaza participated in the Great March of Return. Of the two million people living there, nearly 1.4 million of them are refugees registered with UNRWA.[22] The Great March of Return was organized to bring attention to the "right of return" maintained by those refugees and their descendants from 1948.[23] According to *The Guardian*, within a year since the protests began, 190 Palestinians in Gaza had been killed with an additional 28,000 injured.[24]

The human cost of maintaining the occupation and siege on Gaza is high. In addition to the deaths and injuries sustained by Palestinians, it imposes a human cost on Israeli society. Since the first intifada in 1987, over one thousand Israeli civilians have been killed in the conflict. That figure is double the number of military deaths during the same period. And the psychological effect that such a high rate of civilian casualties has had on Israelis should not be discounted. It creates a mindset where security takes precedence over every other concern. It is equally important to remember that the number of Palestinian fatalities since 1987 is about ten times higher. However it is measured, there can be no doubt that the human price for continuing the occupation is too high for Israelis and Palestinians alike.[25]

Anti-Semitism and Christian-Jewish Relations

How should American Christians think about the conflict between Israelis and Palestinians? We need to understand how problematic our historical engagement has been with both the Jewish and Palestinian communities. In her book *The Misunderstood Jew*, Amy-Jill Levine writes about ways Christian theology has been historically anti-Semitic: "Jesus was a Jew talking to other Jews. . . . Once Jesus's words became placed in the Gospel narratives and addressed to Christian churches, comments spoken *to* Jews became perceived by the church, as well as the synagogue, as comments spoken *against* Jews."[26]

Levine also believes that liberation theology can lead people toward anti-Semitic thoughts and beliefs. When Jesus is framed as a liberator, she explains, there has to be a system that Jesus is liberating people *from*. Historically, Christians perceived the "enemy" of Jesus as the Jews, and thus liberation meant being set free from the presumed evilness of the Jewish people. Judaism, rather than Roman imperialism or colonialism, is seen as the creator of walls and divisions, the system that Jesus is there to demolish. Levine writes, "Taking their cues from the New Testament and nurtured by centuries of the church's anti-Jewish teaching, these theologians . . . find Judaism and Jews to epitomize systemic evil."[27]

James Carroll writes in *Constantine's Sword: The Church and the Jews—A History* about ways the church has not significantly "owned" its role in promoting anti-Semitism. Citing theologies like replacement theology, or supersessionism, which asserts that the old covenant between God and the Jewish people is overridden (or superseded) by the new covenant through Jesus Christ, Carroll says, "Although we cannot assume that Jews and Christians will ever approach the Scriptures in the same way, surely Jews have a right to ask: Must the Christian understanding of the very structure of God's Word include the derogatory 'replacement theology' that is so often found in the New Testament?"[28]

While there are differences of opinion regarding what constitutes anti-Semitism across conservative and liberal divides, commonalities also exist. Beliefs that are detrimental and could lead to physical harm against Jews constitute anti-Semitism. But not every problematic belief manifests anti-Semitism; a person can be inaccurate and wrong, and not be anti-Semitic. Unfortunately, often individuals form strong opinions on limited or one-sided information and although this is problematic, it is not necessarily anti-Semitic. Nonetheless, we must be informed and attentive to when anti-Semitic sentiment, rhetoric, or actions exist.

This is not to say that we can never legitimately critique Israel. Levine concedes that criticism of Israeli policy need not indicate anti-Jewish motivation.[29] Calling Israel to higher ideals because of its self-identification as a "vibrant democracy" and calling for the fair treatment of the approximately 20 percent of its citizens who are Palestinian does not constitute anti-Semitism.[30] And yet, we must also call out violations of human rights and acts of violence by other individuals, groups, and nation states, alongside our critique of Israel. Activists and advocates must not muddy the waters between anti-Semitism and legitimate criticism of Israeli policies.

The reality is that anti-Semitism in the United States and around the world has increased in recent years, and continues to do so. With the rise of neo-Nazis, white nationalists, and other hate groups, significant threats to the Jewish community exist. Christians and those of other belief systems must stand firmly in our solidarity with the Jewish community in response to anti-Semitism and its devastating effects. The October 2018 killings at the Tree of Life synagogue manifest this reality in its worst form.

In essence, while we seek and advocate for justice for Palestinians, calling leaders to account and responding to the human rights abuses we witness in the occupied territories, we must also acknowledge the rootedness of anti-Semitism in Christian history and its remnants in some of today's Christian rhetoric. In our pursuit of justice for Palestinians, we must be diligent to not return to our previous egregious ways. We continue to walk a narrow path as we pursue these two realities.[31]

Christian Zionism

Christian Zionism is a very prevalent movement within the United States and is often based on the historical theology of dispensationalism. According to the International Christian Embassy in Jerusalem, one of the leading Christian Zionist organizations in the world, Christian Zionism can be understood this way:

> The actual theology of Christian Zionism, also known as Biblical Zionism, supports the right of the Jewish people to return to their homeland on scriptural grounds. The biblical foundation for Christian Zionism is found in God's Covenant with Abraham. It was in this covenant that God chose Abraham to birth a nation through which He could redeem the world, and to do this He bequeathed them a land on which to exist as this chosen nation.[32]

One of the results of this belief is unbridled support of the political aspirations of the State of Israel, as the Christian Zionist movement conflates the modern State of Israel with the biblical Israelites and God's chosen people. This often includes support of the Israeli military, Israeli expansionist policies through settlements in the West Bank, and the elevation of Jewish aspirations over and above Palestinian attempts toward self-determination. Some Christian Zionist communities even send missions funds to settlements for swimming pools and playgrounds, often unaware that these building projects are being constructed on Palestinian land.[33] (The history and implications of Christian Zionism are covered more extensively in my book *A Land Full of God: Christian Perspectives on the Holy Land.*)

Palestinian Liberation Theology

I appreciate Levine's concern that quests for liberation from "Jewish oppression" in Palestinian liberation theology can lead to anti-Semitism. This is something to be attentive to, and we should welcome the feedback and contributions of the Jewish community to help us understand these dynamics and to ardently stand firm in our commitments against anti-Semitism.[34]

The founder of Palestinian liberation theology is Palestinian Anglican priest Naim Ateek. While our readings of the sacred texts of the Hebrew Scriptures and the New Testament often come to different conclusions, I believe it is important to understand his perspective as a leading Palestinian Christian voice calling for liberation. He says, "Jesus Christ was a Palestinian [Jew], as we are. He lived in the same land we live in. He breathed the same air we breathe. His language and thought patterns were Semitic, as ours are." Ateek believes that there is a call for justice at the heart of the gospel message: "First, faith in the God of love and justice means that one is already sensitized by the love of God and is committed to doing God's will in the world. Love and justice are two sides of the same coin."[35]

Justice and the quest for both existential and material freedom are imperative in a full expression of the gospel. This is my prayer for Palestinians, Israelis, and all of us who are seeking freedom and liberation:

> The body of Christ must have a holistic understanding of both existential and material freedom in order to be an advocate on behalf of oppressed people around the world. Resting on the truth that justice and righteousness are the foundations of God's throne, evangelicals—alongside so many others—must commit to being advocates of freedom, and to diligently pursuing liberation for all people by being voices for the voiceless and advocates for the disinherited, so that all may one day be free.[36]

Intersectionality and Movements of Liberation

Every year I have the privilege of taking pastors and leaders to Israel, the Palestinian territories, and other parts of the Middle East. In 2017, one guest was one of the leading voices for reconciliation and justice in the

United States. As an African American woman working in the predominantly white evangelical community, she was familiar with the realities affecting communities of color in the United States, including struggles against white supremacy and nationalism. In 2014, she joined dozens of other faith leaders around the country in Ferguson to highlight concerns about the fatal shooting of unarmed African American Michael Brown. During the peaceful protests, the crowd sang hymns and songs from the civil rights movement and heard Christian leaders preach and speak about God's heart for justice and the obligations we have to right systemic injustice. At that moment a young woman standing next to this preacher took her hand and raised their fists in the air, shouting, "From Ferguson to Palestine!"

This story gave me shivers down my spine when I first heard it. Although many people of color in the United States have never been to Israel or Palestine, oppressed communities often share an understanding of suffering that allows them to resonate with each other's realities even before understanding the details. This commonality is increasingly being expressed in movements of intersectionality that look at common themes in how the abuse of power plays out in unjust systems.

In July 2018, *Teen Vogue* published an article called "How Policing in the US and Security in Israel Are Connected."[37] In speaking about the relationship between Ferguson and Israel, the article reports, "Three years before the Ferguson protests, Tim Fitch—the chief of the very same St. Louis County Police Department responsible for firing teargas at activists and concerned citizens—had flown to Israel to receive training from Israeli police, intelligence, and military in a weeklong course on terrorism-focused policing."[38] Often policing techniques for crowd control in the United States are modeled after practices that are utilized toward Palestinians in the West Bank. As we better understand injustices in our own cities and communities related to race, power dynamics, poverty, and other justice issues, this awareness helps us to better understand imbalances of power and injustice in global contexts.

May our responses to the injustices we witness and experience seek to be integrated to address these realities of intersectionality.

American Politics and Theological Imperialism

American policies toward Israel not only further support the ongoing occupation of the Palestinian people; they are also not in the best interest of Israel. The Academy Award–winning film *The Gatekeepers* highlights how the ongoing occupation of the Palestinians is the greatest threat to the long-term security needs of Israel. Palestinians living in East Jerusalem, the West Bank, and Gaza do not experience self-determination and are often subject to human rights abuses. These realities for the more than five million Palestinians living between the Mediterranean and the Jordan are not sustainable and unless resolved will only lead to more violence. All the while, US administrations, Republican and Democrat alike, give billions of dollars every year to Israel for military aid and assistance. For example, prior to leaving office, President Obama signed a historic agreement with Israel promising thirty-eight billion dollars of US funding for military aid over a ten-year period.[39] We should be very concerned about the United States' ongoing military support for Israel without accountability for the human rights abuses mentioned above, such as the expansion of settlements, the illegal separation barrier, the restriction of movement for Palestinians within the West Bank, and the ongoing blockade of Gaza.

These realities have worsened under the Trump administration. Since President Trump took office, the word *occupation* has been completely removed from the human rights report for Israel published by the US State Department. The United States cut almost all funding to UNRWA and humanitarian assistance funding to the Palestinian Authority. The United States de facto acknowledged Israel's annexation of Jerusalem and moved its embassy there from Tel Aviv, one of the only countries in the world to do so. And, in a complete shift in historic US foreign policy, the United States acknowledged the annexation of the Golan Heights from Syria, which has been occupied since the 1967

Arab-Israeli War. In June 2019, to show their appreciation, the Israeli government announced a new settlement in the Golan that would be named "Trump Heights."[40] In November 2019, Secretary of State Mike Pompeo announced another historic shift in US policy by stating that the United States no longer views Israeli settlements in the West Bank as illegal. In early 2020, Israeli politician Benny Gantz agreed to meet with the White House to discuss their plan for Mideast peace, which clearly neglected Palestinian contributions. These are just some of the foreign policy shifts by the US Administration that are having devastating effects on Palestinians and Israelis who long for peace, and that will make a negotiated settlement between Israelis and Palestinians all the more difficult.[41]

The theological and ideological beliefs that undergird these new policy decisions are even more disconcerting, though. In January 2018, Vice President Mike Pence delivered a historic speech to the Israeli Knesset affirming the United States' strong relationship with Israel in no uncertain terms and in language that sounded very much like theological imperialism: "We stand with Israel because we believe in right over wrong, in good over evil, and in liberty over tyranny."[42] What specifically is problematic with this language? It seems to indicate that the "good" Jewish state of Israel (note that 80 percent of Israeli citizens are Jewish and 20 percent are Arab Palestinians) should triumph over "evil." The assumption is that the "evil" forces are Arab Muslims who seek only destruction. Essentially, the vice president compared the American quest for freedom from tyranny with Jewish aspirations to return to their historic homeland. The affirmation of Jewish aspirations is not in and of itself problematic; what is problematic is the complete avoidance of any legitimacy of the same rights for Palestinian Arabs. In the rest of the speech, Pence recognized Jerusalem as the capital of Israel and also promised to eradicate from the world all radical Muslims: "Together with our allies, we will continue to bring the full force of our might to drive radical Islamic terrorism from the face of the Earth. (Applause.)"[43]

Toward Peace

Prospects for peace between Israelis and Palestinians have never seemed more distant. US policies with unilateral support of Israel only diminish the potential for the United States to play any constructive role in brokering peace. How can US Christians get involved? Join movements like Churches for Middle East Peace (CMEP) in our work "to encourage US policies that actively promote a comprehensive resolution to conflicts in the Middle East with a focus on the Israeli-Palestinian Conflict."[44] Sign up for our weekly newsletter to be kept informed of what's happening in the political situation and with churches in the Middle East. Consider coming to one of CMEP's advocacy summits in Washington, DC, where you could have the opportunity to meet with your elected members of Congress and advocate for a holistic solution to the conflict that is honoring to the needs of both Israelis and Palestinians.

If you would like to learn more about the conflict, consider hosting CMEP's five-week video-based curriculum on the Israeli-Palestinian conflict called *The Search for Peace & Justice in the Holy Land*.[45] Other opportunities to engage include hosting Israeli and Palestinian speakers at your church or community through CMEP's Pilgrimage to Peace (P2P) tours that travel all over the United States and Canada. Since 2012, these tours have brought speakers face to face with more than forty thousand people in churches, synagogues, and mosques all over North America. Finally, if you have never had the opportunity to travel to the Holy Land, consider having CMEP create a multinarrative tour experience with MEJDI tours that focuses on creating space for the multiple narratives of the Holy Land, including those of the Israelis, Palestinians, and the three Abrahamic faith traditions of Judaism, Christianity, and Islam.[46] My first trip to Israel changed my life. Perhaps your traveling there will have a similar effect.

What is my prayer in all this? In our quest for justice may we ask for God's mercy and wisdom. May our esteem of the Jewish people and our advocacy for Palestinians not cause harm to the other. But may we also not sit idly by as more than five million Palestinians suffer under the weight of a military occupation that has already lasted more than half a century. Christians have often been "mischief makers in Palestine." May our future engagement be more constructive.[47]

For Further Study

Ateek, Naiman Stifan. *A Palestinian Theology of Liberation: The Bible, Justice, and the Palestinian Israeli Conflict.* Maryknoll, NY: Orbis Books, 2017.

Beller, Steven. *Antisemitism: A Very Short Introduction.* New York: Oxford University Press, 2007.

Bock, Darrell, and Mitch Glaser, eds. *Israel, the Church, and the Middle East: A Biblical Response to the Current Conflict.* Grand Rapids: Kregel, 2018.

Bourke, Dale Hanson. *The Israeli-Palestinian Conflict: Tough Questions, Direct Answers.* Skeptic's Guide. Downers Grove, IL: InterVarsity Press, 2013.

Cannon, Mae Elise, ed. *A Land Full of God: Christian Perspectives on the Holy Land.* Eugene, OR: Cascade Books, 2017.

Carroll, James. *Constantine's Sword: The Church and the Jews—A History.* New York: Houghton Mifflin, 2010.

Carter, Jimmy. *Peace Not Apartheid.* New York: Simon & Schuster, 2007.

Gunner, Göran, and Robert O. Smith, eds. *Comprehending Christian Zionism: Perspectives in Comparison.* Minneapolis: Fortress, 2014.

Isaac, Munther. *The Other Side of the Wall: A Palestinian Christian Narrative of Lament and Hope.* Downers Grove, IL: InterVarsity Press, 2020.

Levine, Amy-Jill. *The Misunderstood Jew: The Church and the Scandal of the Jewish Jesus.* New York: Harper Collins, 2006.

Questions for Discussion

- What ideas about Israel and the politics of the Middle East did you grow up with? Did people in your home or environment have certain perspectives and thoughts about the Palestinians?

- How has the nature of the Israeli-Palestinian conflict shifted over the decades? Are the mechanisms employed in the conflict different now than they were in 1948? In 1967? During the intifadas? And today?

- Have you met any Palestinian or Middle Eastern Christians? Did you learn anything in this chapter about that community?

- How has anti-Semitism affected the relationship between Christians and the Jewish community?

- Have you ever traveled to Israel? What did you see? Did you travel to the West Bank? What stories do you have to tell?

- What human rights considerations were raised in this chapter? How did you first learn about these concerns? What do you hear in the news about this conflict?

- Is there anything about the Middle East that provokes you to want to get more involved? How might God be stirring your heart?

- Consider leading the curriculum mentioned above. How can you encourage further discussions about this within your community?

Religious Freedom

Now the Lord is the Spirit,
and where the Spirit of the Lord is,
there is freedom.

2 CORINTHIANS 3:17

FEBRUARY 15, 2015, marked a significant day in the lives of Egyptian Christians and other followers of the cross living throughout the Arabic-speaking world. ISIS released a "propaganda video" showing the mass execution of twenty-one Egyptian Christian men in Libya, wearing orange jumpsuits with their hands cuffed behind their backs. In the video, men dressed in black stood behind each of the victims, who were then all pushed to the ground and beheaded.

In CNN's live reporting of this incident they used language like "chilling developments" and another "depraved video that is difficult to watch." CNN's conclusion was that it marked ISIS control in Libya. But they did not mention anything about the significance of Christians being specifically targeted for mass murder by ISIS. In other words, CNN labeled the video as "very very worrying" not because of the specific targeting of a religious group by Muslim extremists, but rather because "Libya is right on Europe's doorstep."[1]

In writing about the lives of the twenty-one Egyptian migrant workers killed in Libya, Martin Mosebach says, "The Twenty-One could well have echoed the words of Paul the Apostle: 'for we are made a spectacle unto the world, and to angels, and to men."[2] Identifying the twenty-one Copts as martyrs, Mosebach shares their stories in his book, chronicling their lives as poor farmers outside of Cairo and in rural Upper Egypt. He also explains that the martyrdom of these Egyptians cannot be understood apart from the reality of their Coptic upbringing as minorities in a predominantly Muslim context.

The United Nations condemned the attack, saying in their statement: "This crime once again demonstrates the brutality of ISIL, which is responsible for thousands of crimes and abuses against people from all faiths, ethnicities and nationalities, and without regard to any basic value of humanity."[3] However, in this case, one particular faith was targeted—the faith of those who follow the cross.

What is the state of religious freedom globally? This chapter looks at that question through a geographic lens while highlighting the role religious freedom plays in the US context and around the world.

The State of Religious Freedom Around the World

In 2011, Wilton Park, a strategic think-tank based in the UK, hosted an international forum for discussion about the state of religious freedom around the world.[4] Religious freedom is defined differently by different societies, but essentially it refers to the right of individuals and communities to practice their faith tradition without restriction. According to the Wilton Park report, 70 percent of the world's population lives in countries where there are high or very high levels of restrictions on religious freedom. Contributing factors to religious intolerance include unstable governments, discriminatory laws, religious extremism, fanaticism and terrorism, poverty, and illiteracy. Different nations place varying degrees of importance on the role of religion within their respective civil societies and in their foreign relations. Some societies, including the United States, value religious opinions and influences on conversations about governance and foreign policy. In other contexts like Europe, secularism is upheld as a higher ideal. The report reminds readers, however, that faith and religion are not always used for the sake of good: "They can be a powerful and dangerous vehicles for intolerance, hatred and extremism—and this often with worrying impunity."[5]

Wilton Park recommended several steps for breaking down barriers that can arise because of a lack of understanding and lack of tolerance between people of different religions. One is that faith leaders should acknowledge their role in calling out injustice against other faiths when they see it. Another is holding crosscultural and interfaith dialogue experiences, which can help promote acceptance, tolerance, and the fostering of religious freedom. The report concludes: "At a time of change and political transition in the Middle East, there is good reason to remain particularly watchful of the impact on religious minorities. Religious and other minorities are often the first to bear the brunt of political transition, in particular in countries facing serious economic challenges."[6]

The Pew Research Forum conducted analysis on global religious freedom for their 2016 "Global Uptick in Government Restrictions on Religion" report. Fifty-six percent of countries saw an increase in government restrictions on religious freedom between 2015 and 2016. More specifically, the percentage of countries with "high" or "very high" levels of government restrictions on religious freedom rose from 25 percent in 2015 to 28 percent in 2016. In addition, the harassment of religious minorities around the world is at its highest since survey data began in 2007. About a third of European countries (33 percent) had nationalist parties that made political statements against religious minorities, an increase from 20 percent of countries in 2015. Muslims were targeted in twenty of the twenty-five European countries where nationalist groups were active, and Jews were targeted in ten of those countries.[7]

In 2018, *Christianity Today* reported that both Muslims and Christians have experienced a surge in religiously related attacks and harassment since 2016. Two of the countries listed as having a high intolerance for religious freedom were China and India, whose collective populations make up about 83 percent of the world population.

Christians reported harassment in 144 countries worldwide in 2016, more than for any other religion. Muslims were the second most persecuted religion globally, reporting harassment in 128 countries worldwide in 2016. Of the twenty-five most populous countries in the world, "Russia, India, Indonesia, Turkey, and Egypt are the biggest offenders for government restrictions and social hostilities against religion."[8]

Religious Freedom in the United States

Under the Trump administration, religious freedom is getting a lot of attention in Washington, DC. Significant changes, mostly centered at the State Department, have included downsizing Religion and Global Affairs, monthly religious freedom roundtables, and an annual ministerial on religious freedom with thousands of internationals attending. On one hand, religious actors are getting more emphasis, access to power, and influence within the US government. In reality, as discussed in the earlier chapter on politics and religion, the Trump administration grants more access and power to those who adhere to its religious and political persuasions—namely conservative and fundamentalist evangelicalism.

In 2013, John Kerry (then secretary of state) launched the Office of Religion and Global Affairs (RGA), citing the relevance that religion has in foreign diplomacy. A precursor to the department had been started during Hillary Clinton's tenure as secretary of state. And both of these developments were connected to President Bush's previous "faith-based initiatives."[9] Now, however, under the Trump administration, RGA and its specific work of creating space for persons of faith to inform and consult on matters of state has been in danger.

In the fall of 2017, then–Secretary of State Rex Tillerson notified Bob Corker, a senator from Tennessee at the time, and the Committee on Foreign Relations of his plans to eliminate the RGA special advisor position and fold only a few of its functions into the Office of International Religious Freedom. The loss of this committee could have an effect on churches, missionaries, and the vulnerable across the globe, especially when considering that nearly 84 percent of the world self-identifies as religious. Doug Leonard, the former director of global mission for the Reformed Church in America (RCA), says: "[Religious groups] have the ability to influence the cessation of conflict, to advance peace and justice, and to foster reconciliation. We must not leave these fine tools of diplomacy to state agencies alone. There is a growing awareness among national diplomatic corps that religions and nations would do well to collaborate."[10]

Nearly forty religious leaders signed a letter against the decision to close the RGA office—leaders who are involved in significant work that affects different areas of government work. Under Secretary Kerry, several committees had been formed, inviting religious leaders to consult and advise on how religious considerations could impact US foreign policy. I sat on the group focused on the role of religion in the mitigation of global conflict and had the privilege of coleading a subgroup on the role of religion in civil society in contributing to peacebuilding and the end of violence. My coleader of that subgroup was a senior staff member of the Joint Chiefs of Staff in the Department of Defense (DOD). We made an unusual pairing—a key leader at the DOD along with an evangelical pastor—but in the two years that we met, we made tangible progress in solving both theoretical (future) and real-world problems related to faith, foreign affairs, and peacebuilding. Doug Johnston, founder of the International Center for Religion and Diplomacy (ICRD), said, "Religious leaders and institutions can, and often do, play an important role in addressing political differences that would otherwise result in conflict. . . . We need people in the halls of power communicating directly with decision makers. And US policymakers need us. The world is full of diplomatic and global challenges that require the wisdom and experience of faith leaders and their constituents."[11]

In addition to foreign policy, religious freedom in the United States influences many sectors of our national society. For example, the United States allows for the freedom of religion at work and, according to the ACLU, "prohibits employers with fifteen or more employees from discriminating on the basis of religion," based on Title VII of the Civil Rights Act. If asked, your employer must provide a reasonable accommodation for your religious practices; as the ACLU explains, "In most instances, employers are required by federal law to make exceptions to their usual rules or preferences to permit applicants and employees to observe religious dress and grooming practices."[12] "Religious dress and grooming" can include a Muslim hijab (headscarf), a Sikh turban, or a Christian cross. The United States also has federal protections regarding religious freedom in housing and public schools.

Religious freedom also plays a role in questions like whether or not students should be able to pray in school. The ACLU advises:

> You have the right to express your religious beliefs at school. For example, you may pray individually or in groups and discuss your religious views with your classmates during student activity times like recess or lunch, provided that you are not disruptive. You may express your religious beliefs in your schoolwork if they are relevant to the assignment. You may pass out religious literature to classmates, subject to the same rules that apply to other materials students distribute.[13]

Rules and restrictions on praying in school are different for teachers and faculty, since they have influence over students and could be seen as coercing students to conform to their own religious beliefs. Common violations of these restrictions in public schools include in-class daily prayer led by teachers; distributing Bibles to students; prayer and Scripture readings at awards ceremonies, athletic events, and other school activities; school-day assemblies featuring evangelization and other religious content; coach-organized and coach-led prayer at sporting events; school officials leading and participating in student religious clubs; and school involvement in the planning and promotion of religious baccalaureate services. The ACLU reiterates: "School officials may not preach to students, teach religious doctrine as truth, or otherwise promote religious messages."[14]

The role of religion in the United States is unique in that religion has never been separate from public life; it's simply that the government cannot support a state religion or attempt to ban certain expressions of religion. Wilfred McClay says,

> The United States has achieved in practice what seemed impossible in theory: a reconciliation of religion with modernity, in contrast, as I say, to the Western European pattern. In the United States religious belief has proven amazingly persistent even as the culture has been more and more willing to embrace enthusiastically all or most of the scientific and techno-logical agenda of modernity. Sometimes the two reinforce one another.[15]

Not everyone sees the current state of religious freedom in the United States as something to marvel at. Many Christians, particularly white ones, feel that the United States is at the "end of Christian America." While it is true that this demographic is decreasing in size, it has not in any way decreased in power—and in fact may have more influence with the Trump administration than ever before. In 1976, white Christians comprised 80 percent of Americans and more than half of those (55 percent) were specifically white Protestants.[16] In 2017, however, a Public Religion Research Institute (PRRI) study found that white Christians represented less than half (43 percent) of all Americans, and that younger people were turning to other religions or eschewing religion altogether: "While two-thirds of seniors are white Christians, only around a quarter of people 18-29 are. To varying degrees, this has af-fected almost every Christian denomination—and nearly four in ten young Americans have no religious affiliation at all."[17] The religions with the highest percentage of young people in America are Islam, Hin-duism, and Buddhism.

One immediate effect of this shift is that members of the majority group of white, mostly conservative, Protestant Christians are increas-ingly expressing concern that they are "victims of discrimination."[18] A 2016 report from PRRI and Brookings shows that half of American Christians believe that Christianity is the religion most discriminated against in the United States.[19] The percentage increases to 75 percent when only Republicans who identify as Christians are sampled. And 80 percent of white evangelical Protestants, most of whom voted for

President Trump, think that Christians are discriminated against more than any other religious group in the United States. Seventy-four percent of white evangelical Protestants also agreed with the statement, "Islam is at odds with American values and way of life." According to *Atlantic* writer Emma Green: "If religious people believe their institutions are declining—which, demographically speaking, they are—they may feel more threatened by what they perceive as the growing numbers of people in the country who have a different kind of faith."[20]

On the other side of the coin, some argue that "religious freedom" under the Trump administration is being used to justify the supremacy of Christianity, particularly evangelicalism, in the public sphere. Elevating one religion above others is not that uncommon for a country. Around the world, however, it is often the cause of deep divides, and can exacerbate civil wars and violence. Consider, for example, the growing divide between Muslims and the secular community in France,[21] growing anti-Semitism around the world,[22] and the near annihilation of Christian and minority communities at the hands of Muslim extremists as part of the ISIS movement in places like Iraq and Syria. The question we should be asking is, how can the rights of Christians around the world and in the United States be protected without being elevated over the rights of other religious and minority groups? What do social justice and religious freedom look like when they are integrated and expressed hand in hand?

In an article in *Relevant* magazine, Gabriel Stoutimore defines Christian privilege as the "systemic inherent advantage to Christians solely on the basis of their faith" that is institutional "at either a government, legal, or culturally predominant and normative level." Stoutimore cites examples of Christian privilege:

> the preference of national holidays on the grounds of religious observance with time off from work, no pressure to celebrate non-Christian holidays, the wearing of religious symbolism without being commonly characterized as odd or dangerous, the predominance of representation in lawmaking and governing bodies by those who share your faith, the

ability to avoid having to speak on behalf of your faith or all Christians when one of your own goes bad, the dominance of Christian language in the historical roots of our society and the fundamental influence of Judeo-Christian imagery in the public square.[23]

Are Christians in the United States privileged or discriminated against? In 2016, the website Christian Today published an opinion piece called "The Damaging Myth of Religious Persecution in America." In the article, Ed Cyzewski highlights the dangers of identifying differences of opinion, perspective, religion, and ethics as "religious persecution." While Christians around the world struggle to get government permission to build churches or gather for worship and often experience physical violence and legal discrimination, Christians in the United States are primarily alarmed that conservative understandings of gender and sexuality are no longer social norms held by the wider American population. Cyzewski says, "The focus of perceived 'persecution' in America has been around issues such as prayer in schools, the use of public buildings for church services, same sex marriage, and transgender bathroom laws."[24] New legislation or court decisions that challenge the applicability of conservative Christian social norms to the public sphere are attempts to balance the rights of minority groups and Christians' religious freedom rather than attempts to drive Christian worship underground. American Christians must be careful to not diminish the suffering and persecution of Christians and other minority groups around the world because of the shifting attitudes within US society toward Christianity and religion.

Religious Freedom in France

Of all of the countries in Europe, France is one of the most well known for its intolerance of Muslim religious communities. Proud of its heritage of "secularism," France celebrated the centennial anniversary in 2005 of its secularization law, which "barred the state from officially recognizing, funding or endorsing religious groups."[25] Known as *laïcité*, French secularism has its roots in the 1789 Declaration of the Rights of

Man, Article Ten: "No one may be disturbed on account of his opinions, even religious ones, as long as the manifestation of such opinions does not interfere with the established Law and Order." Other than Napoleon's recognition of the Catholic Church in 1801, the long history of France has been staunchly entrenched in its secular identity, which was reaffirmed in the 1958 French Constitution: "France shall be an indivisible, secular, democratic and social Republic. It shall ensure the equality of all citizens before the law, without distinction of origin, race or religion. It shall respect all beliefs."[26]

While the "respect all beliefs" sounds like religious freedom, the actual expression of religious liberty in France has been contrary to their written commitments. Known as the Foulard Affair, in 1989, two Muslim girls were expelled from school for wearing hijabs, which triggered significant debates on the public display of religious symbols. In 2001, the About-Picard Bill was approved, which attempts to suppress religious movements that may be viewed as cults, if their practices deny their members the same human rights upheld by French society. In 2003 Nicolas Sarkozy created the French Council of the Muslim Faith to regulate Islam in France, but the majority of the council consisted of representatives from Islamic organizations based only in Morocco, Turkey, and Saudi Arabia.[27] These three countries do not represent the breadth of Islamic practices in the Arab world. In addition, in Saudi Arabia, there are many very strict laws and Islamic practices that often discriminate against women and moderate adherents to Islam. In 2004 in France, a law on secularity and conspicuous religious behaviors and symbols in schools was passed, specifically banning Muslim hijabs, Sikh turbans, Jewish kippahs, and Christian crosses. And a 2013 Harris poll in France found that 73 percent of French citizens have negative views of Islam. Ninety percent said wearing a hijab or niqab was incompatible with French culture, and 63 percent said the same of praying five times a day.

One specific example of how Islamophobia plays out in France was the response to the decision of the French sporting goods store

Decathlon to release a new hijab designed for sports and athletic events. The company was already selling them in Morocco, where they were met with wide success, but after the announcement to sell them in France, employees and the corporation received nearly five hundred calls and emails in one morning. In addition, French politicians called for a boycott of the company. Decathlon canceled the sale of the new hijab. "I think it's sad," said sociologist and documentary filmmaker Agnes de Feo. "A brand has been forced to give in as a result of racists. . . . The only positive point is that this collective hysteria has been exposed and no one can deny that Islamophobia exists in France."[28]

Parfums de Vie (Fragrance of Life)

Muslims make up about 8 percent of France's population, and most have traveled from North African countries like Tunisia, Algeria, and Morocco.[29] Many Muslim refugees face severe challenges in French society. In the city of Grasse (most known for being the perfume capital of the world) on the southern coast of France, special schools are funded by the French government to meet the needs of (legal) Muslim refugees from North Africa, but these schools have a difficult time maintaining teachers and have inadequate provisions for the education of the students who attend. The ministry *Parfums de Vie* (Fragrance of Life) was founded in 2008 in Grasse to meet the needs of Muslim students who were being inadequately supported and educated by government schools. Led by devout Christians, the organization seeks to "improve the lives and opportunities available for the underprivileged children and youth of Grasse, through a variety of educational programs and activities." You can visit their guest house and learn more about the work they are doing with students in Grasse.[30]

According to the 2017 European Union Agency for Fundamental Rights survey, acts of discrimination against Muslims across the European Union have been on the rise. In the past five years, 39 percent of Muslim respondents reported experiencing discrimination because of their ethnic or immigrant background, and 35 percent of Muslim women who experienced discrimination attributed it to wearing traditional clothing (by contrast, only 4 percent of men responded similarly).

In addition, 2 percent of Muslim respondents experienced physical violence against them due to their ethnic or immigrant background within the last twelve months. And who were the most common perpetrators of violence against Muslims? Nine percent of violent incidents were perpetrated by police or border guards and 5 percent by right-wing extremist groups.[31]

According to anthropologist Matti Bunzl, today both anti-Semitism and Islamophobia "are rooted in the idea that as 'legalistic religions' neither Judaism nor Islam can integrate into secular society." Bunzl compares the historic problems faced by those who practice Judaism as being similar to those that Muslims are facing today in Europe. He and many others also believe the Israeli-Palestinian conflict has a direct effect on the treatment of Jews and Muslims in European society. "The anti-Semitism found among Arab-Muslims and, to a lesser extent, among Blacks," he says, "is connected to this complex conjuncture of resentment, identification with the Palestinian cause, and the experience of heightened discrimination."[32]

Anti-Semitism in Europe and the United States

As discussed some in the last chapter on Israel and Palestine, the history of Christian anti-Semitism has its roots in the belief that Jews are "Christ killers" who brought about the crucifixion of Jesus. Throughout history, Jews have been scapegoats for various phenomena and natural disasters such as the Black Death pandemic in fourteenth-century Europe. Though some thinking shifted in the wake of the Enlightenment, where an emphasis on individual human rights was helpful to the Jewish people of Europe, the nineteenth century was not kind to them. By 1914, racial and ethnonationalists emphasized that Jews were culturally different and could never be citizens. They were not Europeans, they were viewed as greedy, and they had a stronghold over the economy. When more targeted persecution began in the 1930s, countries were in such economic distress that there was little focus on human rights, and Jews had been identified as "foreign to

Europe." Scholar Steven Beller, author of a short history of anti-Semitism, reminds readers that the "horrors of genocide in the Holocaust" were a direct result of ideologies of anti-Semitism.[33]

As I've mentioned already, anti-Semitism is not merely a phenomenon of the past. According to a 2018 report by the European Union Agency for Fundamental Rights, based on a survey given to Jews living in the European Union, 89 percent of Jewish respondents felt anti-Semitism had increased in their country over the preceding five years. The three most commonly used anti-Semitic statements as identified by respondents were as follows: "Israelis behave like Nazis toward Palestinians" (51 percent), "Jews have too much power" (43 percent), and "Jews exploit Holocaust victimhood for their own purposes" (35 percent). More than a third of the respondents reported that they avoid visiting Jewish events or sites because they do not feel safe. Eighty-nine percent of participants experienced threatening or degrading comments on social media, and almost three quarters experienced personal hostility in the street. And close to 40 percent expressed that they had considered emigrating outside of Europe in the past five years because of the rise of anti-Semitic acts and violence.[34]

We've already looked at some of the ways anti-Semitic rhetoric has been on the rise in the United States. A survey conducted by the Anti-Defamation League in 2017 reveals a bit more about the perceptions of Jews in America. Citing the concern regarding Jewish-American attacks and the rise of anti-Semitic rhetoric, about eight in ten Americans believe that it is important for the government to play a role in mitigating these perspectives. Of those polled, 31 percent of Americans believe that Jews in the United States are more loyal to Israel than they are to the United States. The original trope against Jews as the killer of Jesus was affirmed by 30 percent of the participants in that same poll. And finally, 25 percent of Americans believe that Jews talk too much about the Holocaust.[35]

What do these facts and statistics show us? Discriminatory views and racist perspectives toward Jews continue to be prevalent today and must be fought directly. There is no place in democratic societies for hatred, discrimination, and bigotry toward Jews or any other people group.

Religious Freedom in the Middle East

According to the Pew Forum, social and governmental intolerance to religious freedom is the highest in the Middle East.[36] Here is a brief look at how religious freedom is expressed in Egypt, Syria, Iraq, and Turkey.

Egypt. The Coptic Christian community in Egypt makes up roughly 10 percent of the overall population of more than eighty million people. There is also a small group of Egyptian Protestants who make up less than 1 percent of the population. Islam is the state religion, and Jews and Christians are the only other religious groups besides Muslims for whom the constitution guarantees free practice of religion (freedom of worship). The constitution also prohibits discrimination on the basis of religion for Jews, Christians, and Muslims.[37] Egyptians have their religion listed on their state-issued ID cards. And while freedom of worship is protected, there are still restrictions. For instance, it is illegal for a non-Muslim man to marry a Muslim woman. Because Abrahamic faith traditions are privileged there, it is illegal to criticize them or question their teachings, especially people recognized in Islam as prophets. The religious groups in Egypt whose activities are severely restricted by the government include Mormons, Jehovah's Witnesses, and Baha'is.

During 2017, militant groups continued to target Christian minorities, both Coptic and Protestant, in Egypt. ISIS attacks on two churches on Palm Sunday (April 9) killed forty-five Christians, and twenty-eight Christians were killed by ISIS in northern Sinai while on their way to visit a desert monastery. And even though Egyptian law theoretically protects Christians, in reality they often face social pressure or violence in their everyday lives. For example, there are sometimes protests against church construction, even when legal building permits have been acquired. Christian shops and other properties are frequently vandalized. Police often pressure Christians not to press charges against Muslims for wrongs, arguing that not pressing charges will promote reconciliation and coexistence. In addition, apostasy from Islam is legal, but Muslims who convert to other religions often receive threats from their families and face violence. Sometimes Christian women from rural and impoverished villages are kidnapped and forced to marry Muslim men.[38]

Syria. The ongoing civil war in Syria has had devastating effects on the community there. Christians have typically had a strong relationship with previous totalitarian regimes (and do with the current one) because of the assumed protection of the state against persecution by Muslims and extremist groups. Historically, Christian minority populations under dictatorships like Mubarak in Egypt, Assad in Syria, and Hussein in Iraq, have been protected, at least to a degree. Most Christians in Syria have historically lived in Damascus, Aleppo, Homs, Hama, and Latakia, or in the Hasakah Governorate. Today many of these communities have become broken and displaced. Syria has no official state religion, and all religions have freedom to worship so long as practice "does not disturb the public order." Christians are prohibited from evangelism and proselytizing Muslims, and apostasy from Islam is illegal. Religious activities are also heavily controlled; for instance, religious gatherings outside of an officially recognized house of worship on days apart from regular days of religious observance (Friday for Muslims, Saturday for Jews, Sunday for Christians) require government permits. While ISIS no longer controls territory in Syria, it remains active and continues to target religious minorities. In 2017, ISIS "massacred more than a hundred Christians in the Christian town of Al-Qaryatayn in October, after temporarily capturing it." When ISIS did control territory in Syria (2014–2017), Christians (and other non-Muslim people of the Book) under their rule were subject to the *jizya* tax of $320 per person per year.[39]

Iraq. The persecution of and discrimination against Christians and minority groups in Iraq is some of the worst in the Middle East and around the world. In fact, the violence against these groups in Iraq and other ISIS-affected areas became so severe that the US Congress deemed it a genocide in 2017.[40] The Iraqi people have experienced some of the greatest civilian losses as a result of attacks from ISIS. According to the 2017 Report on International Religious Freedom in Iraq, "From January 1 to June 30, the UN Assistance Mission for Iraq (UNAMI) reported 5,706 civilian casualties resulting from ISIS attacks, including 2,429 persons killed and 3,277 wounded."[41] Iraq once had one of the most thriving Christian communities in the Arab world, but as of 2017, fewer than 250,000 Christians remained, most (200,000) around the Nineveh Plain. The majority (67 percent) of Christians are Chaldean Catholics, with 20 percent belonging to the Assyrian Church of the East. There are about three thousand evangelical Protestants in Iraq (a little over 1 percent of all Iraqi Christians). Islam is the state religion, and, like in other Arab Muslim countries, apostasy from Islam is forbidden by law. The constitution technically guarantees freedom of worship for Muslims, Christians, Yezidis, and Sabean-Mandeans. However, even though violence from Muslim extremists has diminished significantly, reports say that minorities have still "felt pressured by the Muslim majority to adhere to certain Islamic practices, such as wearing the hijab or fasting during Ramadan."[42]

Turkey. Turkey has taken a significant shift religiously toward more militant practices of Islam under the current president, Recep Tayyip Erdoğan. The Turkish constitution does not establish an official state religion and "provides for freedom of conscience, religious belief, conviction, expression, and worship; and prohibits discrimination based on religious grounds" so long as practices do not threaten the "integrity of the state." One of the more proactive limitations on free speech in the context of religion, however, is the penal code's prohibition of imams, priests, rabbis, and other religious leaders "'reproaching or vilifying' the government or the laws of the state while performing their duties." Other limitations include the prohibition of worship in any location that has not specifically been designated for that purpose according to the state. Turkish Christians have experienced increased pressures recently, causing concern: "Various self-defined Islamist groups continued to threaten and vandalize Christian places of worship. In September an unidentified group threw stones at the Armenian Surp Tateos Church in the Narlikapi neighborhood of Istanbul, breaking windows."[43] This is just another example of the increased burdens Christians in the Middle East are carrying.

The future of Christianity in the Middle East. The increased discrimination, even to the point of martyrdom, of Christians in the Middle East has caused some to ask what the future of Christianity is there. In the twentieth century, the number of Middle Eastern Christians in places like Egypt, Israel, Palestine, and Jordan made up about 14 percent of the population. By 2015, the percentage of Christians in the Middle East had declined to only about 4 percent.[44] Christians still play a significant role in the government of Lebanon, but the number of Christians there has also decreased by almost 50 percent over past decades. Some of the demographic decrease has to do with natural birthrates and the reality that Christian families often have fewer children than their Muslim neighbors. But the mass exodus of Christians from Iraq after the defeat of the Saddam Hussein regime also contributed significantly to the current Christian population being less than a quarter of a million today, down from 1.5 million in 2003. The realities affecting Christians in the Middle East range from them simply being a minority in relatively safe Islamic contexts to them being arrested, detained, and imprisoned, as is common in Iran, Egypt, and Saudi Arabia. Just before Christmas in 2018, a group of 114 Christians in Iran were arrested as a form of intimidation and then given court dates to evaluate their behavior and religious practice.[45]

In a 2019 article that cited many of the specific examples and scenarios above, reporter Emma Green raised the question of whether or not Christians would be able to survive and thrive in Muslim-dominated cultures.[46] The answer to that question will also indicate how well or poorly democracy is being expressed in those communities. For their part, the Trump administration, though cutting off foreign aid to Palestinians, is redirecting much of that aid to respond to the genocide of Christians and minority groups in the Middle East. Green reports, "In October [2018], USAID announced even more funding: a new investment of $178 million, bringing the total U.S. government investment to nearly $300 million. For the most part, American money has gone toward rebuilding schools, clinics, and water and electricity systems."[47] This is just one way the current administration is seeking to respond to the plight of Christians in the Middle East.

Other Cases of Religious Freedom Around the World: India and China

Religious freedom is not only decreasing in the Middle East but also in India. Though freedom of religion is recognized under a 1949 constitutional right, the violence against religious minorities in India continues to climb.[48] Amid a crackdown on foreign aid in 2017, Compassion International was forced to close down its operational sites in India after doing ministry among the poor there for forty-eight years, on suspicion of "engaging in religious conversion."[49] The United States Commission on International Religious Freedom (USCIRF) reported that there are several limitations in India that restrict religious freedom. Hindu extremism is on the rise, targeting groups like Dalits, Christians, Muslims, Buddhists, Jains, and Sikhs. In addition, several Indian states have adopted anti-conversion laws or anti–cow slaughter laws aimed at those minority religious groups. The anticonversion law tends to only apply to those who might move from Hinduism to another religion, while those who are not Hindu are free to convert to another religion without punishment.[50] However, the US ambassador for religious freedom, Sam Brownback, and other conservatives have expressed significant concern about the growing anti-Christian sentiment that seems to be in place under the current Indian government.[51]

China has the largest population in the world, and it is estimated that it will also be the country with the most Christians by 2030. The

Communist government of China is rigidly atheist though, making religious practice complicated. The Chinese Communist Party (CCP) recognizes five religions: Buddhism, Daoism, Islam, Catholicism, and Protestantism (without distinguishing further under the two Christian categories). Each of these religions was formerly overseen by the State Administration for Religious Affairs, reorganized in 2018 under the United Front Work Department, which appoints clergy, decides interpretation of doctrine, and makes sure that teachings are in agreement with the government and CCP thinking.[52] When I lived in China in 1998, it was common practice for state officials to attend public worship services to report on and monitor Christian activities. The underground churches in China are rumored to be the fastest growing in the world, with estimates of tens of millions of participants. Underground churches have been a common phenomenon in China since the 1949 Communist Revolution. They are not formally recognized by the government and participants have often been at risk of harassment or even arrest. Many in the government are concerned about the possible Western influences that might come through Christianity. The Council on Foreign Relations reports, "Though the state's regulation of religious practice tends to be cyclical—revival, repression, and back again—religion in China remains inherently political."[53] In addition, there are government officials who are advocating for the construction of a Chinese Christian theology through the lens of government ideals and for the nationalization of Christianity, which would give the state even more oversight and lead to increased repression of religious freedom in China.

Liberty for All

Religious liberty has become a prevailing justice issue in countries all around the world. Several Christian organizations focus on responding to these realities and protecting the rights of Christians and other religious groups to practice their faith freely. Both Open Doors International and International Christian Concern focus specifically on monitoring and responding to the persecution of Christians in violent contexts.[54] Christian Solidarity International is a human rights organization that campaigns for religious liberty and human dignity for all religions.[55] Charter for Compassion reaches more broadly than the Christian community and promotes education and opportunities for people to practice tolerance and compassion in support of the UN Sustainable Development Goals and religious freedom.[56]

China Aid is one organization focused specifically on supporting persecuted Christians there. They also provide information and resources pertaining to the Christian community in China.[57]

What can the church in the United States do? Pray for the persecuted church. Stand in solidarity with groups of other religious traditions who are being persecuted and experiencing suffering. Consider developing relationships with people from different faith traditions and learning about the ways their particular communities are responding to realities like anti-Semitism, Islamophobia, and Christian persecution. These suggestions can get you started in being an advocate for religious freedom in the United States and around the world.

Supporting appropriate government measures that seek to protect the rights of all religious groups around the world is another way US Christians can actively respond. This certainly includes political advocacy in support of congressional acknowledgment of the treatment of Christians and other minority groups in Iraq and other parts of the Middle East. Organizations like In Defense of Christians (IDC) and Churches for Middle East Peace (CMEP) are paving the way for the sustainability of the Christian community in the Arab world and the Middle East.[58]

Both IDC and CMEP provide action alerts and opportunities to engage in political advocacy on behalf of Christians and other persecuted communities in the Middle East.

For Further Study

Bunzl, Matti. *Anti-Semitism and Islamophobia: Hatreds Old and New in Europe*. Chicago: Prickly Paradigm, 2007.

Hurd, Elizabeth Shakman. *Beyond Religious Freedom: The New Global Politics of Religion*. Princeton, NJ: Princeton University Press, 2015.

Mosebach, Martin. *The 21: A Journey into the Land of Coptic Martyrs*. Walden, NY: Plough, 2018.

O'Brien, Brandon J. *Demanding Liberty: An Untold Story of American Religious Freedom*. Downers Grove, IL: InterVarsity Press, 2018.

Wenger, Tisa. *Religious Freedom: The Contested History of an American Ideal*. Chapel Hill: University of North Carolina Press, 2017.

Questions for Discussion

- How familiar were you with issues of religious freedom before reading this chapter? Is there any part of the world that you are more familiar with or connected to?

- What do you think is important about the values of religious freedom? In countries where religious freedom is restricted, what are some of the implications?

- Did any of the stories in this chapter move you? What touched you about what you learned?

- Discuss the current US administration's perspective on religious freedom. How has US policy under the Trump administration served Christians and other minority groups? What are the risks of the current US policies regarding religious freedom?

- What role do you think individual Christians and church communities can play in promoting religious freedom?

A Recommitment to Biblical Justice and Beloved Community

The Lord is close to the brokenhearted
and saves those who are crushed in spirit.

PSALM 34:18

He heals the brokenhearted
and binds up their wounds.

PSALM 147:3

THE ENTIRETY OF THIS BOOK has sought to draw us toward a deeper understanding of God's heart for justice. The God of the Scriptures cares deeply for the poor and oppressed and responds to the cry of the needy. As Psalm 34 and 147 remind us, he is close to the brokenhearted and saves those who are crushed in spirit. Much of this book is about the people who are most affected by the brokenness of the world. Many of the stories told here—stories of oppression, injustice, rejection, isolation, and poverty—are about people who have been crushed in spirit.

In the midst of such harsh realities and pain, what does it mean to have persistent hope? Historian Christopher Lasch wrote: "Hope does not demand a belief in progress. It demands a belief in justice: a conviction that the wicked will suffer, that wrongs will be made right, that the underlying order of things is not flouted with impunity. Hope implies a deep-seated trust in life that appears absurd to most who lack it."[1] *Beyond Hashtag Activism* is seeking the kind of hope that Lasch writes about, a hope that is set firm on the foundation and belief that God is the God who makes things right. He is good. He is powerful. He is just. We rest in the hope that the realities we see in the world today are not the end of the story.

One of my mentors, Mary Nelson, founder and former executive director of Bethel New Life, marched with Dr. Martin Luther King Jr. when he was in Chicago in 1966. She once told me that story. Fannie Lou Hamer, an activist from Mississippi, was at the front of the line with Mary. During one of their marches, a white man approached them and shouted horrible things, his face full of rage and hate. He then spat right in Hamer's face. Mary tells of how Hamer responded: "Jesus loves you," she said. "Jesus loves you."

Hamer's response makes sense when we read these words of hers from another context: "The white man's afraid he'll be treated like he's been treating the Negroes, but I couldn't carry that much hate. It wouldn't have solved any problems for me to hate whites because they hate me. Oh, there's so much hate! Only God has kept the Negro sane."[2] Love drives out fear. Love drives out hatred. One of Martin Luther King Jr.'s most famous quotes reminds us, "Love is the only force capable of transforming an enemy into a friend. . . . I have decided to stick with love. Hate is too great a burden to bear."

My prayer is that this book might encourage us all to be closer to God and also closer to the beloved community that King preached about. A community that is committed to love and not hate. A community that holds on to hope for justice, even in the midst of hopeless situations. A community that rests and trusts in the good news that God is just, and one day he will come again.

Acknowledgments

In MANY WAYS THERE ARE too many individuals, events, and extended parts of my "beloved community" to thank for their contributions to this book. Nonetheless, I would be remiss to not acknowledge a few key people. This is the third project I've had the privilege of working on with Al Hsu and I am grateful for his tireless contributions to bring this book to fruition. It would not have happened without him! All errors are completely my own. I'm grateful to InterVarsity Press for their more than a decade of publishing my work.

Many of the ideas honed in this book were explored with students and colleagues in courses and workshops about social justice at institutions like Bethlehem Bible College in Palestine and Pacific Rim Bible College in Hawaii. I have learned much from conversations about justice within indigenous communities and look forward to learning more.

A few key contributors to this project cannot be ignored. I am indebted to Maddie Roos who was an awesome research assistant.

And to Andrew Wickersham and the CMEP staff—especially Kyle Cristofalo and Katie McRoberts—who provided content, reviews, and support. Nicole Morgan has been a faithful partner in ministry over the past several years and this project was no exception. To Jill Pratt, Alison Glick, Lisa Kennedy, and Jim Maxstadt and the rest of the CMEP team—may God bless the fruit of our labor as we together work toward peace in the Middle East.

To Laura Roy and her husband, Tom. For their friendship and faithful pursuit of justice, forgiveness, and hospitality as an expression of the gospel is nothing short of inspiring.

The joy I've experienced through our friendship with Amanda, Don, and Ben Olson inspires me to stay the course in this hard work of pursuing justice.

I'm grateful to Mark and Joey Hanlon for their unequivocal belief and support in God's call and work in my life over many years.

To Glenn and Margo Balsis, their friendship and spiritual solidarity strengthens me. They prayed over me regularly during this writing the words from Deuteronomy 32:2, "Let my teaching fall like rain and my word settle like dew, like gentle rain on new grass with showers on tender plants." This is my prayer as well.

Finally, to my husband, Paul. After a past of much brokenness and pain, doing life together is the greatest gift.

Notes

Introduction

[1]Lin Taylor, "Child Deaths from Preventable Causes Have Been Cut in Half Since 2000," Global Citizen, September 18, 2018, www.globalcitizen.org/en/content/child-death-preventable; "15,000 under five die from preventable illnesses each day: UN," Medical Xpress, October 19, 2017, https://medicalxpress.com/news/2017-10-fives-die-illnesses-day.html.

[2]"Introduction," "The Statement on Social Justice and the Gospel," published September 4, 2018, https://statementonsocialjustice.com/#introduction.

[3]"Chicago Declaration of Evangelical Social Concern (1973)," Evangelicals for Social Action, accessed December 10, 2018, www.evangelicalsforsocialaction.org/about-esa-2/history/chicago-declaration-evangelical-social-concern/.

1 God's Justice and Prophetic Advocacy

[1]Tracy Balzer, *Thin Places: An Evangelical Journey into Celtic Christianity* (Abilene, TX: Leafwood, 2007), 26.

[2]Balzer, *Thin Places*, 29.

[3]Mae Elise Cannon, *Social Justice Handbook: Small Steps for a Better World* (Downers Grove, IL: InterVarsity Press, 2009), 27.

[4]Jack Jenkins, "Christian Group Plans 'Revival' to Protest 'Toxic Evangelicalism,'" Red Letter Christians, February 10, 2018, www.redletterchristians.org/christian-group-plans-revival-to-protest-toxic-evangelicalism/.

[5]Jack Jenkins, "Red Letter Revival Gives Voice to Evangelicals on the Margins," Baptist Standard, April 11, 2018, www.baptiststandard.com/news/nation/red-letter-revival-gives-voice-evangelicals-margins/.

[6]Gregory Smith and Jessica Martínez, "How the Faithful Voted: A Preliminary 2016 Analysis," Pew Research Center, November 9, 2016, www.pewresearch.org/fact-tank/2016/11/09/how-the-faithful-voted-a-preliminary-2016-analysis/.

[7]Mark Labberton, ed., *Still Evangelical? Insiders Reconsider Political, Social, and Theological Meaning* (Downers Grove, IL: InterVarsity Press, 2018), 5.

[8]Labberton, *Still Evangelical?*, 6.

[9]Vanessa Williamson and Isabella Gelfand, "Trump and Racism: What Do the Data Say?" Brookings, August 14, 2019, www.brookings.edu/blog/fixgov/2019/08/14/trump-and-racism-what-do-the-data-say.

[10]"Introduction," "The Statement on Social Justice and the Gospel," published September 4, 2018, https://statementonsocialjustice.com/#introduction.

[11]Bob Smietana, "Accusing SBC of 'Caving,' John MacArthur Says of Beth Moore: 'Go Home,'" October 19, 2019, Religious News Service, https://religionnews.com/2019/10/19/accusing-sbc-of-caving-john-macarthur-says-beth-moore-should-go-home.

[12]Scot McKnight, "Go Home or At Home?" *Patheos*, October 21, 2019, www.patheos.com/blogs/jesuscreed/2019/10/21/go-home-or-at-home.

[13]Brittney Cooper, "Intersectionality," in *The Oxford Handbook of Feminist Theory*, ed. Lisa Disch and Mary Hawkesworth (London: Oxford University Press, 2016), www

.oxfordhandbooks.com/view/10.1093/oxfordhb/9780199328581.001.0001/oxfordhb
-9780199328581-e-20.

[14]"The Chicago Invitation: Diverse Evangelicals Continue the Journey," Evangelicals for
Social Action, accessed February 2, 2019, www.evangelicalsforsocialaction.org
/chicago-invitation/.

[15]Joshua Gill, "12 Faith Leaders Arrested While Protesting GOP Tax Plan in Senate
Building," *Daily Caller,* December 1, 2017, https://dailycaller.com/2017/12/01/12
-ministers-arrested-while-protesting-gop-tax-plan-in-senate-building/.

[16]Jack Jenkins, "Faith Leaders Arrested as Major Religious Groups Rally Against the
GOP Tax Reform Bill," ThinkProgress, November 30, 2017, https://thinkprogress
.org/faith-leaders-protest-tax-bill-bce14e698ce9/.

[17]Romans 13:1 states that we should be subject to governing authorities because they
have been instituted by God; 1 Peter 2:13-14 says, "Submit yourselves for the Lord's
sake to every human authority, . . . who are sent by him to punish those who do
wrong and to commend those who do right."

[18]Shane Claiborne, "Why We Go to Jail: A Brief History of Christian Civil Disobedience,"
Sojourners, April 2018, https://sojo.net/magazine/april-2018/why-we-go-jail.

[19]The development of these ideas about advocacy occurred through discussions and
conversation in several places, including, but not limited to, my classes on *Social
Justice Handbook* at Pacific Rim Christian University in Honolulu, Hawaii; the May
2017 class on social justice for the peace studies program at Bethlehem Bible
College in Bethlehem, Palestine; my workshop presentation on May 30, 2018,
during the Christ at the Checkpoint conference in Bethlehem, Palestine; and the
Ecumenical Accompaniment Program in Palestine and Israel (EAPPI) Advocacy
Summit hosted by Churches for Middle East Peace (CMEP) on October 20, 2018,
in Washington, DC.

[20]*Phrase Dictionary,* s.v. "Power corrupts; absolute power corrupts absolutely," accessed February 2, 2019, www.phrases.org.uk/meanings/absolute-power-corrupts
-absolutely.html.

[21]Online Library of Liberty, "Lord Acton Writes to Bishop Creighton That the Same
Moral Standards Should Be Applied to All Men, Political and Religious Leaders Included, Especially Since 'Power Tends to Corrupt and Absolute Power Corrupts
Absolutely' (1887)," accessed November 27, 2019, https://oll.libertyfund.org
/quotes/214.

[22]From my teaching at the CMEP EAPPI Advocacy Summit. Notes taken by
Chris Cowan.

[23]Four of these five types of advocacy are discussed extensively in Cannon, *Social
Justice Handbook,* 100-103.

[24]Cannon, *Social Justice Handbook,* 102.

[25]Cara Solomon, "Bringing Slavery's Legacy to Light, One Story at a Time," *Harvard
Law Today,* February 13, 2019, https://today.law.harvard.edu/feature/bringing
-slaverys-legacy-to-light-one-story-at-a-time/.

[26]"About Al-Haq," Al-Haq, updated October 16, 2010, www.alhaq.org/about-al-haq
/about-al-haq.

[27]E. Staehelin-Witt, "Economic Sanctions Against South Africa and the Importance of
Switzerland," Swiss National Science Foundation, November 7, 2013, www.snf
.ch/sitecollectiondocuments/nfp/nfp42p/nfp42p_staehelin-e.pdf.

[28]"Abolition of the Slave Trade," National Archives, accessed February 2, 2019, www
.nationalarchives.gov.uk/pathways/blackhistory/rights/abolition.htm.

[29]"Abolition of the Slave Trade."

[30]Daniel Silas Adamson, "The Christian Family Refusing to Give Up Its Bethlehem Hill
Farm," BBC, June 18, 2014, www.bbc.com/news/magazine-27883685.

[31]Ella David, "The Land of Milk and Honey, and Wanton Destruction," *New Internationalist*, May 28, 2014, https://newint.org/features/web-exclusive/2014/05/28/palestine-israel-tent-of-nations/.

[32]Ilene Prusher, "The Tree Uprooting Heard Around the World," Haaretz, June 12, 2014, www.haaretz.com/.premium-the-tree-uprooting-heard-around-the-world-1.5251560.

2 Politics and the Gospel

[1]Eric Bradner, "Donald Trump: No Apology on 'Blood' Remark Amid GOP Backlash," CNN, updated August 10, 2015, www.cnn.com/2015/08/09/politics/donald-trump-blood-comment-response-2016-sotu/index.html.

[2]John Fea, *Believe Me: The Evangelical Road to Donald Trump* (Grand Rapids: Eerdmans, 2018), 5, 12, 179.

[3]Bob Woodward's book *Fear: Trump in the White House* (London: Simon & Schuster, 2018) spells out in great detail how fear motivated white evangelicals to vote for Donald Trump.

[4]Randall Balmer, "The Real Origins of the Religious Right," *Politico*, May 27, 2014, www.politico.com/magazine/story/2014/05/religious-right-real-origins-107133?o=1.

[5]Fea, *Believe Me*, 7.

[6]Mark Charles and Soong-Chan Rah, *Unsettling Truths: The Ongoing, Dehumanizing Legacy of the Doctrine of Discovery* (Downers Grove, IL: InterVarsity Press, 2019), 63.

[7]Chris Eberle and Terence Cuneo, "Religion and Political Theory," in *Stanford Encyclopedia of Philosophy*, updated January 15, 2015, https://plato.stanford.edu/entries/religion-politics/.

[8]Jordan J. Ballor and Robert Joustra, eds., *The Church's Social Responsibility: Reflections on Evangelicalism and Social Justice* (Grand Rapids: Christian Library, 2015), 26; and J. Howard Pew, "Should the Church 'Meddle' in Civil Affairs?" *Reader's Digest*, May 1966, 49-54.

[9]Adelle Banks, "Museum Highlights 'Slave Bible' That Focuses on Servitude, Leaves Out Freedom," Religion News Service, November 27, 2018, https://religionnews.com/2018/11/27/museum-highlights-slave-bible-that-focuses-on-servitude-leaves-out-freedom/.

[10]Ballor and Joustra, *Church's Social Responsibility*, 27-31; and Richard J. Mouw, "Carl Henry Was Right," *Christianity Today*, January 27, 2010, 30. Original quote from Richard J. Mouw, "The Task of 'Christian Social Ethics,'" *Christianity Today*, January 5, 1968, 5.

[11]Ballor and Joustra, *Church's Social Responsibility*, 27-31; and Mouw, "Carl Henry Was Right," 31-32.

[12]Ballor and Joustra, *Church's Social Responsibility*, 27-31; and Mouw, "Carl Henry Was Right," 34.

[13]Ballor and Joustra, *Church's Social Responsibility*, 27-31; and Mouw, "Carl Henry Was Right," 35.

[14]Adam Stites, "Everything You Need to Know About NFL Protests During the National Anthem," SB Nation, October 19, 2017, www.sbnation.com/2017/9/29/16380080/donald-trump-nfl-colin-kaepernick-protests-national-anthem/.

[15]Mark Maske and Des Bieler, "Jerry Jones Says Cowboys Players 'Disrespecting the Flag' Won't Play," *Washington Post*, October 8, 2017, www.washingtonpost.com/news/sports/wp/2017/10/08/jerry-jones-says-cowboys-players-who-disrespect-the-flag-wont-play/?utm_term=.e0560df8af16.

[16]Erik Ortiz, "New NFL Policy: Teams to Be Fined If Players Kneel During Anthem," NBC News, May 23, 2018, www.nbcnews.com/news/us-news/nfl-announces-new -national-anthem-policy-fines-teams-if-players-n876816.

[17]Lorenzo Reyes, "Colin Kaepernick Featured in Nike's 'Just Do It' 30th Anniversary Ad," *USA Today*, September 3, 2018, www.usatoday.com/story/sports/nfl/2018 /09/03/colin-kaepernick-nike-ad-just-do-protest/1186501002/.

[18]Christian D'Andrea, "What's Next for Colin Kaepernick Now That His Collusion Case Against the NFL Is Settled?" SB Nation, February 18, 2019, www.sbnation .com/nfl/2019/2/18/18226657/colin-kaepernick-future-nfl-quarterback-collusion -case-settlement.

[19]Erwin Lutzer, "Christians and Politics: Serving Two Masters?" Moody Church Media, 2004, accessed March 27, 2019, www.moodymedia.org/articles/christians -and-politics-serving-two-masters/.

[20]Robert Reich, "The Choice of Patriotism," HuffPost, updated June 29, 2017, www .huffpost.com/entry/the-choice-of-patriotism_b_10718824.

[21]Fea, *Believe Me*, 182.

3 Global Poverty

[1]History.com editors, "'Live Aid' Concert Raises $127 Million for Famine Relief in Africa," History, updated July 27, 2019, www.history.com/this-day-in-history/live -aid-concert.

[2]Interview with Sidney Muisyo, February 3, 2019.

[3]Interview with Sidney Muisyo.

[4]Esteban Ortiz-Ospina and Max Roser, "Global Extreme Poverty," Our World in Data, updated March 27, 2017, https://ourworldindata.org/extreme-poverty.

[5]"Health Situation and Trend Assessment—Poverty," World Health Organization, ac- cessed April 29, 2019, www.searo.who.int/entity/health_situation_trends/data/chi /multidimensional-poverty/en/.

[6]"Goal: Reduce Child Mortality," UNICEF, accessed April 29, 2019, www.unicef.org /mdg/childmortality.html.

[7]"Children: Reducing Mortality," World Health Organization, September 19, 2019, www.who.int/news-room/fact-sheets/detail/children-reducing-mortality.

[8]Homi Kharas, Kristofer Hamel, and Martin Hofer, "Rethinking Global Poverty Re- duction in 2019," Brookings, December 13, 2018, www.brookings.edu/blog/future -development/2018/12/13/rethinking-global-poverty-reduction-in-2019/.

[9]Kharas, Hamel, and Hofer, "Rethinking Global Poverty."

[10]"11 Facts About Global Poverty," Do Something, accessed May 21, 2019, www.do something.org/us/facts/11-facts-about-global-poverty.

[11]"Poverty Overview," The World Bank, updated October 2, 2019, www.worldbank .org/en/topic/poverty/overview.

[12]"Poverty Overview."

[13]"Poverty Overview."

[14]"Global Inequality," Inequality, accessed February 17, 2019, https://inequality.org /facts/global-inequality/#global-wealth-inequality.

[15]"Global Inequality."

[16]"Rapid, Climate-Informed Development Needed to Keep Climate Change from Pushing More than 100 Million People into Poverty by 2030," The World Bank, No- vember 8, 2015, www.worldbank.org/en/news/feature/2015/11/08/rapid-climate -informed-development-needed-to-keep-climate-change-from-pushing-more -than-100-million-people-into-poverty-by-2030.

[17]Jessinia Ruff, "5 Ways Climate Change Affects People Living in Poverty," One Day's Wages, June 9, 2017, www.onedayswages.org/2017/06/09/5-ways-climate-change -affects-poverty/.

[18]Gabe Bullard, "See What Climate Change Means for the World's Poor," *National Geographic,* December 1, 2015, https://news.nationalgeographic.com/2015/12/151 201-datapoints-climate-change-poverty-agriculture/.

[19]"Climate Change," Christian Aid, accessed March 15, 2019, www.christianaid.org .uk/campaigns/climate-change-campaign.

[20]"Sustainable Development Goal 1," UN Sustainable Development Goals Knowledge Platform, accessed March 15, 2019, https://sustainabledevelopment.un.org/sdg1.

[21]"Transforming Our World: The 2030 Agenda for Sustainable Development," UN Sustainable Development Goals Knowledge Platform, accessed April 29, 2019, https:// sustainabledevelopment.un.org/post2015/transformingourworld.

[22]"Sustainable Development Goal 1."

[23]Fred Pearce, "Is It Possible to Reduce CO2 Emissions and Grow the Global Economy?," The Guardian, April 14, 2016, www.theguardian.com/environment/2016/apr/14 /is-it-possible-to-reduce-co2-emissions-and-grow-the-global-economy.

[24]Melissa Denchak, "Paris Climate Agreement: Everything You Need to Know," Na- tional Resources Defense Council, December 12, 2018, www.nrdc.org/stories/paris -climate-agreement-everything-you-need-know#sec-beyond.

[25]Daniel Drezner, "'The End of Poverty': Brother, Can You Spare $195 Billion?" *New York Times,* April 24, 2005, www.nytimes.com/2005/04/24/books/review/the -end-of-poverty-brother-can-you-spare-195-billion.html.

[26]William Gates, "On Development, Sachs Was Wrong. And Right," World Economic Forum, May 22, 2014, www.weforum.org/agenda/2014/05/fighting-poverty-taking -risks-jeffrey-sachs-bill-gates-mvp-idealist-nina-munk-book/.

[27]Matthew Brennan, "World Vision's Approach to Community Development," World Vision, May 17, 2013, www.worldvision.org/blog/world-vision-approach-community -development.

[28]"Ministry Mission Statement," Compassion International, accessed April 29, 2019, www.compassion.com/mission-statement.htm.

[29]Brennan, "World Vision's Approach to Community Development."

[30]Interview with Sidney Muisyo.

[31]Bruce Wydick, Paul Glewwe, and Laine Rutledge, "Does International Child Spon- sorship Work? A Six-Country Study of Impacts on Adult Life," *Journal of Political Economy* 121, no. 2 (2013): 393-436, www.journals.uchicago.edu/doi/pdfplus/10 .1086/670138.

[32]Interview with Sidney Muisyo.

[33]Shannon Jung, "Who Gets to Eat? Consumption, Complicity, and Poverty," *Journal of Lutheran Ethics,* June 1, 2010, www.elca.org/JLE/articles/292.

4 Domestic Poverty

[1]"About Us," Safe Families for Children, accessed May 20, 2019, https://safe-families .org/about/.

[2]"The Population of Poverty USA," Poverty USA, 2016, https://povertyusa.org/facts.

[3]Bill Fay, "Poverty in the United States," Debt.org, accessed May 20, 2019, www.debt .org/faqs/americans-in-debt/poverty-united-states/.

[4]"The Population of Poverty USA."

[5]Lisa Dettling, Joanne Hsu, Lindsay Jacobs, Kevin Moore, and Jeffrey Thompson, "Recent Trends in Wealth-Holding by Race and Ethnicity: Evidence from the Survey of Consumer Finances," Board of Governors of the Federal Reserve System,

September 27, 2018, www.federalreserve.gov/econres/notes/feds-notes/recent -trends-in-wealth-holding-by-race-and-ethnicity-evidence-from-the-survey -ofconsumer-finances-20170927.htm.

[6]Mary Daly, Bart Hobijn, and Joseph Pedtke, "Disappointing Facts About the Black-White Wage Gap," Federal Reserve Bank of San Francisco, September 5, 2017, www .frbsf.org/economic-research/publications/economic-letter/2017/september /disappointing-facts-about-black-white-wage-gap/.

[7]Shannon Luders-Manuel, "The Inequality Hidden Within the Race-Neutral G.I. Bill," JSTOR Daily, September 18, 2017, https://daily.jstor.org/the-inequality-hidden -within-the-race-neutral-g-i-bill/.

[8]Chuck Collins, Dedrick Asante-Muhammed, Emanuel Nieves, and Josh Hoxie, "The Ever-Growing Gap: Failing to Address the Status Quo Will Drive the Racial Wealth Divide for Centuries to Come," Institute for Policy Study, August 8, 2016, https:// ips-dc.org/report-ever-growing-gap/.

[9]Ale Bishaw and Kirby Posey, "Poverty Rate Lower in Rural America Than Urban Center," United States Census Bureau, November 30, 2017, www.census.gov /library/stories/2017/11/income-poverty-rural-america.html.

[10]"2017 Poverty Rate in the United States," United States Census Bureau, September 13, 2018, www.census.gov/library/visualizations/2018/comm/acs-poverty-map .html.

[11]Derek Thompson, "Busting the Myth of 'Welfare Makes People Lazy,'" *The Atlantic*, March 8, 2018, www.theatlantic.com/business/archive/2018/03/welfare-childhood /555119.

[12]Michael Katz, *The Undeserving Poor* (New York: Oxford University Press, 2013).

[13]Mae Elise Cannon, "Poverty-Cycles," in *The Social Justice Handbook: Small Steps for a Better World* (Downers Grove, IL: InterVarsity Press, 2008), 205.

[14]Jeff Truesdell, "They Attempted Suicide and Survived," *People*, October 28, 2019, 66.

[15]Editorial Board, "America Is Losing Ground to Death and Despair," *Washington Post*, November 30, 2018, www.washingtonpost.com/opinions/america-is-losing -ground-to-death-and-despair/2018/11/30/77c6b38e-f45a-11e8-bc79-68604ed88 993_story.html?noredirect=on&utm_term=.6387180c3ef8.

[16]"Ending America's Opioid Crisis," White House, accessed May 21, 2019, www.white house.gov/opioids/.

[17]"Suicide Statistics," American Foundation for Suicide Prevention, accessed May 21, 2019, https://afsp.org/about-suicide/suicide-statistics/.

[18]Carly Hoilman, "A Crisis of Despair: Christian Mental Health Professional Reveals the Reason Behind Recent Surge in Suicides and Drug-Related Deaths," Faithwire, March 6, 2019, www.faithwire.com/2019/03/06/a-crisis-of-despair-christian -mental-health-professional-reveals-the-reason-behind-recent-surge-in-suicides -and-drug-related-deaths/.

[19]Hoilman, "A Crisis of Despair."

[20]Hoilman, "A Crisis of Despair."

[21]Hoilman, "A Crisis of Despair."

[22]Learn more at www.afsp.org.

[23]Albert Hsu, *Grieving a Suicide: A Loved One's Search for Comfort, Answers, and Hope*, rev. ed. (Downers Grove, IL: InterVarsity Press, 2017).

[24]Hsu, *Grieving a Suicide*. In addition, the BBC did an auditory documentary in October 2018 called *After Suicide*, sharing the stories of those left behind: Caroline Donne, prod., *After Suicide* (London: BBC World Service, 2018), www.bbc.co.uk /sounds/play/w3csxyky.

[25]Matt Black, Wes Moore, and Eben Shapiro, "States of Vulnerability," *TIME*, accessed May 27, 2019, http://time.com/poorest-states-america-photos/.

[26] Angus Deaton, "The U.S. Can No Longer Hide from Its Deep Poverty Problem," *New York Times,* June 24, 2018, www.nytimes.com/2018/01/24/opinion/poverty-united -states.html.

[27] Deaton, "The U.S. Can No Longer Hide."

[28] Bill Fay, "Poverty in the United States." Debt.org, accessed November 27, 2019, www .debt.org/faqs/americans-in-debt/poverty-united-states.

[29] David Cutler and Jonathan Gruber, "The Affordable Care Act Is Constitutional," Annals of Internal Medicine, May 1, 2012, http://annals.org/aim/fullarticle/1134706 /affordable-care-act-constitutional.

[30] Tara Isabella Burton, "Meet the Bishops, Rabbis, and Pastors Taking a Stand Against Obamacare Repeal," Vox, June 21, 2017, www.vox.com/identities/2017/6/21/15847780 /faith-leaders-respond-aca-repeal-religion-protest-interfaith-activism.

[31] "The Case Against ObamaCare," Republican National Committee, March 23, 2011, www.gop.com/the-case-against-obamacare/.

[32] Julie Rovner, "Why Do So Many People Hate Obamacare So Much?" NPR, December 13, 2017, www.npr.org/sections/health-shots/2017/12/13/570479181/why -do-so-many-people-hate-obamacare-so-much.

[33] Richard Foster, "Estimated Financial Impact of the 'Patient Protection and Affordable Care Act,' as Amended," Department of Health and Human Services, Centers for Medicare and Medicaid Services, April 22, 2010, https://abcnews .go.com/images/Politics/OACT_memo_on_financial_impact_100423.pdf.

[34] Myriam Renaud, "Three Reasons White Evangelicals Hate Obamacare," University of Chicago Divinity School, April 12, 2018, https://divinity.uchicago.edu/sightings /three-reasons-white-evangelicals-hate-obamacare.

[35] Kate Shellnutt, "Bearing Burdens After Obamacare: The Future of Christian Healthcare Sharing," *Christianity Today,* February 2, 2017, www.christianitytoday .com/ct/2017/february-web-only/future-of-christian-healthcare-ministries-after -obamacare.html

[36] Mike Obel, "Why Health Care Sharing Ministry Memberships Now Top 1 Million," Fox Business, June 26, 2018, www.foxbusiness.com/features/why-health-care -sharing-ministries.

[37] Shellnutt, "Bearing Burdens After Obamacare."

[38] Timothy Stoltzfus Jost, "Health Care in the United States and the Affordable Care Act," *Human Rights* 43, no. 4 (2018): 6.

[39] Fay, "Poverty in the United States."

[40] Stacy Singh, "A Christian Response to Poverty Aims for Long-Term Restoration," Institute for Faith, Work, & Economics, January 31, 2018, https://tifwe.org/christian -poverty-long-term/.

[41] Learn more at Derek Jacobs, "Promoting Economic Development: Empowering the Church to Empower the Community," Ministry Matters, May 1, 2009, www.ministry matters.com/reach/entry/423/promoting-economic-development-empowering -the-church-to-empower-the-community.

[42] Singh, "A Christian Response to Poverty."

[43] Rebecca Vallas and Melissa Boteach, "The Top 10 Solutions to Cut Poverty and Grow the Middle Class," Center for American Progress, September 17, 2014, www .americanprogress.org/issues/poverty/news/2014/09/17/97287/the-top-10-solutions -to-cut-poverty-and-grow-the-middle-class/.

5 White Supremacy and American Christianity

[1] Mae Elise Cannon, Spiritual Renewal Week, John Brown University, January 24, 2017, www.youtube.com/watch?v=cx95QPPTGuo.

[2]History.com editors, "Bleeding Kansas," History, updated October 19, 2018, www .history.com/topics/19th-century/bleeding-kansas.

[3]"Our History," John Brown University, accessed May 26, 2019, https://catalog.jbu .edu/content.php?catoid=6&navoid=483.

[4]Mae Elise Cannon, "Black Christian Leaders Changing the World (Part 2 of 3)," HuffPost, updated December 6, 2017, www.huffpost.com/entry/black-christian -leaders-c_b_6717794.

[5]Leada Gore, "'Last Lynching in America' Shocked Mobile in 1981, Bankrupted the KKK," AL.com, updated March 7, 2019, www.al.com/news/2018/04/last_lynching _in_america_shock.html.

[6]"The National Memorial for Peace and Justice," Equal Justice Initiative, accessed May 28, 2019, https://museumandmemorial.eji.org/memorial.

[7]Robin J. DiAngelo, *White Fragility: Why It's So Hard for White People to Talk About Racism* (Boston: Beacon, 2018), 1.

[8]James Forbes, from conversation hosted by Sojourners Faith Table on January 4, 2019, in Washington, DC.

[9]Eddie Glaude Jr., from conversation hosted by Sojourners Faith Table on January 4, 2019, in Washington, DC.

[10]Daniel Hill, *White Awake: An Honest Look at What It Means to Be White* (Downers Grove, IL: InterVarsity Press, 2017), 130.

[11]Marianne Bertrand and Sendhil Mullainathan, "Are Emily and Greg More Employable Than Lakisha and Jamal? A Field Experiment on Labor Market Discrimination," NBER Working Paper Series (Cambridge, MA: National Bureau of Economic Research, 2003), www.nber.org/papers/w9873.pdf.

[12]Katie Sanders, "Do Job-Seekers with 'White' Names Get More Callbacks Than 'Black' Names?" Pundit Fact, March 15, 2015, www.politifact.com/punditfact/statements /2015/mar/15/jalen-ross/black-name-resume-50-percent-less-likely-get-respo/.

[13]Mae Elise Cannon, *Social Justice Handbook: Small Steps for a Better World* (Downers Grove, IL: InterVarsity Press, 2008), 242.

[14]Hill, *White Awake*, 55.

[15]Carl Skutsch, "The History of White Supremacy in America," *Rolling Stone,* August 19, 2017, www.rollingstone.com/politics/politics-features/the-history-of-white -supremacy-in-america-205171/.

[16]Harriet McLeod, "Charleston Church Shooter Pleads Guilty to State Murder Counts," Reuters, April 10, 2017, www.reuters.com/article/us-south-carolina -shooting-roof/charleston-church-shooter-pleads-guilty-to-state-murder-counts -idUSKBN17C15W.

[17]Mae Elise Cannon, "Charleston: 5 Things White Christians Can Do in Solidarity with Our Brothers and Sisters of Color," HuffPost, June 22, 2016, www.huffpost .com/entry/charleston-5-things-white-christians-can-do-in-solidarity-with-our -brothers-and-sisters-of-color_b_7628862.

[18]Dara Lind, "Unite the Right, the Violent White Supremacist Rally in Charlottesville, Explained," Vox, August 14, 2017, www.vox.com/2017/8/12/16138246/charlottes ville-nazi-rally-right-uva.

[19]"Anti-Semitic Incidents Remained at Near-Historic Levels in 2018; Assaults Against Jews More Than Doubled," Anti-Defamation League (press release), April 30, 2019, www.adl.org/news/press-releases/anti-semitic-incidents-remained-at-near -historic-levels-in-2018-assaults.

[20]Christopher Mele, Campbell Robertson, and Sabrina Tavernise, "11 Killed in Synagogue Massacre; Suspect Charged with 29 Counts," *New York Times,* October 27, 2018, www.nytimes.com/2018/10/27/us/active-shooter-pittsburgh-synagogue -shooting.html.

[21]Julie Turkewitz and Kevin Roose, "Who Is Robert Bowers, the Suspect in the Pitts-burgh Synagogue Shooting?" *New York Times*, October 27, 2018, www.nytimes.com/2018/10/27/us/robert-bowers-pittsburgh-synagogue-shooter.html.

[22]"For Immediate Release: Churches for Middle East Peace (CMEP) Stands in Soli-darity with the Jewish Community in the Face of Tragedy and Condemns Anti-Semitism," October 28, 2018, https://cmep.org/wp-content/uploads/2019/02/10.28.18-PR.pdf, used with permission from Delaware Churches for Middle East Peace (DCMEP).

[23]Tal Kopan, "What Donald Trump Has Said About Mexico and Vice Versa," CNN, August 31, 2016, www.cnn.com/2016/08/31/politics/donald-trump-mexico-statements/index.html.

[24]Eric C. Redmond, Walter B. Redmond Jr., and Charis A. M. Redmond, "#Charlottesville: Some Gospel Thinking on White Supremacy," *Themelios* 42, no. 3 (2017): 494-504, http://tgc-documents.s3.amazonaws.com/themelios/Themelios-42-3.pdf#page=62.

[25]Redmond, Redmond Jr., and Redmond, "#Charlottesville," 494-504.

[26]William H. Frey, "The US Will Become 'Minority White' in 2045, Census Projects," Brookings, March 14, 2018, www.brookings.edu/blog/the-avenue/2018/03/14/the-us-will-become-minority-white-in-2045-census-projects/.

[27]Glaude Jr., conversation.

[28]Robert Jones, "The End of White Christian America: Understanding America's Identity Crisis" (lecture and PowerPoint presentation, Chicago Invitation, Chicago, IL, September 14, 2018), slides 5 and 11.

[29]Jones, "The End of White Christian America," slides 6 and 12.

[30]Jones, "The End of White Christian America," slide 17.

[31]Domenico Montanaro, "How the Browning of America Is Upending Both Political Parties," NPR, October 12, 2016, www.npr.org/2016/10/12/497529936/how-the-browning-of-america-is-upending-both-political-parties.

[32]Jones, "The End of White Christian America," slide 28.

[33]Lisa Sharon Harper and Robert Jones, quoted in Eliza Griswold, "Evangelicals of Color Fight Back Against the Religious Right," *New Yorker*, December 26, 2018, www.newyorker.com/news/on-religion/evangelicals-of-color-fight-back-against-the-religious-right.

[34]Quoted in DiAngelo, *White Fragility*, ix.

[35]DiAngelo, *White Fragility*, x, 2.

[36]DiAngelo, *White Fragility*, 153.

[37]DiAngelo, *White Fragility*, 145-46.

[38]*Traitors*, season 1, episode 5, "Jackson," directed by Alex Winckler, written by Bath-sheba Doran, featuring Emma Appleton and Luke Treadway, aired on February 17, 2019, on Netflix.

[39]Learn more at www.jvmpf.org/ronald-clifton-potter/.

[40]Soong-Chan Rah, "In Whose Image: The Emergence, Development, and Challenge of African-American Evangelicalism" (ThD diss., Duke Divinity School, 2016), 191, https://dukespace.lib.duke.edu/dspace/bitstream/handle/10161/12925/Rah_divinity.duke_0066A_10056.pdf.txt?sequence=4.

[41]Kevin DeYoung, "Racial Reconciliation: What We (Mostly, Almost) All Agree On, and What We (Likely) Still Don't Agree On," The Gospel Coalition, April 17, 2018, www.thegospelcoalition.org/blogs/kevin-deyoung/racial-reconciliation-mostly-almost-agree-likely-still-dont-agree/.

[42]Randy White, "I Don't Understand the Evangelical Response to Ferguson," Randy White Ministries, accessed February 25, 2019, https://randywhiteministries.org/articles/dont-understand-evangelical-response-ferguson/.

[43]White, "I Don't Understand the Evangelical Response to Ferguson."

[44]Jarvis Williams, "Racial Reconciliation, the Gospel, and the Church," 9Marks, September 25, 2015, www.9marks.org/article/racial-reconciliation-the-gospel-and -the-church/.

[45]Williams, "Racial Reconciliation, the Gospel, and the Church."

[46]"The Legacy Museum: From Enslavement to Mass Incarceration," Equal Justice Initiative, accessed May 28, 2019, https://museumandmemorial.eji.org/museum.

[47]"What Is Epigenetics?" National Institutes of Health U.S. National Library of Medicine, accessed June 20, 2019, https://ghr.nlm.nih.gov/primer/howgeneswork /epigenome; Nagy A. Youssef, Laura Lockwood, Shaoyong Su, Guang Hao, and Bart P. F. Rutten, "The Effects of Trauma, with or Without PTSD, on the Transgenerational DNA Methylation Alterations in Human Offsprings," *Brain Sciences* 8, no. 5 (May 2018): 83, www.ncbi.nlm.nih.gov/pmc/articles/PMC5977074/.

[48]Benedict Carey, "Can We Really Inherit Trauma?" *New York Times,* December 10, 2018, www.nytimes.com/2018/12/10/health/mind-epigenetics-genes.html.

[49]"Sankofa Journey," The Evangelical Covenant Church, accessed May 28, 2019, https:// covchurch.org/resources/sankofa-journey/.

[50]Sheryl Gay Stolberg, "At Historic Hearing, House Committee Explores Reparations" *New York Times,* June 19, 2019, www.nytimes.com/2019/06/19/us/politics/slavery -reparations-hearing.html.

[51]P. R. Lockhart, "Writer Ta-Nehisi Coates Gives Mitch McConnell a Thorough History Lesson on Reparations," Vox, June 19, 2019, www.vox.com/identities/2019/6/19 /18691735/ta-nehisi-coates-mitch-mcconnell-reparations-history-racism-slavery.

[52]Ed Pilkington, "'Stain of Slavery': Congress Debates Reparations to Atone for America's Original Sin," *The Guardian,* June 19, 2019.

[53]"H.R.40—Commission to Study and Develop Reparation Proposals for African-Americans Act," Congress.gov, accessed November 27, 2019, www.congress.gov /bill/116th-congress/house-bill/40.

[54]See more at http://liberatingevangelicalism.org/program/workshops/.

[55]Redmond, Redmond Jr., and Redmond, "#Charlottesville," 494-504.

[56]Redmond, Redmond Jr., and Redmond, "#Charlottesville," 494-504.

6 Racial Violence, Police Brutality, and the Age of Incarceration

[1]Sean Flynn, "The Tamir Rice Story: How to Make a Police Shooting Disappear," *GQ,* July 14, 2016, www.gq.com/story/tamir-rice-story.

[2]Michael Pearson, "Tamir Rice Shooting: Cleveland to Pay $6 Million to Settle Family's Lawsuit," CNN, April 25, 2016, www.cnn.com/2016/04/25/us/tamir-rice -settlement/index.html.

[3]From a personal interview with Sarah King on May 23, 2019.

[4]Clifton E. Olmstead, *History of Religion in the United States* (Upper Saddle River, NJ: Prentice-Hall, 1960), 183.

[5]Emily Babay, "Unintentional Shootings Involving Children in Philadelphia," *Philadelphia Inquirer,* June 30, 2016, www.inquirer.com/philly/blogs/real-time /Accidental-shootings-involving-children-in-Philadelphia.html; Vince Lattanzio, "Boy, 6, Shot 10 Times in Germantown Doing Better, Shooters Still at Large," NBC Philadelphia, updated August 18, 2016, www.nbcphiladelphia.com/news/local/Boy -Shot-10-Times-in-Germantown-Doing-Better-Shooters-Still-at-Large-390501901 .html; Stephanie Farr, "Stray Bullets: 'Where Were the Angels?'" *Philadelphia Inquirer,* September 30, 2016, www.inquirer.com/news/inq/5-weeks-this-summer-4 -philly-kids-were-hit-by-stray-bullets-20160930.html.

⁶Farr, "Stray Bullets."

⁷Farr, "Stray Bullets."

⁸Emily Babay and Chris Palmer, "1 Arrested, 1 Sought in Germantown Ave. Gun Battle that Left Young Father Dead," *Philadelphia Inquirer,* August 19, 2016, www .inquirer.com/philly/news/20160820_1_arrested__1_sought_in_Germantown_Ave __gun_battle_that_left_young_father_dead.html.

⁹Personal interview with Sarah King.

¹⁰Personal interview with Sarah King.

¹¹Alex Kotlowitz, *An American Summer: Love and Death in Chicago* (New York: Doubleday, 2019), 7, 278; Aamer Madhani, "At Least 72 Shot, 13 Killed in Chicago over Violent Summer Weekend, Police Department Says," *USA Today,* updated August 7, 2018, www.usatoday.com/story/news/2018/08/06/chicago-violence-leaves-71-shot -11-dead-weekend/914141002/.

¹²Kotlowitz, *An American Summer,* 11.

¹³Kotlowitz, *An American Summer,* 20.

¹⁴Implicit bias is the manifestation of assumptions or negative stereotypes about different people groups often attributed to them without knowledge.

¹⁵Yolanda T. Mitchell, and Tiffany L. Bromfield, "Gun Violence and the Minority Experience." National Council on Family Relations, Family Focus: Understanding Gun Violence from a Family Perspective, January 10, 2019, www.ncfr.org/ncfr -report/winter-2018/gun-violence-and-minority-experience.

¹⁶Emma Long, "The Historians' View: What Are the Real Issues in the US Gun Control Debate?" History Extra, August 1, 2018, www.historyextra.com/period/modern/us -gun-control-debate-issues-explained-arguments-america-law-history/.

¹⁷Ray Sanchez, "'My School Is Being Shot Up': The Massacre at Marjory Stoneman Douglas, Moment by Moment," CNN, February 18, 2018, www.cnn.com/2018/02/18 /us/parkland-florida-school-shooting-accounts/index.html.

¹⁸"Mission & Story," March for Our Lives, accessed May 24, 2019, https://march forourlives.com/mission-story/.

¹⁹Kate Storey, "How Gun Laws—and Gun Norms—Have Changed Since the Parkland Shooting," *Esquire,* February 14, 2019, www.esquire.com/news-politics/a26290650 /parkland-shooting-one-year-later-gun-law-changes/.

²⁰*New York Times* reporters, "March for Our Lives Highlights: Students Protesting Guns Say 'Enough Is Enough,'" *New York Times,* March 24, 2018, www.nytimes .com/2018/03/24/us/march-for-our-lives.html.

²¹Perri Konecky, "The Most Powerful Signs from March for Our Lives," Popsugar, March 24, 2018, www.popsugar.com/news/Best-Signs-Slogans-March-Our -Lives-44695118.

²²Casey Chapter, "How Have Florida's Gun Laws Changed Since Parkland?" WJCT, February 14, 2019, https://news.wjct.org/post/how-have-floridas-gun-laws-changed -parkland.

²³Chapter, "How Have Florida's Gun Laws Changed?"

²⁴Storey, "How Gun Laws—and Gun Norms—Have Changed."

²⁵Sue McMillin, "The Red Flag Bill Again Thrusts Colorado's Sheriffs into the Gun Debate," *Colorado Sun,* March 14, 2019, https://coloradosun.com/2019/03/14/red -flag-bill-colorado-sheriffs-gun-rights-debate/.

²⁶Storey, "How Gun Laws—and Gun Norms—Have Changed."

²⁷John Eligon, "An Alabama Mall Shooting, a Black Man's Death, and a Debate Over Race and Guns," *New York Times,* November 29, 2018, www.nytimes.com/2018 /11/29/us/alabama-mall-shooting.html.

²⁸Eligon, "An Alabama Mall Shooting."

[29]Kate Shellnutt, "Packing in the Pews: The Connection Between God and Guns," *Christianity Today*, November 8, 2017, www.christianitytoday.com/news/2017 /november/god-gun-control-white-evangelicals-texas-church-shooting.html.

[30]Andrew L. Whitehead, Landon Schnabel, and Samuel L. Perry, "Gun Control in the Crosshairs: Christian Nationalism and Opposition to Stricter Gun Laws," *Socius*, January 1, 2018, https://journals.sagepub.com/doi/10.1177/2378023118790189.

[31]Shellnutt, "Packing in the Pews."

[32]Eliza Griswold, "God, Guns, and Country: The Evangelical Fight Over Firearms," *New Yorker*, April 19, 2019, www.newyorker.com/news/on-religion/god-guns-and -country-the-evangelical-fight-over-firearms.

[33]"Trayvon Martin Shooting Fast Facts," CNN, May 7, 2018, www.cnn.com/2013/06 /05/us/trayvon-martin-shooting-fast-facts/index.html.

[34]Material in this section is adapted from Mae Elise Cannon, "Why White Evangelical Churches Don't Wear Hoodies," HuffPost, October 2, 2013, www.huffpost.com /entry/why-white-evangelical-chu_b_3696440.

[35]"Herstory," BlackLivesMatter.com, accessed September 18, 2019, https://blacklives matter.com/herstory.

[36]Larry Buchanan, et al. "What Happened in Ferguson?" *New York Times*, August 10, 2015, www.nytimes.com/interactive/2014/08/13/us/ferguson-missouri-town -under-siege-after-police-shooting.html.

[37]"Ferguson Unrest: From Shooting to Nationwide Protests," BBC News, August 10, 2015, www.bbc.com/news/world-us-canada-30193354.

[38]J. David Goodman, "Difficult Decisions Ahead in Responding to Police Chokehold Homicide," *New York Times*, August 4, 2014, www.nytimes.com/2014/08/05 /nyregion/after-eric-garner-chokehold-prosecuting-police-is-an-option.html ?smid=pl-share.

[39]Mark Morales, "NYPD Files Formal Departmental Charges Against Officers in Eric Garner Case," CNN, July 22, 2018, www.cnn.com/2018/07/21/us/nypd-eric-garner -departmental-charges/index.html.

[40]Oliver Laughland and John Swaine, "Six Baltimore Officers Suspended over Police-Van Death of Freddie Gray," *Guardian US*, April 20, 2015, www.theguardian.com /us-news/2015/apr/20/baltimore-officers-suspended-death-freddie-gray.

[41]David Graham, "The Mysterious Death of Freddie Gray," *Atlantic*, April 22, 2015, www.theatlantic.com/politics/archive/2015/04/the-mysterious-death-of -freddie-gray/391119/.

[42]Richard Gonzalez, "DOJ Won't Prosecute Baltimore Officers in Freddie Gray Case," NPR, September 12, 2017, https://www.npr.org/sections/thetwo-way/2017/09 /12/550550977/doj-won-t-prosecute-baltimore-officers-in-freddie-gray-case.

[43]Andrea McDaniels, "Civil Unrest Related to Freddie Gray Death Caused Depressive Symptoms Among Mothers in Affected Neighborhoods, Study Finds," *Baltimore Sun*, July 10, 2017, www.baltimoresun.com/health/bs-hs-stress-freddie-gray -20170720-story.html.

[44]Andy Mannix and Chao Xiong, *Star Tribune*, June 21, 2017, www.startribune.com /case-file-in-philando-castile-shooting-to-be-made-public-today/429659263/.

[45]Tessa Nelson, "Two Years After the Police Killing of Philando Castile, Justice Continues to Be Denied," ACLU, July 6, 2018, www.aclu.org/blog/racial-justice/two -years-after-police-killing-philando-castile-justice-continues-be-denied.

[46]Pat Pheifer and Claude Peck, "Aftermath of Fatal Falcon Heights Officer-Involved Shooting Captured on Video," *Star Tribune*, July 7, 2016, www.startribune.com /aftermath-of-officer-involved-shooting-captured-on-phone-video/385789251/.

[47]Dominique Gilliard, *Rethinking Incarceration: Advocating for Justice That Restores* (Downers Grove, IL: InterVarsity Press, 2018), 5.

[48]Gilliard, *Rethinking Incarceration*, 28.

[49]Gilliard, *Rethinking Incarceration*, 21, 25, 26.

[50]Gilliard, *Rethinking Incarceration*, 63.

[51]Gilliard, *Rethinking Incarceration*, 64, 65.

[52]Gilliard, *Rethinking Incarceration*, 73.

[53]Gilliard, *Rethinking Incarceration*, 81.

[54]Gilliard, *Rethinking Incarceration*, 94.

[55]"A New Deal: Finding Promise in Prisoners," *Economist*, March 19, 2018, www
.economist.com/united-states/2008/03/19/a-new-deal.

[56]"Catherine Hoke, Defy Ventures," Hearts on Fire, accessed May 25, 2019, www
.heartsonfire.org/catherine-hoke-defy-ventures.

[57]Written communication between the author and Micky ScottBey Jones on May 24,
2019. More information about Micky can be found at www.mickyscottbeyjones
.com/about. Used with permission.

[58]Victoria M. Massie, "Department of Justice: Baltimore Cops 'Coerced Sex in
Exchange for Immunity from Arrest,'" Vox, August 11, 2016, www.vox.com/2016
/8/10/12429214/baltimore-police-investigation-justice-department-sexual-mis
conduct.

[59]Jennifer Reed, "The Cato Institute's National Police Misconduct Reporting Project,"
2010 Annual Report (Washington, DC: Cato Institute, 2013), www.leg.state.nv.us
/Session/77th2013/Exhibits/Assembly/JUD/AJUD338L.pdf.

[60]"#SAYHERNAME," African American Policy Forum, accessed May 24, 2019, http://
aapf.org/shn-campaign.

[61]Kimberlé Williams Crenshaw and Andrea J. Ritchie, "Say Her Name: Resisting Police
Brutality Against Black Women: July 2015 Update," African American Policy Forum
and Center for Intersectionality and Social Policy Studies, 2015, http://static1.square-
space.com/static/53f20d90e4b0b80451158d8c/t/560c068ee4b0af26f72
741df/1443628686535/AAPF_SMN_Brief_Full_singles-min.pdf.

[62]"About," The Marshall Project, accessed May 25, 2019, www.themarshallproject.org
/about?via=navright.

[63]"Bryan Stevenson," TED, accessed May 25, 2019, www.ted.com/speakers/bryan
_stevenson.

7 Global Immigration and Battles at the Border

[1]Diane Cole, "Study: What Was the Impact of the Iconic Photo of the Syrian Boy?"
NPR, January 13, 2017, www.npr.org/sections/goatsandsoda/2017/01/13/509650251
/study-what-was-the-impact-of-the-iconic-photo-of-the-syrian-boy.

[2]Kristine Phillips, "How a Photographer Captured the Image of a Migrant Mother and
Her Children Fleeing Tear Gas," *Washington Post*, November 27, 2018, www
.washingtonpost.com/world/2018/11/26/how-photographer-captured-image
-migrant-mother-her-children-fleeing-tear-gas/?utm_term=.1c15f2518505.

[3]Alan Gomez and Gregory Korte, "Trump Ramps Up Rhetoric on Undocumented
Immigrants: 'These Aren't People. These Are Animals,'" *USA Today*, May 16,
2018, www.usatoday.com/story/news/politics/2018/05/16/trump-immigrants
-animals-mexico-democrats-sanctuary-cities/617252002/.

[4]Karen Gonzalez, *The God Who Sees: Immigrants, the Bible, and the Journey to Belong*
(Harrisonburg, VA: Herald Press, 2019), 55.

[5]Gretchen Frazee, "4 Myths about How Immigrants Affect the U.S. Economy," PBS
Newshour, November 2, 2018., www.pbs.org/newshour/economy/making-sense/4
-myths-about-how-immigrants-affect-the-u-s-economy.

[6]James K. Hoffmeier, *The Immigration Crisis: Immigrants, Aliens, and the Bible* (Wheaton, IL: Crossway, 2009), 16, 17.

[7]Hoffmeier, *The Immigration Crisis*, 17-18.

[8]Hoffmeier, *The Immigration Crisis*, 153-154.

[9]Hoffmeier, *The Immigration Crisis*, 155.

[10]Hoffmeier, *The Immigration Crisis*, 156-57.

[11]Hoffmeier, *The Immigration Crisis*, 160.

[12]M. Daniel Carroll R., review of *The Immigration Crisis: Immigrants, Aliens, and the Bible*, by James K. Hoffmeier, *Denver Journal*, January 7, 2010, https://denverseminary .edu/resources/news-and-articles/the-immigration-crisis-immigrants-aliens-and -the-bible/.

[13]Carroll R., review of *The Immigration Crisis*.

[14]Carroll R., review of *The Immigration Crisis*.

[15]M. Daniel Carroll R., *Christians at the Border: Immigration, the Church, and the Bible* (Grand Rapids: Baker, 2008), 47-48, 71.

[16]Carroll R., *Christians at the Border*, 134.

[17]Carroll R., *Christians at the Border*, 5.

[18]"What Is the Quote on the Statue of Liberty?" How Tall Is the Statue of Liberty?, accessed June 7, 2019, www.howtallisthestatueofliberty.org/what-is-the-quote-on -the-statue-of-liberty/.

[19]"Chinese Exclusion Act (1882)," National Archives, accessed June 7, 2019, www .ourdocuments.gov/doc.php?flash=false&doc=47.

[20]"Early American Immigration Policies," U.S. Citizenship and Immigration Services, updated September 4, 2015, www.uscis.gov/history-and-genealogy/our-history /agency-history/early-american-immigration-policies.

[21]D'Vera Cohn, "How U.S. Immigration Laws and Rules Have Changed Through History," Pew Research Center, September 30, 2015, www.pewresearch.org/fact -tank/2015/09/30/how-u-s-immigration-laws-and-rules-have-changed-through -history/.

[22]Willa Frej, "How U.S. Immigration Policy Has Changed Since 9/11," HuffPost, September 9, 2016, www.huffpost.com/entry/us-immigration-since-911_n_57d054 79e4b0a48094a71bc0.

[23]"Timeline of the Muslim Ban," ACLU Washington, June 2018, www.aclu-wa.org /pages/timeline-muslim-ban.

[24]William Saletan, "Of Course It's a Muslim Ban," *Slate*, January 31, 2017, https://slate .com/news-and-politics/2017/01/trumps-executive-order-on-immigration-is-a -muslim-ban.html.

[25]"What Makes Trump's Revised Travel Ban Different?" Al Jazeera, March 6, 2017, https://www.aljazeera.com/news/2017/03/trump-revised-travel-ban-170306 210329013.html.

[26]"Timeline of the Muslim Ban."

[27]Nolan McCaskill, "Trump: Muslim Ban Would Have Stopped 9/11," *Politico*, August 3, 2016, www.politico.com/story/2016/08/donald-trump-muslim-ban-september11 -226637.

[28]Pamela Engel, "Trump's Immigration Ban Doesn't Include the Country Most of the 9/11 Hijackers Came From," *Business Insider*, January 30, 2017, www.business insider.com/trumps-muslim-ban-saudi-arabia-911-2017-1.

[29]Ioan Grillo, "The Migrant Caravan as Political Bandwagon," *Time*, November 1, 2018, http://time.com/5441423/migrant-caravan-politics/.

[30]Kirk Semple, "What Is the Migrant Caravan and Why Does Trump Care?" *New York Times*, October 18, 2018, www.nytimes.com/2018/10/18/world/americas/trump -migrant-caravan.html.

³¹Semple, "What Is the Migrant Caravan and Why Does Trump Care?"

³²Julia Ainsley and Courtney Kube, "What Are 5,600 Troops Going to Do at the Border? Maybe Not Much," NBC News, November 12, 2018, www.nbcnews.com /politics/immigration/what-are-5-200-troops-going-do-border-maybe-not-n934501.

³³Ryan Browne and Barbara Starr, "Pentagon Puts Cost of Border Troops at $72 Million—for Now," CNN, November 20, 2018, www.cnn.com/2018/11/20/politics /border-troop-cost-estimate/index.html.

³⁴Barbara Starr and Zachary Cohen, "Pentagon No Longer Calling Border Mission 'Operation Faithful Patriot,'" CNN, November 7, 2018, www.cnn.com/2018/11/07 /politics/pentagon-changes-name-of-mission-at-border/index.html.

³⁵Dara Lind, "How a March at the US-Mexico Border Descended into Tear Gas and Chaos," Vox, November 26, 2018, www.vox.com/policy-and-politics/2018/11/26 /18112474/tear-gas-border-patrol-caravan-rocks.

³⁶Lindsay Schnell, "2nd Guatemalan Child Who Died in US Immigration Custody Identified," KCEN TV, December 25, 2018, www.kcentv.com/article/news/nation -world/2nd-guatemalan-child-who-died-in-us-immigration-custody-identified /507-624820963.

³⁷Dara Lind, "The Trump Administration's Separation of Families at the Border, Explained," Vox, June 15, 2018, www.vox.com/2018/6/11/17443198/children-immigrant -families-separated-parents; John Kruzel, "No, Donald Trump's Separation of Im- migrant Families Was Not Barack Obama's Policy," Pundit Fact, June 19, 2018, www .politifact.com/punditfact/statements/2018/jun/19/matt-schlapp/no-donald -trumps-separation-immigrant-families-was/.

³⁸Kruzel, "No, Donald Trump's Separation of Immigrant Families."

³⁹Lind, "The Trump Administration's Separation of Families."

⁴⁰Jenny Yang, "Why Christians Shouldn't Be So Quick to Shut the Door on Immigrants and Refugees," *Relevant,* May 25, 2018, https://relevantmagazine.com/current/why -christians-shouldnt-be-so-quick-to-shut-the-door-on-immigrants-and-refugees/.

⁴¹Linda Qiu, "The Many Ways Trump Has Said Mexico Will Pay for the Wall," *New York Times,* January 11, 2019, www.nytimes.com/2019/01/11/us/politics/trump -mexico-pay-wall.html.

⁴²Nick Miroff, "Arrests Along Mexico Border Surged Again in May, Blowing Past 'Breaking Point,'" *Washington Post,* June 5, 2019, www.washingtonpost.com/immigration/arrests -along-mexico-border-surged-again-in-may-blowing-past-breaking-point/2019/06/05 /6d21585e-87a7-11e9-a491-25df61c78dc4_story.html?utm_term=.9a9eebd9ffa1.

⁴³"What Is DACA and Who Are the DREAMers?" Anti-Defamation League, accessed June 7, 2019, www.adl.org/education/resources/tools-and-strategies/table-talk /what-is-daca-and-who-are-the-dreamers.

⁴⁴"DACA," Immigrant Legal Resource Center, accessed June 7, 2019, www.ilrc.org /daca.

⁴⁵"DACA (Deferred Action for Childhood Arrivals)," Immigration Equality, accessed June 7, 2019, www.immigrationequality.org/get-legal-help/our-legal-resources /path-to-status-in-the-u-s/daca-deferred-action-for-childhood-arrivals/#.XD5 EOM9KhQJ.

⁴⁶Presbyterian Office of Public Witness, "Success!—H.R. 6 American Dream and Promise Act of 2019," email, June 5, 2019.

⁴⁷Maria Sacchetti, "Trump Administration Cancels English Classes, Soccer, Legal Aid for Unaccompanied Child Migrants in US Shelters," *Washington Post,* June 5, 2019, www.washingtonpost.com/immigration/trump-administration-cancels -english-classes-soccer-legal-aid-for-unaccompanied-child-migrants-in-us -shelters/2019/06/05/df2a0008-8712-11e9-a491-25df61c78dc4_story.html.

[48]David Platt, "We're Called to Serve Immigrants," *Relevant*, February 27, 2019, https://relevantmagazine.com/culture/global-culture/were-called-to-serve-immigrants-regardless-of-their-legal-status/.

[49]"About Us," Christians for Comprehensive Immigration Reform, accessed June 7, 2019, www.faithandimmigration.org/about-us/.

[50]Emily Miller, "Faith Leaders Denounce Trump Proclamation Denying Asylum Outside Border Crossings," *Word & Way*, November 12, 2018, https://wordandway.org/2018/11/12/faith-leaders-denounce-trump-proclamation-denying-asylum-outside-border-crossings/.

[51]Emma Green, "Religious Leaders Condemn Family Separations—but Not Necessarily Trump," *Atlantic*, June 19, 2018, www.theatlantic.com/politics/archive/2018/06/why-religious-conservatives-are-calling-out-trump-on-family-separation-at-the-border/563060/.

[52]Judith McDaniel, "The Sanctuary Movement, Then and Now," *Religion & Politics*, February 21, 2017, https://religionandpolitics.org/2017/02/21/the-sanctuary-movement-then-and-now/.

[53]Scott Pelley, "Churches, Synagogues Openly Defy Trump's Immigration Crackdown," CBS, May 21, 2017, www.cbsnews.com/news/churches-synagogues-openly-defy-trump-immigration-crackdown/.

[54]Catherine Shoichet, "An Undocumented Immigrant Who Lived for 11 Months in a Sanctuary Church Has Been Deported," CNN, November 30, 2018, www.cnn.com/2018/11/30/us/undocumented-immigrant-sanctuary-church-deported/index.html.

[55]Pelley, "Churches, Synagogues Openly Defy Trump's Immigration Crackdown."

[56]"U.S. Code §1324. Bringing In and Harboring Certain Aliens," Cornell Law School Legal Information Institute, accessed June 7, 2019, www.law.cornell.edu/uscode/text/8/1324.

[57]From a phone discussion between Chris Pierson and the author on June 5, 2019.

[58]"United Nations Volunteers," UNHCR, accessed June 7, 2019, www.unhcr.org/en-us/united-nations-volunteers.html.

[59]"Our Team," Border Angels, June 7, 2019, www.borderangels.org/our-team/.

[60]Email from Meredith Owen, Deputy Director of Policy and Advocacy, Immigration and Refugee Program, Church World Service, "Seeking Organizational Endorsements for World Refugee Day Resolution," June 6, 2018.

[61]Owen, "Seeking Organizational Endorsements".

[62]"Refugees Welcome," Refugees Welcome International, accessed June 7, 2019, www.refugees-welcome.net/#refugees-welcome-2.

[63]"Send Your Letter of Hope Today," CARE, accessed June 7, 2019, https://my.care.org/site/SPageNavigator/CARE_SpecialDelivery.html.

[64]"Support Syria's Heroes," The White Helmets, accessed June 7, 2019, www.whitehelmets.org/en/.

[65]"Syrian Refugee Crisis: Facts, FAQs, and How to Help," World Vision, updated March 15, 2019, www.worldvision.org/refugees-news-stories/syrian-refugee-crisis-facts.

[66]"U.S. Offices," World Relief, accessed June 7, 2019, https://worldrelief.org/us-offices.

8 Divisions of Race and Ethnicity Around the World

[1]Terry George, dir., *Hotel Rwanda* (Beverly Hills, CA: MGM, 2005), www.imdb.com/title/tt0395169/plotsummary?ref_=tt_stry_pl.

[2]Marilyn Lake and Henry Reynolds, *Drawing the Global Colour Line: White Men's Countries and the International Challenge of Racial Equality* (Cambridge, UK: Cambridge University Press, 2008), 347.

[3]Lake and Reynolds, *Drawing the Global Colour Line*, 348.

[4]Lake and Reynolds, *Drawing the Global Colour Line*, 349.

[5]"Myanmar Military Leaders Must Face Genocide Charges—UN Report," UN News, August 27, 2018, https://news.un.org/en/story/2018/08/1017802.

[6]"Myanmar Rohingya: What You Need to Know About the Crisis," BBC News, April 24, 2018, www.bbc.com/news/world-asia-41566561.

[7]"Bangladesh FM: Violence Against Rohingya 'Is Genocide,'" Al Jazeera, September 10, 2017, www.aljazeera.com/news/2017/09/bangladesh-fm-violence-rohingya-genocide-170911023429604.html.

[8]"Who Are the Rohingya?" Al Jazeera, April 18, 2018, www.aljazeera.com/indepth/features/2017/08/rohingya-muslims-170831065142812.html.

[9]Jennifer Williams, "South Sudan's Civil War Has Raged for 5 Years. Now the Leaders of the Two Sides Are Meeting," Vox, June 20, 2018, www.vox.com/world/2018/6/20/17483232/south-sudan-civil-war-meeting-ethiopia-riek-machar-salva-kiir-peace-talks.

[10]Megan Specia, "383,000: Estimated Death Toll in South Sudan's War," *New York Times*, September 26, 2018, www.nytimes.com/2018/09/26/world/africa/south-sudan-civil-war-deaths.html.

[11]Adam Taylor, "What Became of the Arab Spring's Ousted Dictators?" *Washington Post*, December 4, 2017, www.washingtonpost.com/news/worldviews/wp/2017/12/04/what-became-of-the-arab-springs-ousted-dictators/?utm_term=.11ea3388294f.

[12]"The Arab Winter," *Economist*, January 9, 2016, www.economist.com/middle-east-and-africa/2016/01/09/the-arab-winter.

[13]Johnny Harris and Max Fischer, "Syria's War: Who Is Fighting and Why," YouTube, Vox News, 2017, accessed October 2018, www.youtube.com/watch?v=JFpanWNgfQY.

[14]"Syria's Civil War Explained from the Beginning," Al Jazeera, April 14, 2018, www.aljazeera.com/news/2016/05/syria-civil-war-explained-160505084119966.html.

[15]Kathy Gilsinan, "The Confused Person's Guide to the Syrian Civil War," *Atlantic*, October 29, 2015, www.theatlantic.com/international/archive/2015/10/syrian-civil-war-guide-isis/410746/.

[16]"Iraq Emergency," UNHCR, accessed February 20, 2019, www.unhcr.org/en-us/iraq-emergency.html.

[17]"Syria Regional Refugee Response," Refugees Operational Data Portal, accessed February 20, 2019, https://data2.unhcr.org/en/situations/syria#_ga=2.180605927.1775932278.1560288686-986405880.1560288686.

[18]"Syria Emergency," UNHCR, updated April 19, 2018, www.unhcr.org/en-us/syria-emergency.html.

[19]"Syria Emergency."

[20]Office of the Press Secretary, "Government Assessment of the Syrian Government's Use of Chemical Weapons on August 21, 2013," The White House: Barack Obama, August 30, 2013, https://obamawhitehouse.archives.gov/the-press-office/2013/08/30/government-assessment-syrian-government-s-use-chemical-weapons-august-21.

[21]Jeremy Diamond and Barbara Starr, "Trump Launches Military Strike Against Syria," CNN, April 7, 2017, www.cnn.com/2017/04/06/politics/donald-trump-syria-military/index.html.

[22]"As Syria Conflict Enters Ninth Year, Humanitarian Crisis 'Far from Over,' Security Council Hears," UN News, March 27, 2019, https://news.un.org/en/story/2019/03/1035611.

[23]"As Syria Conflict Enters Ninth Year."

[24]Jonathan Spyer, "Syria's Civil War Is Now 3 Civil Wars," *Foreign Policy*, March 18, 2019, https://foreignpolicy.com/2019/03/18/syrias-civil-war-is-now-3-civil-wars/.

[25]Jeremy Courtney, "Withdrawal From Syria: What It Means for Allies, Refugees, and ISIS." Preemptive Love (blog), October 8, 2019, https://preemptivelove.org/blog/withdrawal-from-syria.

[26]Jeremy Courtney, "Withdrawal From Syria."

[27]"Statement on Abduction of Bishops in Syria," Churches for Middle East Peace, April 26, 2013, https://cmep.org/wp-content/uploads/2019/02/4.26.13-PS.pdf.

[28]"U.S. Bombing in Syria: Escalating Violence Will Not Bring Peace," Churches for Middle East Peace, April 7, 2017, https://cmep.org/wp-content/uploads/2019/02/4.7.17-PR.pdf.

[29]"How—and Why—to End the War in Yemen," *Economist*, November 30, 2017, www.economist.com/leaders/2017/11/30/how-and-why-to-end-the-war-in-yemen?zid=308&ah=e21d923f9b263c5548d5615da3d30f4d.

[30]"Key Facts About the War in Yemen," Al Jazeera, March 25, 2018, www.aljazeera.com/news/2016/06/key-facts-war-yemen-160607112342462.html.

[31]"Yemen Crisis: Why Is There a War?" BBC, March 21, 2019, www.bbc.com/news/world-middle-east-29319423.

[32]"Yemen War: No End in Sight," Amnesty International, updated March 14, 2019, www.amnesty.org/en/latest/news/2015/09/yemen-the-forgotten-war/.

[33]Michelle Nichols, "U.N. Warns Half Yemen's People Could Soon Be on Brink of Famine," Reuters, October 23, 2018, www.reuters.com/article/us-yemen-security-famine-un/u-n-warns-half-yemens-people-could-soon-be-on-brink-of-famine-idUSKCN1MX33U.

[34]Nichols, "U.N. Warns."

[35]Declan Walsh, "The Tragedy of Saudi Arabia's War," *New York Times*, October 26, 2018, www.nytimes.com/interactive/2018/10/26/world/middleeast/saudi-arabia-war-yemen.html.

[36]Walsh, "The Tragedy of Saudi Arabia's War."

[37]CFR.org editors, "U.S.-Saudi Arabia Relations," Council on Foreign Relations, December 7, 2018, www.cfr.org/backgrounder/us-saudi-arabia-relations.

[38]Tracy Wilkinson, "Is Saudi Arabia Really a Crucial Strategic Ally for the U.S.?" *LA Times*, October 28, 2018, www.latimes.com/nation/la-na-pol-us-saudi-ally-20181023-story.html.

[39]CFR.org editors, "U.S.-Saudi Arabia Relations."

[40]"Churches for Middle East Peace (CMEP) Praises Passage of Resolution Removing U.S. Armed Forces from Yemen," Churches for Middle East Peace, April 5, 2019, https://cmep.org/wp-content/uploads/2019/04/4.5.19-Public-Statement-House-Yemen-Resolution.pdf.

[41]Peter Baker and Mark Landler, "Trump Vetoes Measure to Force End to U.S. Involvement in Yemen War," *New York Times*, April 16, 2019, www.nytimes.com/2019/04/16/us/politics/trump-veto-yemen.html.

[42]Baker and Landler, "Trump Vetoes Measure to Force End."

[43]Mohamad Bazzi, "The United States Could End the War in Yemen if It Wanted To," *Atlantic*, September 30, 2018, www.theatlantic.com/international/archive/2018/09/iran-yemen-saudi-arabia/571465/.

[44]You can learn more by watching this March 2019 webinar with me and Scott Paul, Oxfam America's policy expert on Yemen: "Greatest Humanitarian Crisis of Our Time: What's Happening in Yemen?" Churches for Middle East Peace, 2019, https://www.youtube.com/watch?v=ZCCcKUcOGM8&feature=youtu.be.

⁴⁵Churches for Middle East Peace, "Ecumenical Letter to Congressional Leadership on Ending U.S. Support for Civil War in Yemen," June 12, 2019, https://cmep.org /wp-content/uploads/2019/06/Christian-Leaders-letter-Yemen-2019-1.pdf.

⁴⁶Timothy Longman, *Christianity and Genocide in Rwanda* (New York: Cambridge University Press, 2010), 3-5.

⁴⁷Mae Elise Cannon, *Social Justice Handbook: Small Steps for a Better World* (Downers Grove, IL: InterVarsity Press, 2009), 164.

⁴⁸"Rwanda: Justice After Genocide—20 Years On," Human Rights Watch, March 28, 2014, www.hrw.org/news/2014/03/28/rwanda-justice-after-genocide-20-years.

⁴⁹Longman, *Christianity and Genocide in Rwanda*, 10.

⁵⁰See "The Humanitarian Crisis in Yemen," CRS, www.crs.org/media-center/current -issues/yemen-crisis-facts-and-how-help; and "Yemen," Save the Children, www .savethechildren.org/us/what-we-do/where-we-work/greater-middle-east-eurasia /yemen.

⁵¹"Yemen," Islamic Relief USA, http://irusa.org/yemen/.

⁵²Laura Mouanoutoua, "Frontline Report: The Rohingya Refugee Crisis," World Relief, June 27, 2018, https://worldrelief.org/blog/frontline-report-the-rohingya -refugee-crisis.

⁵³"Mission and History," United States Holocaust Memorial Museum, accessed June 10, 2019, www.ushmm.org/information/about-the-museum/mission-and-history.

⁵⁴Longman, *Christianity and Genocide in Rwanda*, 11.

⁵⁵"The Righteous Among the Nations," Yad Vashem, accessed June 10, 2019, www .yadvashem.org/righteous.html.

⁵⁶Mae Elise Cannon, Lisa Sharon Harper, Troy Jackson, and Soong-Chan Rah, *Forgive Us: Confessions of a Compromised Faith* (Grand Rapids: Zondervan, 2014), 187.

⁵⁷"Anti-Semitic Incidents Remained at Near-Historic Levels in 2018; Assaults Against Jews More Than Doubled," Anti-Defamation League, April 30, 2019, www.adl.org /news/press-releases/anti-semitic-incidents-remained-at-near-historic-levels-in -2018-assaults.

⁵⁸Cannon, Harper, Jackson, and Rah, *Forgive Us*, 203.

9 #MeToo, Women in the Workplace, and Women in the Church

¹Eliana Dockterman, Haley Sweetland Edwards, and Stephanie Zacharek, "The Silence Breakers," *TIME*, December 18, 2017, https://time.com/time-person-of-the -year-2017-silence-breakers/.

²Eliza Griswold, "Silence Is Not Spiritual: The Evangelical #MeToo Movement," *New Yorker*, June 15, 2018, www.newyorker.com/news/on-religion/silence-is-not -spiritual-the-evangelical-metoo-movement.

³Manya Brachear Pashman and Jeff Coen, "After Years of Inquiries, Willow Creek Pastor Denies Misconduct Allegations," *Chicago Tribune*, March 23, 2018, www .chicagotribune.com/news/breaking/ct-met-willow-creek-pastor-20171220-story .html.

⁴Nancy Ortberg, "Sequence Matters," *Nancy Ortberg* (blog), March 24, 2018, www .nancyortberg.com/.

⁵Ortberg, "Sequence Matters."

⁶Bob Smietana, "Bill Hybels Accused of Sexual Misconduct by Former Willow Creek Leaders," *Christianity Today*, March 22, 2018, www.christianitytoday.com /news/2018/march/bill-hybels-misconduct-willow-creek-john-nancy-ortberg.html.

[7]Bob Smietana, "Bill Hybels Resigns from Willow Creek," *Christianity Today*, April 10, 2018, www.christianitytoday.com/news/2018/april/bill-hybels-resigns-willow -creek-misconduct-allegations.html.

[8]Laurie Goodstein, "He's a Superstar Pastor. She Worked for Him and Says He Groped Her Repeatedly," *New York Times*, August 5, 2018, www.nytimes.com/2018/08/05 /us/bill-hybels-willow-creek-pat-baranowski.html.

[9]Bob Smietana, "Willow Creek Elders and Pastor Heather Larson Resign over Bill Hybels," *Christianity Today*, August 8, 2018, www.christianitytoday.com/news/2018 /august/willow-creek-bill-hybels-heather-larson-elders-resign-inves.html.

[10]Kate Shellnutt, "Willow Creek Investigation: Allegations Against Bill Hybels Are Credible," *Christianity Today*, February 28, 2019, www.christianitytoday.com /news/2019/february/willow-creek-bill-hybels-investigation-iag-report.html.

[11]Scot McKnight, "About Willow Creek: What Do I Think?" *Jesus Creed* (blog), June 27, 2018, www.patheos.com/blogs/jesuscreed/2018/06/27/about-willow-creek -what-do-i-think/.

[12]"Process Updates," Willow Creek Community Church, accessed June 15, 2019, www .willowcreek.org/en/about/process-updates.

[13]Andrea Smith, *Conquest: Sexual Violence and American Indian Genocide* (Cambridge, MA: South End Press, 2005), 1.

[14]Smith, *Conquest*, 2.

[15]Charisse Jones and Kumea Shorter-Gooden, *Shifting: The Double Lives of Black Women in America* (New York: Perennial, 2003), 2, 8.

[16]Jones and Shorter-Gooden, *Shifting*, 8-10.

[17]Mehreen Kasana, "These 'Church Too' Tweets Are a Powerful Reminder That Sexual Abuse Isn't Limited to Hollywood," Bustle, November 21, 2017, www.bustle.com/p /these-church-too-tweets-are-a-powerful-reminder-that-sexual-abuse-isnt -limited-to-hollywood-5535716.

[18]Emily Joy, "#ChurchToo," Emily Joy Poetry, accessed June 15, 2019, http://emilyjoy poetry.com/churchtoo.

[19]Phone conversation with author, January 18, 2019.

[20]"About the Campaign," #SilenceisnotSpiritual, accessed June 15, 2019, www.silence isnotspiritual.org/about-us.

[21]"Statement: Breaking the Silence on Violence Against Women and Girls," #Silence isnotSpiritual, accessed June 15, 2019, www.silenceisnotspiritual.org/statement.

[22]Rachael Denhollander, "Why Survivors Aren't Surprised by Sexual Abuse Inside Southern Baptist Churches," interview by Judy Woodruff, *PBS News Hour*, June 12, 2019, www.pbs.org/newshour/show/why-survivors-arent-surprised-by-sexual -abuse-inside-southern-baptist-churches.

[23]Kate Shellnutt, "10 Women Who Are Changing the Southern Baptist Response to Abuse," *Christianity Today*, May 17, 2019, www.christianitytoday.com/ct/2019 /june/sbc-abuse-survivors-advocates-profiles.html?utm_source=ctweekly -html&utm_medium=Newsletter&utm_term=20161641&utm_content=65465 5494&utm_campaign=email.

[24]"Statistics About Sexual Violence," National Sexual Violence Resource Center (2015), www.nsvrc.org/sites/default/files/publications_nsvrc_factsheet_media -packet_statistics-about-sexual-violence_0.pdf.

[25]Matthew J. Breiding, Sharon G. Smith, Kathleen C. Basile, Mikel L. Walters, Jieru Chen, and Melissa T. Merrick, "Prevalence and Characteristics of Sexual Violence, Stalking, and Intimate Partner Violence Victimization—National Intimate Partner and Sexual Violence Survey, United States, 2011," Centers for Disease Control and Prevention, Surveillance Summaries 63, no. SS08 (2014): 1-18.

[26]"Statistics About Sexual Violence."

[27]William D. Cohan, "Remembering (and Misremembering) the Duke Lacrosse Case," *Vanity Fair*, March 10, 2016, www.vanityfair.com/news/2016/03/duke-lacrosse-case-fantastic-lies-documentary.

[28]Ashley Cote, Lori Gardinier, David Lisak, and Sarah Nicksa, "False Allegations of Sexual Assault: An Analysis of Ten Years of Reported Cases," *Violence Against Women* 16, no. 12 (December 2010): 1318-34, https://web.archive.org/web/20180101025446/https://icdv.idaho.gov/conference/handouts/False-Allegations.pdf.

[29]Katie Heaney, "Almost No One Is Falsely Accused of Rape," *New York*, October 5, 2018, www.thecut.com/article/false-rape-accusations.html.

[30]Cote, Gardinier, Lisak, and Nicksa, "False Allegations."

[31]Catherine Clark Kroeger and James R. Beck, eds., *Women, Abuse, and the Bible* (Grand Rapids: Baker Books, 1996), 232.

[32]Kroeger and Beck, *Women, Abuse, and the Bible*, 233.

[33]Kroeger and Beck, *Women, Abuse, and the Bible*, 235.

[34]Nicole King, "Southern Baptist Convention and Sexual Abuse," *Morning Edition*, NPR, June 14, 2019, www.npr.org/2019/06/14/732628096/southern-baptist-convention-and-sexual-abuse.

[35]"Caring Well: A Report from the SBC Sexual Abuse Advisory Group," Southern Baptist Church, June 2019, https://caringwell.com/wp-content/uploads/2019/06/SBC-Caring-Well-Report-June-2019.pdf.

[36]Joe Carter, "The FAQs: Southern Baptists Release Urgent Report on Sexual Abuse," The Gospel Coalition, June 12, 2019, www.thegospelcoalition.org/article/faqs-southern-baptist-release-critical-report-sexual-abuse/.

[37]"Gender Inequality and Women in the US Labor Force," International Labour Organization, accessed October 13, 2019, www.ilo.org/washington/areas/gender-equality-in-the-workplace/WCMS_159496/lang--en/index.htm.

[38]"Gender Inequality and Women."

[39]Claire Zillman, "The Fortune 500 Has More Female CEOs Than Ever Before," *Fortune*, May 16, 2019, http://fortune.com/2019/05/16/fortune-500-female-ceos/.

[40]Chai R. Feldblum and Victoria A. Lipnic, "Select Task Force on the Study of Harassment in the Workplace," U.S. Equal Employment Opportunity Commission, June 2016, www.eeoc.gov/eeoc/task_force/harassment/upload/report.pdf.

[41]Eliza Griswold, "Silence Is Not Spiritual: The Evangelical #MeToo Movement." *The New Yorker*, June 15, 2018, www.newyorker.com/news/on-religion/silence-is-not-spiritual-the-evangelical-metoo-movement.

[42]Peggy Orenstein, *Flux: Women on Sex, Work, Love, Kids, and Life in a Half-Changed World* (New York: Anchor Books, 2000), 288.

[43]Karen Swallow Prior, "The Problem with 'Don't Eat Alone with Women': Good Character Is Better than Strict Rules," Vox, April 1, 2017, www.vox.com/first-person/2017/4/1/15142744/mike-pence-billy-graham-rule.

[44]Caitlin Gibson, "The End of Leaning In: How Sheryl Sandberg's Message of Empowerment Fully Unraveled," *Washington Post*, December 20, 2018, www.washingtonpost.com/lifestyle/style/the-end-of-lean-in-how-sheryl-sandbergs-message-of-empowerment-fully-unraveled/2018/12/19/9561eb06-fe2e-11e8-862a-b6a6f3ce8199_story.html?noredirect=on&utm_term=.aea580140b31.

[45]Nikki Toyama and Tracey Gee, eds., *More Than Serving Tea: Asian American Women on Expectations, Relationships, Leadership and Faith* (Downers Grove, IL: InterVarsity Press, 2006), 192.

[46]Material in this section is adapted from Mae Elise Cannon, "Christian Women: Gifted to Lead," HuffPost, updated December 6, 2017, www.huffpost.com/entry/christian-women-gifted-to-lead_b_6932880.

⁴⁷Bob Smietana, "The #MeToo Movement Has Educated Pastors. And Left Them with More Questions," *Christianity Today*, September 18, 2018, www.christianitytoday.com/news/2018/september/metoo-domestic-violence-sexual-abuse-pastors-lifeway-2018.html.

⁴⁸Sally Canning and Tammy Schultz, "What We Long for the Church to Face About Sexual Violence," *Christianity Today*, December 11, 2018, www.christianitytoday.com/edstetzer/2018/december/what-we-long-for-church-to-face-about-sexual-violence.html.

⁴⁹Katlyn Smith, "We Are Here to Gather Our Courage," *Daily Herald*, December 14, 2018, www.dailyherald.com/news/20181213/we-are-here-to-gather-our-courage-wheaton-college-summit-addresses-sex-abuse-in-evangelical-churches.

⁵⁰Morgan Lee, "Max Lucado Reveals Past Sexual Abuse at Evangelical #MeToo Summit," *Christianity Today*, December 13, 2018, www.christianitytoday.com/news/2018/december/metoo-evangelicals-abuse-beth-moore-caine-lucado-gc2-summit.html.

⁵¹Eugene Hung, "4 Ways Churches Can Respond to the #MeToo Movement," *Sojourners*, November 1, 2017, https://sojo.net/articles/4-ways-churches-can-respond-metoo-movement.

⁵²"Our Mission," GRACE, June 15, 2019, https://www.netgrace.org/.

⁵³Lisa Sharon Harper, "#metoo #churchtoo #silenceisnotspiritual," *Freedom Road Podcast*, January 31, 2018, https://freedomroad.us/2018/02/podcastepisode1/.

10 The Liberation of Women Around the World

¹"Togo Country Profile," BBC, May 10, 2018, www.bbc.com/news/world-africa-14106781.

²"Sad and Sobering Reality That Women Continue to Be Deprived of Basic and Fundamental Rights, Special Assembly Session Told," United Nations (press release), June 8, 2000, www.un.org/press/en/2000/20000608.ga9723.doc.html.

³"Togo," Compassion, accessed June 15, 2019, www.compassion.com/about/where/togo.htm.

⁴United Nations Development Program (UNDP), "Gender Inequality Index," November 15, 2013, http://hdr.undp.org/en/content/gender-inequality-index.

⁵Florence Massena, "Women in Togo Are at the Core of Development and Political Change," Equal Times, November 21, 2018. www.equaltimes.org/women-in-togo-are-at-the-core-of?lang=en#.XQeuwdNKjOR.

⁶"Goal 5: Achieve Gender Equality and Empower All Women and Girls," UN Sustainable Development Goals, accessed June 15, 2019, www.un.org/sustainabledevelopment/gender-equality/.

⁷"Female Genital Mutilation," UNICEF, updated October 2019, https://data.unicef.org/topic/child-protection/female-genital-mutilation/.

⁸"Female Genital Mutilation."

⁹"Child Marriage," UNICEF, updated October 2019, https://data.unicef.org/topic/child-protection/child-marriage/#status.

¹⁰Nawal M. Nour, "Health Consequences of Child Marriage in Africa," *Emerging Infectious Diseases* 21, no. 11 (November 2006): 1644-49, www.ncbi.nlm.nih.gov/pmc/articles/PMC3372345.

¹¹"HIV/AIDS," World Health Organization, updated July 25, 2019, www.who.int/news-room/fact-sheets/detail/hiv-aids.

¹²Gita Ramjee and Brodie Daniels, "Women and HIV in Sub-Saharan Africa," *AIDS Research and Therapy* 10, no. 30 (December 2013), https://doi.org/10.1186/1742-6405-10-30.

[13]Donna Barne and Divyanshi Wadhwa, "Year in Review: 2018 in 14 Charts," The World Bank, December 21, 2018, www.worldbank.org/en/news/feature/2018/12/21/year-in-review-2018-in-14-charts.

[14]"Beijing+25: Celebrating 25 Years of Championing Women's Rights," UN Women, accessed June 15, 2019, www.unwomen.org/en/get-involved/beijing-plus-25.

[15]One movement that you may want to check out that supports the United Nations initiative and promotes men and women working together to end inequality of the sexes is called He for She: www.heforshe.org/en/movement.

[16]Matt Reynolds, "*Christianity Today*'s 2019 Book Awards," *Christianity Today*, December 11, 2018, www.christianitytoday.com/ct/2019/january-february/christianity-today-2019-book-awards.html.

[17]"Forced Labour, Modern Slavery and Human Trafficking," International Labour Organization, September 2017, www.ilo.org/global/topics/forced-labour/lang—en/index.htm.

[18]Marilyn Jones, "Rachel Goble Helps Stop Sex Trafficking of Impoverished Children," *Christian Science Monitor*, January 25, 2013, www.csmonitor.com/World/Making-a-difference/2013/0125/Rachel-Goble-helps-stop-sex-trafficking-of-impoverished-children.

[19]*The SOLD Project*, Vimeo, Dokument Films, 2010, https://vimeo.com/12978458.

[20]"Our Programs," Freely in Hope, accessed June 16, 2019, www.freelyinhope.org/our-programs/.

[21]"Nadia Murad—from Rape Survivor in Iraq to Nobel Peace Prize," BBC News, October 5, 2018, www.bbc.com/news/world-europe-45759669.

[22]"About," Nadia's Initiative, accessed June 16, 2019, https://nadiasinitiative.org/about/.

[23]Eliza Anyangwe and Stephanie Busari, "Denis Mukwege: The Man Who Mends Women," CNN, October 5, 2018, www.cnn.com/2017/10/19/africa/denis-mukwege-congo-doctor-rape/index.html.

[24]Pete Jones and Fiona Lloyd-Davies, "Congo: We Did Whatever We Wanted, Says Soldier Who Raped 53 Women," *Guardian US*, April 11, 2013, www.theguardian.com/world/2013/apr/11/congo-rapes-g8-soldier.

[25]Reid Mene, "11 Feminine Body Types That Societies Thought Were 'Sexy' Throughout History," *IJR*, February 3, 2015, https://ijr.com/society-considered-idolized-female-body-types-throughout-history; and "Body Types Through History," Science of People, accessed November 19, 2019, www.scienceofpeople.com/ideal-body-types-throughout-history.

[26]Nikki Toyama and Tracey Gee, eds., *More Than Serving Tea: Asian American Women on Expectations, Relationships, Leadership and Faith* (Downers Grove, IL: InterVarsity Press, 2006), 91.

[27]Jennifer Latson, "How Karen Carpenter's Death Changed the Way We Talk About Anorexia," *TIME*, May 23, 2016, https://time.com/3685894/karen-carpenter-anorexia-death/.

[28]Roxanne Gay, *Hunger: A Memoir of (My) Body* (New York: Perennial, 2017), 149.

[29]"Sexual & Reproductive Health & Rights," Global Fund for Women, accessed June 15, 2019, www.globalfundforwomen.org/sexual-reproductive-health-rights/.

[30]"Sexual & Reproductive Health & Rights."

[31]David M. Freeman, "Anti-Rape Condoms: Will Jagged Teeth Deter World Cup Sex Assaults? Rape-AXe Hopes So," CBS News, June 21, 2010, www.cbsnews.com/news/anti-rape-condoms-picture-will-jagged-teeth-deter-world-cup-sex-assaults-rape-axe-hopes-so/.

[32]Katy Kelleher, "Penis-Shredding Condom Can't Actually Prevent Rape," Jezebel, May 11, 2010, https://jezebel.com/penis-shredding-condom-cant-actually-prevent-rape-5536082.

[33]Jacque Wilson, "Could Condoms Change the World?" CNN, May 29, 2013, www .cnn.com/2013/05/29/health/haiti-condom-donation/index.html.

[34]"The World's Abortion Laws," Center for Reproductive Rights, June 15, 2019, https:// reproductiverights.org/worldabortionlaws.

[35]David Welna, "Senate Backs Embryonic Stem Cell Research," NPR, April 12, 2007, www.npr.org/templates/story/story.php?storyId=9533574.

[36]Rachel Held Evans, "I'm a Pro-Life Christian. Here's Why I'm Voting for Hillary Clinton," Vox, August 4, 2016, www.vox.com/2016/8/4/12369912/hillary-clinton-pro-life.

[37]"Snowflake: What Is Embryo Adoption?" Night Light, accessed June 15, 2019, www .nightlight.org/snowflakes-embryo-adoption-donation/embryo-adoption/.

[38]"Abortion," ACLU, accessed June 15, 2019, www.aclu.org/issues/reproductive -freedom/abortion.

[39]Alia E. Dastagir, "When It Comes to Abortion, Conservative Women Aren't a Monolith," *USA Today*, updated May 28, 2019, www.usatoday.com/story/news /nation/2019/05/22/abortion-law-republican-and-conservative-women-dont-all -agree/3749202002/.

[40]David Railton, "What Are Stem Cells and Why Are They Important?" Medical News Today, February 18, 2019, www.medicalnewstoday.com/articles/200904.php.

[41]Mae Elise Cannon Fisk, "The New Baby Boom," *The Covenant Companion*, October 2004, http://covchurch.org/wp-content/uploads/sites/2/2010/05/0410-Baby-Boom.pdf.

[42]"Clarifying the Difference Between Cord Blood and Embryonic Stem Cells," New England Cord Blood Bank, Inc., April 10, 2015, www.cordbloodbank.com /umbilical-embryonic-stem-cells/.

[43]Gabriel Power, "Six Things Women in Saudi Arabia Still Can't Do," *The Week*, June 5, 2018, www.theweek.co.uk/60339/things-women-cant-do-in-saudi-arabia.

[44]Alexia Underwood, "Here Are Some of the Ways Women Made Strides in 2018," Vox, December 4, 2018, www.vox.com/2018/12/4/18114868/women-rights-advancements -world-2018.

[45]Nicholas Kristof and Sheryl WuDunn, *Half the Sky: Turning Oppression into Opportunity for Women Worldwide* (New York: Random House, 2009), 252.

[46]Carolyn Custis James, *Half the Church: Recapturing God's Global Vision for Women* (Grand Rapids: Zondervan, 2011), 19.

[47]James, *Half the Church*, 177.

[48]James, *Half the Church*, 19.

11 Marriage and Sexuality

[1]"About ECO—Our Story," ECO, accessed June 16, 2019, www.eco-pres.org/who-we -are/our-story/.

[2]Jeremy Steele, "United Methodists' LGBT Vote Will Reshape the Denomination," *Christianity Today*, February 21, 2019, www.christianitytoday.com/news/2019 /february/united-methodists-lgbt-vote-umc-general-conference-denomina.html. Meg Anderson, "United Methodist Church Announces Proposal to Split over Gay Marriage," NPR, January 4, 2020, https://www.npr.org/2020/01/04/793614135 /united-methodist-church-announces-proposal-to-split-over-gay-marriage.

[3]Elizabeth Dias and Timothy Williams, "United Methodists Tighten Ban on Same-Sex Marriage and Gay Clergy," *New York Times*, February 26, 2019, www.nytimes .com/2019/02/26/us/united-methodists-vote.html.

[4]Jenell Pluim, "Action on Involuntary Removal from Membership of FCCM," Gather, May 31, 2019, https://gather.covchurch.org/wp-content/uploads/2019/06/Agenda -Item-10.b.-Action-on-Involuntary-Removal-from-Membership-of-FCCM_Public _v3.pdf.

[5]Matthew Nightingale, "Living the Truth," Medium, July 22, 2016, https://medium .com/@mattnightingale/living-the-truth-d2058f937516.

[6]Matthew Nightingale and Luanne Nightingale, "Choosing Gratitude and Hope," Tedx-SonomaCounty, November 21, 2016, www.youtube.com/watch?v=eHJs04-YIYc.

[7]Mae Elise Cannon, interview with Amanda Olson, Chicago, December 3, 2018.

[8]Phone conversation with the author, January 18, 2019.

[9]An excellent book about the relationship between the descendants of Hagar and Sarah is called *Arabs in the Shadow of Israel: The Unfolding of God's Prophetic Plan for Ishmael's Line* by Tony Maaalouf (Grand Rapids: Kregel Academic, 2003).

[10]Nell Sunukjian, "Women in Jesus' Genealogy," The Good Book Blog, Biola University, Talbot School of Theology, November 20, 2013, www.biola.edu/blogs/good -book-blog/2013/women-in-jesus-genealogy.

[11]Gilbert Bilezikian, *Beyond Sex Roles: What the Bible Says About a Woman's Place in Church and Family* (Grand Rapids: Baker Academic, 2006), 206.

[12]Andrew Cornes, quoted in David Instone-Brewer, *Divorce and Remarriage in the Church: Biblical Solutions for Pastoral Realities* (Downers Grove, IL: InterVarsity Press, 2003), 94.

[13]Instone-Brewer, *Divorce and Remarriage*, 99.

[14]Rebecca F. Miller, "When Does the Bible Allow Divorce?" *Christianity Today*, April 27, 2016, www.christianitytoday.com/women/2016/april/when-does-bible-allow -divorce.html.

[15]Miller, "When Does the Bible Allow Divorce?"

[16]Miller, "When Does the Bible Allow Divorce?"

[17]Miller, "When Does the Bible Allow Divorce?"

[18]Miller, "When Does the Bible Allow Divorce?"

[19]St. Luke the Evangelist Catholic Church, "Was Sex Only Meant for Procreation?" excerpted from *The Catholic Church's Teaching on Sexual Morality Issues* by Father Eamon Tobin, accessed June 16, 2019, https://stlukescatholic.com/was-sex-only -meant-for-procreation.

[20]"Was Sex Intended Solely for Procreation?" Beyond Today, accessed June 17, 2019, www.ucg.org/bible-study-tools/booklets/marriage-and-family-the-missing -dimension/was-sex-intended-solely-for-procreation.

[21]Paul Carter, "5 Surprising Things That the Bible Says About Sex," The Gospel Co-alition, August 15, 2018, https://ca.thegospelcoalition.org/columns/ad-fontes /5-surprising-things-that-the-bible-says-about-sex/.

[22]David P. Gushee, *Changing Our Mind* (Canton, MI: David Crumm Media, 2014), 60-62.

[23]Robert A. J. Gagnon, *The Bible and Homosexual Practice: Texts and Hermeneutics* (Nashville: Abingdon, 2001), 74-75.

[24]Gushee, *Changing Our Mind*, 62.

[25]Gagnon, *The Bible and Homosexual Practice*, 78.

[26]Gushee, *Changing Our Mind*, 64.

[27]Dave Hill, "76 Things Banned in Leviticus (and Their Penalties)," *Dave Does the Blog* (blog), June 13, 2012, https://hill-kleerup.org/blog/2012/06/13/76-things-banned -in-leviticus-and-their-penalties.html.

[28]Gagnon, *The Bible and Homosexual Practice*, 114-17.

[29]Gagnon, *The Bible and Homosexual Practice*, 117.

[30]Gushee, *Changing Our Mind*, 72.

[31]Gagnon, *The Bible and Homosexual Practice*, 254-55, 337.

[32]Mark Achtemeier, *The Bible's Yes to Same-Sex Marriage: An Evangelical's Change of Heart* (Louisville, KY: Westminster John Knox, 2014), 94-95.

[33]Gushee, *Changing Our Mind*, 75.

[34]Private conversation with the author, February 2018.

[35]Gushee, *Changing Our Mind*, 79.

[36]Achtemeier, *The Bible's Yes to Same-Sex Marriage*, 99.

[37]Gagnon, *The Bible and Homosexual Practice*, 303.

[38]Glenn Stanton, "10 Things Everyone Should Know About a Christian View of Homosexuality," Focus on the Family, July 22, 2019, www.focusonthefamily.com/about/focus-findings/sexuality/10-things-everyone-should-know-about-a-christian-view-of-homosexuality.

[39]"About Us," Institute for the Study of Sexual Identity, accessed June 16, 2019, https://sexualidentityinstitute.org/.

[40]Mark Yarhouse, "Understanding Gender Dysphoria," *Christianity Today*, July/August 2015, 48, https://sexualidentityinstitute.org/Papers/UnderstandingTransgenderPhenomenon.pdf.

[41]Yarhouse, "Understanding Gender Dysphoria," 48-49.

[42]Yarhouse, "Understanding Gender Dysphoria," 49.

[43]Yarhouse, "Understanding Gender Dysphoria," 49.

[44]Yarhouse, "Understanding Gender Dysphoria," 49.

[45]Yarhouse, "Understanding Gender Dysphoria," 49.

[46]Yarhouse, "Understanding Gender Dysphoria," 50.

[47]"Obergefell v. Hodges," Oyez, accessed June 17, 2019, www.oyez.org/cases/2014/14-556.

[48]David Masci, "Same-Sex Marriage Around the World," Pew Research Center, May 17, 2019, www.pewforum.org/fact-sheet/gay-marriage-around-the-world/.

[49]"Sexual & Reproductive Health & Rights," Global Fund for Women, June 16, 2019, www.globalfundforwomen.org/sexual-reproductive-health-rights/.

[50]Rosamund Hutt, "This Is the State of LGBTI Rights Around the World in 2018," We Forum, June 14, 2018, www.weforum.org/agenda/2018/06/lgbti-rights-around-the-world-in-2018/.

[51]Hutt, "This Is the State of LGBTI Rights."

[52]Joshua Kors, "'God Hates Fags': Q&A with Pastor Fred Phelps," HuffPost, August 8, 2010, www.huffpost.com/entry/god-hates-fags-qa-with-pa_b_689430.

[53]Amy Orr-Ewing, "If Christians Are Supposed to Love Everyone, Why Do They Hate Homosexuals?" Zacharias Trust, accessed June 16, 2019, www.zachariastrust.org/if-christians-are-supposed-to-love-everyone-why-do-they-hate-homosexuals.

[54]"Who We Are," Larkin Street Youth Services, accessed June 17, 2019, https://larkinstreetyouth.org/who-we-are/#section-about-us.

[55]Gushee, *Changing Our Mind*, 36.

12 The Middle East, Israel, and Palestine

[1]Churches for Middle Eastern Peace (CMEP), Session 2, "Ties to the Land: Christianity in Israel and Palestine," in *The Search for Peace & Justice in the Holy Land*, n.d., https://cmep.org/curriculum/.

[2]Churches for Middle Eastern Peace, Session 4, "50+ Years Too Long: The Effects of the Ongoing Occupation on Israeli and Palestinian Society," *The Search for Peace & Justice in the Holy Land*, n.d., https://cmep.org/curriculum/.

[3]Churches for Middle Eastern Peace, "50+ Years Too Long."

[4]Churches for Middle Eastern Peace, "50+ Years Too Long."

[5]Churches for Middle Eastern Peace "50+ Years Too Long."

[6]Churches for Middle Eastern Peace "50+ Years Too Long."

[7]Churches for Middle Eastern Peace "50+ Years Too Long."

[8]"What We Do," United Nations Relief and Work Agency, June 17, 2019, www.unrwa
.org/what-we-do.

[9]Hady Amr, "In One Move, Trump Eliminated US Funding for UNRWA and the US
Role as Mideast Peacemaker," Brookings, September 7, 2018, www.brookings.edu
/blog/order-from-chaos/2018/09/07/in-one-move-trump-eliminated-us-funding
-for-unrwa-and-the-us-role-as-mideast-peacemaker/.

[10]"Israel: Background and U.S. Relations," Congressional Research Service (CRS) Reports, July 31, 2018, www.everycrsreport.com/files/20180731_RL33476_28b29ca05
7430acc86b3b2f2e5f8cb174d03025d.html.

[11]"The Separation Barrier," B'Tselem, November 11, 2017, www.btselem.org
/separation_barrier.

[12]Churches for Middle Eastern Peace, "50+ Years Too Long."

[13]"The Human Right to Water and Sanitation," United Nations (media release), accessed June 17, 2019, www.un.org/waterforlifedecade/pdf/human_right_to_water
_and_sanitation_media_brief.pdf.

[14]Natan Odenheimer, "Israel—A Regional Water Superpower," *Jerusalem Post*, May 13,
2017, www.jpost.com/Magazine/A-regionalwater-superpower-484996.

[15]Peggy McInerny, "Water and Collective Punishment Policies in the Occupied Palestinian Territory," UCLA International Institute, March 21, 2017, https://international
.ucla.edu/Institute/article/173493.

[16]Mae Elise Cannon and Jessica Hill, "Life Inside the Gaza Blockade," *Sojourners*,
July 2017, https://sojo.net/magazine/july-2017/life-inside-gaza-blockade.

[17]Merrit Kennedy, "U.N. Says Gaza Is 'De-Developing' Even Faster Than Expected,"
NPR, July 11, 2017, www.npr.org/sections/thetwo-way/2017/07/11/536656901/u
-n-says-gaza-is-de-developing-even-faster-than-expected.

[18]Kennedy, "U.N. Says Gaza Is 'De-Developing' Even Faster Than Expected."

[19]"Gaza Strip," Gisha, June 17, 2019, www.gisha.org/UserFiles/File/publications
/Gaza_Infographic_Eng.pdf.

[20]"Water Crisis," B'Tselem, November 11, 2017, www.btselem.org/water.

[21]"Gaza Strip," Gisha.

[22]"Where We Work," UNRWA, January 1, 2018, www.unrwa.org/where-we-work
/gaza-strip.

[23]Daniel Estrin, "4 Palestinians Killed Along Gaza Border in 'Great March of Return'
Protest," NPR, March 31, 2019, www.npr.org/2019/03/31/708551097/4-palestinians
-killed-along-gaza-border-in-great-march-of-return-protest.

[24]Oliver Holmes and Josh Holder, "190 Killed and 28,000 Injured in a Year of
Bloodshed," *The Guardian*, March 29, 2019, www.theguardian.com/world/ng
-interactive/2019/mar/29/a-year-of-bloodshed-at-gaza-border-protests.

[25]Churches for Middle Eastern Peace, "50+ Years Too Long."

[26]Amy-Jill Levine, *The Misunderstood Jew: The Church and the Scandal of the Jewish
Jesus* (New York: Harper Collins, 2006), 111.

[27]Levine, *The Misunderstood Jew*, 168.

[28]James Carroll, *Constantine's Sword: The Church and the Jews—A History* (New York:
Houghton Mifflin, 2010), 564.

[29]Levine, *The Misunderstood Jew*, 171.

[30]"PM Netanyahu Addresses UN General Assembly," Israel Ministry of Foreign Affairs,
September 27, 2018, https://mfa.gov.il/MFA/PressRoom/2018/Pages/PM
-Netanyahu-addresses-UN-General-Assembly-27-September-2018.aspx.

[31]Material in this section is adapted from Mae Elise Cannon, "Anti-Semitism Versus
Legitimate Criticism of the State of Israel," Religion News Service, March 7,
2019, https://religionnews.com/2019/03/07/anti-semitism-versus-legitimate
-criticism-of-the-state-of-israel/.

³²Malcolm Hedding, "Christian Zionism 101," International Christian Embassy Jerusalem, June 17, 2019, https://int.icej.org/media/christian-zionism-101.

³³Judy Maltz, "Inside the Evangelical Money Flowing into the West Bank," Haaretz, December 9, 2018, www.haaretz.com/israel-news/.premium.MAGAZINE-inside-the-evangelical-money-flowing-into-the-west-bank-1.6723443.

³⁴I write about this extensively in the book I coedited with Andrea Smith, *Evangelical Theologies of Liberation and Justice* (Downers Grove, IL: InterVarsity Press, 2019), in my chapter called "Strange Freedom: Existential and Social Liberation from a Christian Perspective," comparing African American struggles for liberation to those of the Palestinian people. The foundation of an evangelical theology of liberation rests in the belief that Christ is our Savior and the liberator from sin and from physical oppression.

³⁵Naiman Stifan Ateek, *A Palestinian Theology of Liberation: The Bible, Justice, and the Palestinian Israeli Conflict* (Maryknoll, NY: Orbis, 2017), 45, 47.

³⁶Cannon and Smith, *Evangelical Theologies of Liberation and Justice*, 248.

³⁷Lincoln Anthony Blades, "How Policing in the U.S. and Security in Israel Are Connected," *Teen Vogue*, July 25, 2018, www.teenvogue.com/story/how-policing-in-the-us-and-security-in-israel-are-connected.

³⁸Blades, "How Policing in the U.S. and Security in Israel Are Connected."

³⁹Peter Baker and Julie Hirschfield Davis, "U.S. Finalizes Deal to Give Israel $38 Billion in Military Aid," *New York Times*, September 13, 2016, www.nytimes.com/2016/09/14/world/middleeast/israel-benjamin-netanyahu-military-aid.html.

⁴⁰Oren Liebermann, "Israel Announces New Golan Heights Settlement Named 'Trump Heights,'" CNN, June 17, 2019, www.cnn.com/2019/06/17/politics/trump-heights-golan-settlement-us-israel-scli-intl/index.html.

⁴¹I write more about the historic changes in US foreign policy toward Israel in this article: Mae Elise Cannon, "Blessed Are the Peacemakers, but What About the Troublemakers?" *The Christian Citizen*, May 15, 2019, https://christiancitizen.us/a-road-to-peace-or-trouble-one-year-after-u-s-moves-its-embassy-to-jerusalem/.

⁴²"Remarks by Vice President Mike Pence in Special Session of the Knesset," White House, January 22, 2018, www.whitehouse.gov/briefings-statements/remarks-vice-president-mike-pence-special-session-knesset/.

⁴³"Remarks by Vice President Mike Pence."

⁴⁴"Vision and Mission," Churches for Middle East Peace, accessed June 17, 2019, https://cmep.org/about/vision-and-mission/.

⁴⁵"Small Group Resources," Churches for Middle East Peace, June 17, 2019, https://cmep.org/curriculum/.

⁴⁶"Trips to Middle East," Churches for Middle East Peace, accessed June 17, 2019, https://cmep.org/events/travel/.

⁴⁷See my chapter "Mischief Making in Palestine" in *Comprehending Christian Zionism: Perspectives in Comparison*, ed. Göran Gunner and Robert O. Smith (Minneapolis: Fortress, 2014).

13 Religious Freedom

¹CNN staff, "ISIS Video Appears to Show Beheadings of Egyptian Coptic Christians in Libya," CNN, February 16, 2015, www.cnn.com/2015/02/15/middleeast/isis-video-beheadings-christians/index.html.

²Martin Mosebach, *The 21: A Journey into the Land of Coptic Martyrs* (Walden, NY: Plough, 2018), 7.

³CNN staff, "ISIS Video Appears to Show Beheadings."

[4]"Wilton Park Conference Report: Promoting Religious Freedom around the World," Wilton Park, July 3-5, 2011, www.wiltonpark.org.uk/wp-content/uploads/wp1108 -report.pdf.

[5]"Wilton Park Conference Report," 2, 8.

[6]"Wilton Park Conference Report," 9.

[7]"Global Uptick in Government Restrictions on Religion in 2016," Pew Research Center, June 21, 2018, www.pewforum.org/2018/06/21/global-uptick-in-gov ernment-restrictions-on-religion-in-2016/.

[8]Griffin Jackson, "Global Religious Freedom Takes Its Biggest Hit in Over a Decade," *Christianity Today*, June 21, 2018, www.christianitytoday.com/news/2018/june /global-religious-freedom-christian-persecution-pew-research.html.

[9]History.com editors, "President George W. Bush Announces Plan for 'Faith-Based Initiatives,'" History, updated July 28, 2019, www.history.com/this-day-in -history/president-george-w-bush-announces-plan-for-faith-based-initiatives.

[10]Mae Elise Cannon, "Dear Secretary Tillerson: Don't Downsize Religion in Foreign Affairs," *Christianity Today*, September 2017, www.christianitytoday.com/women /2017/september/secretary-tillerson-dont-downsize-religion-foreign-affairs.html.

[11]Cannon, "Dear Secretary Tillerson."

[12]"Know Your Rights: Religious Freedom," ACLU, accessed June 6, 2019, www.aclu .org/know-your-rights/religious-freedom.

[13]"Know Your Rights: Religious Freedom."

[14]"Know Your Rights: Religious Freedom."

[15]Wilfred McClay, "Religion and Secularism: The American Experience," (lecture at Pew Forum Faith Angle Conference, Key West, Florida, December 3, 2007), www .pewforum.org/2007/12/03/religion-and-secularism-the-american-experience/.

[16]James Wilson, "We're at the End of White Christian America. What Will That Mean?" *Guardian US*, September 20, 2017, www.theguardian.com/us-news/2017 /sep/20/end-of-white-christian-america.

[17]Wilson, "We're at the End of White Christian America."

[18]Emma Green, "Most American Christians Believe They're Victims of Discrimination," *Atlantic*, June 30, 2016, www.theatlantic.com/politics/archive/2016/06 /the-christians-who-believe-theyre-being-persecuted-in-america/488468/.

[19]Robert P. Jones, Daniel Cox, E. J. Dionne Jr., William A. Galston, Betsy Cooper, and Rachel Lienesch, "How Immigration and Concerns About Cultural Changes Are Shaping the 2016 Election," PRRI/Brookings, June 23, 2016, www.prri.org/wp -content/uploads/2016/06/PRRI-Brookings-2016-Immigration-survey-report.pdf.

[20]Green, "Most American Christians Believe They're Victims of Discrimination."

[21]Pascal-Emmanuel Gobry, "'Secular' Is a French Word for 'Anti-Muslim,'" Bloomberg, February 23, 2018, www.bloomberg.com/opinion/articles/2018-02-23/france-s -emmanuel-macron-isn-t-fighting-ant-muslim-bias.

[22]Jonathan Weisman, "Anti-Semitism Is Rising. Why Aren't American Jews Speaking Up?" *New York Times*, March 17, 2018, www.nytimes.com/2018/03/17/sunday -review/anti-semitism-american-jews.html.

[23]Gabriel Stoutimore, "Does Christian Privilege Really Exist? (In America It Depends on Your Skin Color)," *Relevant*, April 6, 2018, https://relevantmagazine.com /current/christian-privilege-really-exist-america-depends-skin-color/.

[24]Ed Cyzewski, "The Damaging Myth of Religious Persecution in America," Christian Today, September 14, 2016, https://www.christiantoday.com/article/the-damaging -myth-of-religious-persecution-in-america/95416.htm.

[25]"100th Anniversary of Secularism in France," Pew Research Center, December 5, 2005, www.pewforum.org/2005/12/09/100th-anniversary-of-secularism-in -france/.

26"100th Anniversary of Secularism in France."

27Karina Piser, "A New Plan to Create an 'Islam of France,'" *Atlantic*, March 29, 2018, www.theatlantic.com/international/archive/2018/03/islam-france-macron /556604/.

28"Decathlon Cancels Plans to Sell Sport Hijab in France," Al Jazeera, February 27, 2019, www.aljazeera.com/news/2019/02/decathlon-cancels-plans-sell-sport-hijab -france-190227163950355.html.

29Piser, "A New Plan to Create an 'Islam of France.'"

30"Villa Des Parfums," accessed June 18, 2019, https://www.villadesparfums.com/our -story.

31Michael O'Flaherty, dir., "Second European Union Minorities and Discrimination Survey. Muslims—Selected Findings," European Union Agency for Fundamental Rights (Luxembourg: Publications Office of the European Union, 2017), 24, 46, https://fra.europa.eu/sites/default/files/fra_uploads/fra-2017-eu-minorities -survey-muslims-selected-findings_en.pdf.

32Matti Bunzl, *Anti-Semitism and Islamophobia: Hatreds Old and New in Europe* (Chicago: Prickly Paradigm, 2007), 51, 67, 81.

33Steven Beller, *Antisemitism: A Very Short Introduction* (New York: Oxford University Press, 2007), 84, 89.

34Michael O'Flaherty, dir., "Experiences and Perceptions of Antisemitism," European Union Agency for Fundamental Rights (Luxembourg: Publications Office of the European Union, 2018), 11, 22, https://fra.europa.eu/sites/default/files/fra_uploads /fra-2018-experiences-and-perceptions-of-antisemitism-survey_en.pdf.

35"Anti-Semitism in the United States," Anti-Defamation League, accessed June 6, 2019, www.adl.org/what-we-do/anti-semitism/anti-semitism-in-the-us.

36"Global Uptick in Government Restrictions on Religion in 2016," Pew Research Center, June 21, 2018, http://www.pewforum.org/2018/06/21/global-uptick-in -government-restrictions-on-religion-in-2016/.

37"2017 Report on International Religious Freedom: Egypt," U.S. Department of State, May 29, 2018, https://www.state.gov/reports/2017-report-on-international -religious-freedom/egypt/.

38Lela Gilbert, "Egypt's Silent Epidemic of Kidnapped Christian Girls," *Jerusalem Post*, December 5, 2018, www.jpost.com/Opinion/Egypts-silent-epidemic-of-kidnapped -Christian-girls-573614.

39"2017 Report on International Religious Freedom: Syria," U.S. Department of State, www.state.gov/reports/2017-report-on-international-religious-freedom /syria/.

40Peter Feaver and Will Inboden, "We Are Witnessing the Elimination of Christian Communities in Iraq and Syria," Foreign Policy, September 6, 2017, https://foreign policy.com/2017/09/06/we-are-witnessing-the-elimination-of-christian-commu nities-in-iraq-and-syria/.

41"2017 Report on International Religious Freedom: Iraq," U.S. Department of State, www.state.gov/reports/2017-report-on-international-religious-freedom /iraq/.

42"2017 Report on International Religious Freedom: Iraq."

43"2017 Report on International Religious Freedom: Turkey," U.S. Department of State, https://www.state.gov/reports/2017-report-on-international-religious -freedom/turkey/.

44Eliza Griswold, "Is This the End of Christianity in the Middle East?" *New York Times*, July 22, 2015, www.nytimes.com/2015/07/26/magazine/is-this-the-end-of -christianity-in-the-middle-east.html.

[45]Patrick Wintour, "Persecution of Christians 'Coming Close to Genocide' in Middle East—Report," *Guardian US,* May 2, 2019, www.theguardian.com/world/2019/may/02/persecution-driving-christians-out-of-middle-east-report.

[46]Emma Green, "The Impossible Future of Christians in the Middle East" *The Atlantic,* May 23, 2019, www.theatlantic.com/international/archive/2019/05/iraqi-christians-nineveh-plain/589819.

[47]Green, "The Impossible Future of Christians in the Middle East."

[48]Ewelina U. Ochab, "Religious Freedom Is on the Decrease in India," *Forbes,* January 12, 2019, www.forbes.com/sites/ewelinaochab/2019/01/12/religious-freedom-is-on-the-decrease-in-india/#1b8c36e0403b.

[49]Ellen Barry and Suhasini Raj, "Major Christian Charity Is Closing India Operations Amid a Crackdown," *New York Times,* March 7, 2017, www.nytimes.com/2017/03/07/world/asia/compassion-international-christian-charity-closing-india.html.

[50]Ochab, "Religious Freedom Is on the Decrease in India."

[51]Doug Bandow, "India Will Never Be Great Until It Protects Religious Freedom," *The American Conservative,* May 2, 2019, www.theamericanconservative.com/articles/india-will-never-be-great-until-it-protects-religious-freedom/.

[52]Eleanor Albert, "Christianity in China," Council on Foreign Relations, October 11, 2018, www.cfr.org/backgrounder/christianity-china.

[53]Albert, "Christianity in China."

[54]See www.opendoors.org and www.persecution.org for more on these organizations.

[55]"About Us," Christian Solidarity International, accessed June 18, 2019, https://csi-usa.org/about-us#mission.

[56]Charter for Compassion, https://charterforcompassion.org/.

[57]China Aid, www.chinaaid.org/.

[58]More information about In Defense of Christians (IDC) can be found at https://in-defenseofchristians.org/ and about Churches for Middle East Peace (CMEP) can be found at www.cmep.org.

Epilogue

[1]Quoted in John Fea, *Believe Me: The Evangelical Road to Donald Trump* (Grand Rapids: Eerdmans, 2018), 184.

[2]Quoted in Fea, *Believe Me,* 188.

About the Author

REV. DR. MAE ELISE CANNON is the executive director of Churches for Middle East Peace (CMEP) and an ordained minister in the Evangelical Covenant Church (ECC). Cannon formerly served as the senior director of advocacy and outreach for World Vision US on Capitol Hill in Washington, DC; as consultant to the Middle East for child advocacy issues for Compassion International in Jerusalem; as the executive pastor of Hillside Covenant Church located in Walnut Creek, California; and as director of development and transformation for extension ministries at Willow Creek Community Church in Barrington, Illinois.

Cannon holds an MDiv from North Park Theological Seminary, an MBA from North Park University's School of Business and Nonprofit Management, and an MA in bioethics from Trinity International University. She received her first doctorate in American history with a minor in Middle Eastern studies at the University of California (Davis) focusing on the history of the American Protestant church in Israel and Palestine and her second doctorate in ministry in spiritual formation from Northern Theological Seminary. Her work has been highlighted in *The New York Times,* CNN, *Chicago Tribune, Christianity Today, Leadership Magazine, The Christian Post, Jerusalem Post, EU Parliament Magazine, Huffington Post, The Washington Post, Newsweek,* and other international media outlets.

Also by Mae Elise Cannon

Social Justice Handbook
SMALL STEPS FOR A BETTER WORLD

Mae Elise Cannon
Foreword by John Perkins

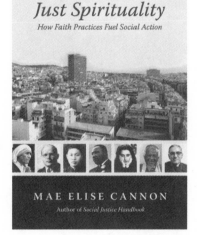

Just Spirituality
How Faith Practices Fuel Social Action

MAE ELISE CANNON
Author of *Social Justice Handbook*